JOYCE KILMER
Poems, Essays and Letters

TWO VOLUMES IN ONE
VOLUME ONE: *Memoir and Poems*

JOYCE KILMER'S *Complete Works*

JOYCE KILMER: Poems, Essays and
Letters, *Edited with* a Memoir *by*
ROBERT CORTES HOLLIDAY

VOLUME ONE:
MEMOIR AND POEMS

VOLUME TWO:
PROSE WORKS

VOLUME THREE:
THE CIRCUS: And Other Essays

By ALINE KILMER

CANDLES THAT BURN

VIGILS

HUNTING A HAIR SHIRT: And
Other Spiritual Adventures

© *Underwood & Underwood*

JOYCE KILMER, AGE 30

LAST CIVILIAN PORTRAIT

JOYCE
KILMER

EDITED WITH A MEMOIR BY
ROBERT CORTES HOLLIDAY

TWO VOLUMES IN ONE
VOLUME ONE
Memoir and Poems

DOUBLEDAY, DORAN & COMPANY, INC.
Garden City   1942   New York

147432

To the memory of
JOYCE KILMER

ACKNOWLEDGMENT

Many persons have contributed exceedingly valuable service to the preparation of these volumes. Credit has been gratefully acknowledged, wherever feasible, in the course of the text. To make anything like a full record, however, of the names of that remarkable society, the ardent and devoted friends of Joyce Kilmer, would require a chapter. Though particular reference should be made in this place to the invaluable assistance of: Kilmer's lifelong friend and lawyer, Louis Bevier, Jr.; his especial friend, Thomas Walsh; and his office associate, John Bunker.

Permission has been most cordially granted by the editors of the following magazines for the reprinting of the poems from France: *Scribner's Magazine, Good Housekeeping, The Saturday Evening Post, America,* and *The Bookman.* Essays and miscellaneous pieces have been gathered, with the warm approval of the editors of these publications, from these sources: *The Bookman, The New York Times Sunday Magazine, The Bellman, The Catholic World, Poetry: A Magazine of Verse,*

ACKNOWLEDGMENT

The Smart Set, Munsey's Magazine and *Puck*— a curiously assorted company, highly expressive of the catholicity of the mind these pages reflect.

The article on Hilaire Belloc, originally one of Kilmer's lectures, was first printed in the American edition of Belloc's "Verses." The early poems have been chosen from Kilmer's first book, "A Summer of Love," now out of print, rights to which are held by Mrs. Aline Kilmer. Poems not otherwise credited have been reprinted from the volumes already published by George H. Doran Company.

R. C. H.

New York, 1918.

CONTENTS VOLUME ONE

CONTENTS

CONTENTS

The Table of Contents for Volume Two will be found at the middle of the book.

ILLUSTRATIONS

VOLUME ONE

VOLUME TWO

MEMOIR

MEMOIR

IT IS the felicity of these pages that they cannot be dull. It is their merit, peculiar in such a memoir, that they cannot be sad. It is their novelty that they can be restricted in appeal only by the varieties of the human species. It is their good fortune that they can be extraordinarily frank. It is their virtue that they cannot fail to do unmeasurable good. And it is their luck to abide many days.

With their subject how could it be otherwise? They make not a wreath, but a chronicle, and in their assembled facts tell a bright chapter in the history of our time. If there is one word which more than any other should be linked with the name of this gallant figure now claimed (and rightly) by so many elements of the nation, that word certainly is "American." A character and a career so racy, typical of all that everybody likes to believe that at our best we are, can hardly be matched, I think, outside of stories.

I

Joyce Kilmer was reported in the papers as having said, just before he sailed for France, that he was "half Irish," and that was why he belonged with the boys of the Sixty-ninth. His birth was not exactly eloquent of this fact. Though, indeed, he was, as will appear, a much more ardent Irishman than many an Irishman born—that is, in the sense of keenly savouring those things which are fine in the Irish character, and with characteristic gusto feeling within himself an affinity with them. Later, in a letter from France to his wife, he was more explicit on this point:

As to the matter of my own blood (you mentioned this in a previous letter) I did indeed tell a good friend of mine who edits the book-review page of a Chicago paper that I was "half Irish." But I have never been a mathematician. The point I wished to make was that a large percentage—which I have a perfect right to call half—of my ancestry was Irish. For proof of this, you have only to refer to the volumes containing the histories of my mother's and my father's families. Of course I am American, but one cannot be pure American in blood unless one is an Indian. And I have the good fortune to be able to claim, largely because of the wise matrimonial selections of my progenitors on both sides, Irish blood. And don't let anyone publish a statement contrary to this.

He also, in a letter from France, quoted with much relish the remark of Father Francis P. Duffy

that he was "half German and half human."
English and Scotch strains made up another half
or three quarters. The English goes straight back
to one Thomas Kilburne, church warden at Wood-
dilton, near Newmarket, in Cambridgeshire, who
came to Connecticut in 1638. The "e" was lost
apparently in Massachusetts, and the word became,
as in his mother's maiden name, Kilburn.

Soldier blood, too, flowed in his veins—though it
is likely that this fact for the first time occurred to
him, if at all, when his nature rose white-hot to
arms. He was, so to say, a Colonial Dame on both
sides, as members of both his father's and his mother's family fought in the American Revolution; and
members of his father's family in the French and
Indian wars.

Alfred Joyce Kilmer (as he was christened) was
born at New Brunswick, New Jersey, December 6,
1886, son of Annie Kilburn and Frederick Kilmer.
Though he seems always to have been, in familiar
address and allusion, called Joyce, the Alfred did
not disappear from his address and signature until
he began, as more or less of a professional writer,
to publish his work, when it went the way of the
Newton in Mr. Tarkington's name, and the Enoch
in Mr. Bennett's. Then "Joyce Kilmer" acquired a

fine humorous disdain for what he regarded as the
florid note in literary signatures of three words (or,
worse still to his mind, the A. Joyce kind of thing);
and he enjoyed handing down, with much relish of
the final and judicial character of his utterance, the
opinion that the proper sort of a trademark, so to
say, for success in letters was something short,
pointed, easy to say and to remember, such as Rud-
yard Kipling, Mark Twain, O. Henry, Joseph
Conrad, and so on through illustrations carried, at
length, to intentionally infuriating numbers.

As a small boy, Kilmer is described by those who
knew him then as the "funniest" small boy they
ever saw, by which is meant, apparently, that he was
an odd spectacle. And this, of course, is so altogether in line with literary tradition that it would
have been odd if he had not been an oddity in the
way of a spectacle. He wore queer clothes, it seems,
ordinary stockings with bicycle breeches, and that
sort of thing. He didn't altogether fit in somehow,
couldn't find himself, was somewhat of an outsider
among the juvenile clans; he was required to fight
other boys a good deal; he evidenced a pronounced
inability to comprehend anything at all of arith-
metic; and somewhere between eight and twelve (so
the report goes) he contracted a violent passion for

[20]

a lady, of about thirty-five, who was his teacher at school; a passion which endured for a considerable time, and became a hilarious legend among the youth about him of jocose humour.

It is told that at "Prep" school, when this goal seemed rather unlikely of his attainment, he made up his mind to stand at the head of his class; and with something like the later Kilmerian exercise of will he accomplished his purpose.

Kilmer attended Rutgers College from 1904 to 1906, and received his B.A. from Columbia in 1908. His University life seems to have been, in outward effect, fairly normal. There is no ready evidence that he "shone" particularly, and none that he failed to "shine." He was not deported by the authorities, and he was not unanimously hailed the idol of his classmates. He became a member of Delta Upsilon fraternity: and he was, of course, active in college journalism. Then as always he appears to have been zestful in living well, to have counted sufficient to the day the excellence thereof, and to have been too warm with life to be calculating in expenditures. He retained in the years that followed—and it seems to have been the college memory he retained most distinctly—a humorous recollection of his consuming his allowance on an abundance of rich viands during the first few days of each month, and being reduced to the necessity of living precariously on a meagre ration of crackers and sandwiches thereafter—until next income day.

Characteristic of the vehement manner in which he went after life, as a Sophomore Kilmer became engaged to Miss Aline Murray, of New Jersey, a step-daughter of Henry Mills Alden, editor of *Harper's Magazine*. Upon leaving Columbia he took up the business of making a living in the way of an elder American intellectual tradition, by teaching school in a (more or less) rural community. He returned to New Jersey and began his career as instructor of Latin at Morristown High School. So slight a lad he was, even several years after this time, that it is difficult to picture him in the disciplinary adventures of the classic figure of this calling. His problems at Morristown doubtless were dissimilar to those of his early, Hoosier, prototype. He married and became a householder. His son, Kenton, was born. In religion he had been bred an Episcopalian, and during this period in New Jersey (it is told) he acted as a lay reader in this church.

He soon concluded, apparently, that pedagogy was, so to say, no life for a boy. At the conclusion of a year's teaching he tore up the roots he had planted, and, together with the young lady he had married, and the son born to them, and with a few youthful poems in his pocket, he advanced upon the metropolis, even in the classic way, on the ancient quest of conscious talent.

The rapidity and brilliance of Joyce Kilmer's success has altogether obscured his very democratic beginnings. As his initial occupation in New York, he obtained, by a lucky chance, employment as editor of a journal for horsemen, though of horses he had no particular knowledge—to be exact, no such knowledge whatever. Here finding little to do, and discovering one day in a desk drawer a bulky manuscript, he decided—as he was editor—to edit it. This, apparently, he did with youthful energy. The little job he mentioned with some satisfaction to his employer, a fine portly sportsman with a crimson face and an irascible temper. The young editor explained that the manuscript evidently had been written by a man familiar with horses, but one apparently innocent of the art of literary composition. "Young man," bellowed his employer, "I would have you understand I have been through the best veterinary college in the world, and I have been a veterinary myself for over forty years." His wife, he added, was his amanuensis, and he guessed she knew something about writing. The editorship came to an abrupt termination.

Then followed a brief sojourn, at a salary of (I think) eight dollars a week, as retail salesman in the book store of Charles Scribner's Sons, a dignity which the young littérateur wore with humorous dignity for exactly two weeks. A distinct mental impression of him of this time presents him as decidedly like an Eton boy in general effect, and it seems that a large white collar and a small-size high hat should have gone with him to make the picture quite right. One who met him then felt at once a gracious, slightly courtly, young presence. He gave forth an aroma of excellent, gentlemanly manners. He frequently pronounced, as an indication that he had not heard you clearly, the word "Pardon?"— with a slight forward inclination of his head, which, altogether, was adorable. His smile, never far away, when it came was winning, charming. It broke like spring sunshine, it was so fresh and warm and clear. And there was noticeable then in his eyes a light, a quiet glow which marked him as a spirit not to be forgotten. So tenderly boyish was he in effect that his confreres among the book clerks accepted with difficulty the story that he was married.

[24]

MEMOIR

When it was told that he had a son they gasped their incredulity. And when one day this extraordinary elfin sprite remarked that at the time of his honeymoon he had had a beard they felt (I remember) that the world was without power to astonish them further.

As a retail salesman, however, this exceedingly interesting young man did not make a high mark. One's general impression of him "on the floor" is a picture of a happy student, standing, entranced, frequently with his back to the door (which theoretically he should have been watching for incoming customers), day after day engrossed in perusing a rare edition of "Madame Bovary." One sensational feat of business he did as a clerk perform. Misreading, in his newness to these hieroglyphics, the cypher in which in stores the prices of books are marked on the fly leaves of the volumes, he sold to a lady a hundred-and-fifty-dollar book for a dollar and a half. This transaction being what is termed a "charge sale," not a "cash sale," and amid some excitement the matter being immediately rectified, disaster for the amateur salesman was averted.

At Scribner's a close friendship was, almost at once, formed between the youthful poet and another then unpublished writer acting at that time in the same capacity of clerk—a friendship which was never diminished by the numerous shiftings of Kilmer's fields of activity, the multitudinous, diverse and ardent interests which he acquired in an ever-mounting measure, and the steady addition of numberless friends of all classes who eagerly yielded him their devotion. It was rather a friendship which was continually cemented by increasing and closer bonds. It was a part of Kilmer's spirit to make his first friend in his literary life a sharer as far as was possible in each new success of his own. One among many, innumerable, instances of this was his contriving, by his influence with the editor (at that time another intimate, Louis H. Wetmore), to work his friend into a position somewhat rivaling his own at the period (1912-1913) when he was the bright and shining star reviewer for the *New York Times Review of Books*. The regular Tuesday lunching together of these two friends when their offices were widely separated became, at least in their own fancy, an American literary institution. The two were united in all the symbols of affection between men. And at seasons of rejoicing and adversity the Kilmer house was to his friend as his own. It is to this one who among all of Joyce Kilmer's friends owes him the greatest debt of friendship has come

[26]

the supreme trust of writing, within the power of his
many and conscious limitations, this Memoir, and
editing these volumes.

Dropping the very small bird which he held in his
hand in the way of a secure salary, the spectacular
bookseller, somewhat to twist the figure, plunged
again into uncharted seas, and became a lexico-
grapher, as an editorial assistant in the work of preparing a new edition of the Standard Dictionary.
He blithely began his Johnsonian labours by defining ordinary words assigned to him, at a pay of five
cents for each word defined. This is a very different thing indeed from receiving a rate of five cents
a word for writing. It is a task at which you can
obtain an average of perhaps ten or twelve dollars
a week, though some weeks "stickers" will hold you
back. It soon became apparent, evidently, that it
was advisable to put this very capable pieceworker
on a salary; and he was rapidly promoted, with corresponding increases in remuneration (reaching an
amount of something like four times his initial earn-
ings), to more advanced phases of the work: research into dates of birth (involving correspondence
with living celebrities); research into the inception
of inventions (as, for example, the introduction of
the barrier into horse racing); together with the

defining of words of contemporary origin, in, for instance, the nomenclature of aviation. In this last mentioned department, it was his office to call upon authorities, such as the Wright brothers, and upon presentation of his credentials to receive precise information. He interviewed famous tobacco importers, and coffee merchants; compiled in the New York Public Library material about fans; unearthed for use as an illustration a picture of a strange bird; or was assigned to collect for this purpose designs of ancient mouldings.

If lexicography was Kilmer's venerable occupation, by political faith he was at the time, this very young, young man, a socialist. He subscribed for and frequently contributed to the *Call* newspaper. And the height of his effervescence was in addressing meetings of the proletariat. He was, it must be said, a burning "young radical." He frequented, to some extent, a club of that name. And with a joyous consciousness of being in the character of his surroundings he ate meals at the Rand School of Social Science. He rapidly acquired a wonderful string of queer acquaintances, in whose idiosyncrasies he took immense delight. Some, not of the persuasion, fancied that as an adherent of the socialist party he was merely enam-

[28]

oured of an intellectual idea. At any rate, whenever in conversation he spoke of socialism, as he
frequently did, his graceful, amiable young features assumed a very firm and earnest aspect.
Exactly the point of transition, if there was any
decided point, I cannot recall, but from the proletariat he passed to the literati. A "man of letters" became a great word with him. And he looked rather
proudly about as he said it, as a Scot might speak
of the doughty deeds of the Scotch. He was wont
to refer, too, to the "intellectual aristocracy." His
luncheon engagements were now mostly with this
order of humanity, and his anecdotes featured such
figures as Richard Le Gallienne and Bliss Carman
—men whose personalities delighted his heart beyond measure.

How absurdly juvenile he looked. But you would
have noted, as you observed him, that he had a very
fine head, something like that of Arthur Symons
(without the moustache), I thought; or, according
to Mr. Le Gallienne's sympathetic picture in *The
Bookman:* "Though the resemblance was perhaps
only a spiritual expression, his then thin, austere
young face, with those strangely strong and gentle
eyes (eyes that seemed to have an independent,
dominating existence), reminded me of Lionel

Johnson, for whom he had already a great admiration, and whose religion he was afterwards to em-
brace." Or, again, he seemed as if he might be a
comely youth out of ancient Greece. I think that
what I mean is that he was so unlike all other young
men anyone had ever seen walking about, so much
brighter and purer, or some indescribable thing,
that he did not seem altogether real. A feeling
which I think was shared by many, and which I
have never quite been able to make articulate, Mr.
Le Gallienne has most happily expressed with his
own easy charm; that is the "hint of destiny" in this
"very concentrated, intense young presence—masculine intense, not feminine:"

We have all met young people who give us that
—beautiful, brilliant, lovely natured, so superabundant in all their qualities (and particularly perhaps
in some quality of emanating light)—as to make
them suggest the supernatural, and touched, too,
with the finger of a moonlight that has written
"fated" upon their brows. Probably our feeling is
nothing more mysterious than our realisation that
temperaments so vital and intense must inevitably
tempt richer and swifter fates than those less wild
winged.

Above all, this young gentleman was the portrait
of a poet, even (in those days) of the type of liter-

[30]

ary sophistication which is (or was) called decadent! There was about him a perceptible aroma of
literary self-consciousness. He had begun to con-
tribute to magazines and newspapers the verses
which he soon gathered into a first volume, "A
Summer of Love" (an "author's book," as the trade
term has it), verses patently derivative in character
(as whose early verses are not?), showing the influences of various masters.

He had already become a bit of a celebrity, arriving at twenty-five in *Who's Who*. In conversation he spoke with striking fluency and precision,
and a rather amusing effect of authority; all of
which, together with a ready command, rather incongruous for his years, of very apt words little employed in speech, gave a general impression, I
fancy, of something of an infant prodigy. He
wrote in a letter of this time of the poems of Coventry Patmore:

I have come to regard them with intense admiration. Have you read them? Patmore seems to me
to be a greater poet than Francis Thompson. (Kilmer, had by the way, just given a lecture at Columbia University on Francis Thompson.) He has
not the rich vocabulary, the decorative erudition,
the Shelleyan enthusiasm, which distinguish the
"Sister Songs" and the "Hound of Heaven," but

[31]

he has a classical simplicity, a restraint and sincerity which make his poems satisfying. Some of his shorter poems, such as "Alexander and Lycon" and "The Toys," approach Landor in their Greek economy. Of course, the "Angel in the House," and many other of his poems, are marred by Tennysonian influences. But the "Unknown Eros" is a work of stupendous beauty. It is certainly supreme among modern religious poems. That part of it devoted to Eros and Psyche is remarkably daring and remarkably fine. Psyche symbolizes the soul, and Eros the love of God. Their amour is described with realistic minuteness, even with humorous flippancy, and yet the whole poem is alive with religious feeling.

The finding of Patmore, by the way, was what might be called a finger-post in Kilmer's life. The fortunate introduction was performed by, it is my impression, Kilmer's friend Thomas Walsh.

If in cold print to-day there is a slightly preposterous didactic quality in these remarks of this youthful character, it should be instantly noted as a tribute to the charm that was his that in the presence of so much handsomeness and grace, combined with so much flexibility of mind and agile humour, even this was an engaging thing.

There was to Kilmer nothing whatever dry-as-dust about the erudite business of lexicography; instead his impressionable nature found among his co-workers a rich, a colourful, an exciting school of humanity. He glowed continually with affectionate amusement at the motley band of literary adventurers, intellectual soldiers of fortune, who apparently were his colleagues. One, the most motley perhaps of all (the long cherished dream of whose ancient bachelor life it was one day to write a popular song), touched, for the first time, I think, the deepest spring of his song—his profound and wideranging humanity.

> Some people ask: "What cruel chance
> Made Martin's life so sad a story?"
> Martin? Why, he exhaled romance,
> And wore an overcoat of glory.

II

And then, lo! the aesthete became a churchman. After a couple of years or so of lexicographic employment, work on the dictionary was completed, and Kilmer entered what, with immense gusto, he described as "religious journalism." He became literary editor of *The Churchman.*

He had completed a very thorough course in uptown New York apartment house life (living, I

think, in rapid succession in some half dozen speci-
mens of "the great stone box cruelly displayed
severe against the pleasant arc of sky") ; and now
removing to the suburban village of Mahwah, New
Jersey, in the Ramapo foothills, he entered upon his
career as one of the world's most accomplished com-
muters. He used to say, with a spacious gesture of
the arm and a haughty inflation of the chest, that it
was no life at all, no life at all, for a man not to
swing around an orbit of at least sixty miles a day
between his office and his home. His home, even so!

I never have seen a vagabond who really liked to
    roam
All up and down the streets of the world and not to
    have a home.

What more exhilarating experience than the
owning of a home! And one paid one's installments
on the building loan with the fine pride of a man
exercising a noble prerogative. Yes, he often
walked to Suffern along the Erie track, and medi-
tated on "what a house should do, a house that has
sheltered life,"

That has put its loving wooden arms around a man
    and his wife,
A house that has echoed a baby's laugh and held up
    his stumbling feet.

As became a churchman, he began to hold forth to his companion on the train to and from the city on the fascinations of the Anglican poets. Either his enthusiasm for the subject resulted in a series of articles on the theme, or an assignment for such a series of articles resulted in his enthusiasm, I don't know which. The significant point is that it was just as like to have been either way about. "Passon Hawker"—Robert Stephen Hawker—Vicar of Morwenstow, a coast life-guard in a cassock—who can recite off hand the deeds of his piety and his valour? Well, on the Erie smoker he became one of the most romantic figures of story. Robert Herrick, in a manner of speaking, went home many a night on the Twelve-Forty-Five (Robert Herrick, that is, with his "Unbaptized Rhimes" left out), and Bishop Coxe returned on the Seven-Fifty-Six in the morning.

Kilmer had already done a few book reviews for *The Nation* and for the *New York Times;* but at *The Churchman* he acquired such a proficiency at this exercise that he was able, jocularly, to regard Arnold Bennett, as a literary journalist, as a "mere amateur." The real reward of "religious journalism," however, it soon developed, was the opportunity of writing a feature which the secular might

[35]

call an editorial, but the proper name of which this
editor pronounced, in the tone and with the manner
of one who was consciously engaged in something
grand, gloomy and peculiar, as a "meditation."

The real meditations of Joyce Kilmer, however,
were not "meditations" so called, and partook in no
wise of the nature of editorials. He had been, in the
main, a graceful troubadour who thrummed pleasant things to his lady-love, and had a bright eye to
his singing robes. He had thought it rather fine,
too, that refrain in imitation of Richepin:

> May booze be plenty, bulls be few,
> The poet is the beggars' king.

He had even been much taken, artistically, with the
thought of absinthe:

> O little green god in your crystal shrine,
> Your heavenly dream-shower shed!

It was when his business took him near to God,
when his exploring spirit, upon a peak in Darien,
beheld that:

> Poems are made by fools like me,
> But only God can make a tree,

that he began to be a poet. "Trees," which more
than all the rest he had written put together made

[36]

his reputation, appeared in *Poetry: A Magazine of Verse* in August, 1913.

At about this period it was that he was altogether born again. Then, doubtless in castigatory reaction against his own aesthetic and "decadent" wild oats, entered into his fibre that sovereign disdain for the intellectual flub-dub which later gave such a delightful note of "horse-sense" to all his humorous thought—the Johnsonian sting ("and don't you think you were an ass?") which found its earliest biting expression in the verses "To a Young Poet Who Killed Himself."

"I've been leading a rather active life, for several days," was with a gay salute of the hand, a frequent Kilmerian remark. In 1912 the direction of the *New York Times Review of Books* fell into the hands of a high-spirited young man, a Max-Beerbohmian character, with a decided taste for gaiety in reviews, Mr. Wetmore, who conducted that organ through what is known in New York journalistic tradition as its "meteoric period." Mr. Wetmore's wit perceived in Kilmer his happiest rocket. Not only given his head but egged on by his editor to strive for sublime heights of fantasy, this fairly unknown contributor shot in a series of reviews which for readability was, the applause now indicated, an altogether new thing in the book pages of an American newspaper. "This is a bad book, a very bad book, indeed," so ran the style. "It is bad because it makes this reviewer feel old and fat and bald." If, together with their humorous assumption of a jovial cocksureness of manner, the literary judgments expressed were, of necessity, snap-shot judgments, there was nothing snap-shot nor assumed about a certain quality in them which in general effect was the most striking of all, namely, the reflection in a very positive way of a radiantly clean and wholesome young nature, abounding in mental and spiritual health.

As one of the general prime movers in, and for a number of years Corresponding Secretary of The Poetry Society of America, Kilmer engaged on the side in activities which for many another would have been in themselves almost a whole job. A fervent Dickensonian, he was for a long period president and (one felt) the animating principle of the American Dickens Fellowship. He accumulated offices to such an extent that I am doubtful if anyone but himself knew exactly how many employments he had altogether, or at any one moment. He conducted the Poetry department of *The Literary Digest* for something like nine years, an obligation which he continued to fulfill even from Camp Mills, Long Island, to the time when he sailed for France. For a time he conducted a similar department in *Current Literature,* and also did a quarterly article on poetry for, I think, the *Review of Reviews.* Among his earlier essays in the lecture field was a paper on "The Drama as an Instrument of Sex Education," read before a regular meeting of the Society of Sanitary and Moral Prophylaxis held at the New York Academy of Medicine, in December, 1913. The society with the playful name, I recollect, got seriously interested in the matter of sex education as then expounded. Their views on the drama in this connection were enlarged by acquisition of the idea that though " 'The Great Love' is, in my opinion, one of the most skilfully constructed plays presented on the New York stage for many a year, I am quite serious in saying that as a factor in sex education, it is a thousand times inferior to 'Bertha the Beautiful Cloak Model.' "

As Kilmer was always decidedly what is termed a ready writer, what I should attempt to describe as a natural writer (a startling exception to the rule that easy writing makes hard reading), so he appeared to have the gift of speaking readily in public. On frequent occasions, at any rate in his early talks, he neglected altogether to prepare any outline beforehand, and even sometimes to choose a subject. Every now and then, I have known him repeatedly to say to his companion at dinner, without, however, any trace at all of nervousness: "Now, look here: Put your mind on this. Stop all that gossip. Tell me what I'm to talk about. I have to begin" (looking at his watch) "in twenty-five minutes."

He was particularly active in the affairs of the Authors' Club, and was a member of the Vagabonds, the Columbia University Club and the Alianza Puertorriguena. In 1913 he ceased, officially, to be a churchman. For a brief period he contemplated the prospect of a professorship, lecturing on English Literature at the University of the South, Sewanee, Tennessee. Then, to his great delight, he became a newspaper man—as he continually put it, with much relish in the part, "a hard newspaper man." He became a special writer for the *New York Times Sunday Magazine*. I am sure he saw himself in fancy as one of those weather-beaten characters bred in the old-time newspaper school of booze, profanity and hard knocks, his only text-book the police-court blotter and the moulder of his youth a particularly brutal night city-editor. He maintained, with humorous arrogance against

opposing argument, the thesis that every great
writer had got his "training" as a newspaper man.
He delighted to point, as illustrations of this, to
Dickens, to Thackeray, and to a lot more, who, in
any strict sense of the word, were not "newspaper
men" at all. Hard pressed, he even stood ready to
make some such hilariously sweeping assertion as
that George Eliot, Shakespeare, Tennyson and
Robert Browning were, properly perceived, "newspaper men."

At any rate, this hard newspaper man had to
begin with a comical equipment for his task: he
would never learn to typewrite and he knew nothing
of shorthand. Or rather, he was remarkably well
equipped, as one of the outstanding traits of his
character was the fearless zest with which, so to say,
he took the hurdles of life, and a peculiar faculty in
triumphing over such obstacles as his own limitations. He rapidly invented a curious system of
abbreviations and marks to remind him of points,
which served him as an interviewer as effectively as
any knowledge of stenography could have done.
He energetically entered upon his occupation as a
feature writer with the customary themes of the
"Sunday story." He interviewed, figuratively
speaking, the man who had discovered the missing

link, and he got from the latest inventor of perpetual motion all the arresting details of his machine. And a lively part of the early Sunday morning ritual at his home was the advance calculating with a tape measure of the week's income from space writing.

It was later that he created his own highly successful type of literary interview. An intelligent perception of the business, a perception which is not general, perhaps is required fully to appreciate the fact that in this department of newspaper work he was an exceedingly skillful journalist. The secret of his really brilliant success in this field lay in large part in his instinct for luring the distinguished subject of his interview into provocative statements, enabling him to employ such heads as: "Is O. Henry a Pernicious Literary Influence?" "Godlessness Mars Most Contemporary Poetry," "Americans Lack Loyalty To Their Writers," "Shackled Magazine Editors Harm Literature," "Declares Our Rich Authors Make Cheap Literature" and "Says American Literature Is Going To the Dogs."

At the time of the death of James Whitcomb Riley, Kilmer hurried to the Catskills for his interview with Bliss Carman. On his way back to the

[42]

city, by way of his home at Mahwah, he dashed with his usual impetuosity in front of the moving train he was seeking to board, was knocked down and hurled or dragged a considerable distance, and taken to the Good Samaritan Hospital at Suffern, New York, with three ribs fractured and other injuries; where, wiring immediately to New York for his secretary, he dictated an interview as engaging and as full of journalistic craft as any he ever wrote. He seemed much more intent on his Sunday story, it is reported by H. Christopher Watts, who was acting as his secretary at that time, than on his predicament.

I did not see Kilmer at this time myself, but I have an idea that, when he had relieved his mind of the anxiety concerning his article, he entered into the spirit of his experience with much relish. It isn't every day that one gets hit by a train, nor everybody that has three ribs broken. Exhilarating kind of thing, when you see it that way! I remember one time when I was practically in hospital myself he went to a good deal of trouble to come to see me. He seemed to admire my predicament very much, and, beaming upon me, remarked in high good humour that it must be an entertaining thing to be so completely at the mercy of circum-

[43]

stances over which you had no control. When shall
we look upon his like again!

III

I really doubt very much whether anybody ever
enjoyed food more than Kilmer. The slender
youth had become a decidedly stocky young man,
who ate mammoth meals with prodigious satisfaction. He delighted upon sitting down to breakfast
to maintain, with almost savage earnestness (such
was the amusing effect), that the most fitting dish
for that meal was steak. As a matter of fact, however, his habit was to miss his breakfast altogether
through haste to catch his train, except for a cup of
coffee and a piece of buttered toast which, when he
missed the 'bus, he ate, a mouthful every dozen or
so leaps, on his way down the hill (almost a mountain) to the station. Sundays, however, with the
whole day at home, he apparently regarded among
other things as a sort of barbecue. Looking over
the morning table it was his custom to inquire with
the air of a man making a fairly satisfactory beginning, what was scheduled for dinner.

Kilmer never ate any lunch, as the ordinary world
understands the word—about the first hour of the
afternoon he went (when his means had become

such that he could afford it) to a sort of Thanksgiving or Christmas dinner every day. How proceeding directly to his office he did any work afterward, was always considerable of a mystery to me. And lunching alone he doubtless regarded as a misanthropic perversion. His luncheons and his frequent dinners in town alone represented what many would regard as a rather arduous social life, which however arduous, however, never failed to include the weekly luncheon with his mother, Mrs. Kilburn-Kilmer. As an epilogue, so to say, to his meal it was his wont to have, speaking his order slowly so as to suck the full flavour of the idea, "a large black cigar."

One time being in the city with his family for a period after the birth of one of his children, he gave a series of Sunday morning breakfasts at a fashionable restaurant (it was a pleasant crotchet with him that he was "a fashionable young man"), entertainments which were distinguished by, first, the fact the guests so abundantly represented the world of journalism that they filled a good portion of the room, and, secondly, by the circumstance of their lingering at the board until mid-day diners began to arrive.

How a poet could *not* be a glorious eater, it was one of Kilmer's whims to say, he could not see; for

[45]

the poet was happier than other men by reason of his acuter senses, and as his eyes delighted in the beauty of the world, so should his palate thrill with pleasure in the taste of the earth's bounteous yield for the sustenance of men. The romance, too, of the things we eat he felt lustily.

> Rich spices from the Orient,
> And fruit that knew Italian skies.

He had another, and a decidedly quaint, notion of food. He firmly believed that hearty eating was an adequate physical compensation for loss of sleep. He was fond of declaring his faith in this fantastic idea by means of a story of some "ancient receptive child" (friend of his) who managed to bring up a family of seven (or so) children by ill-paid hack-work occupying most of the day and night—a noble success due entirely to noble meals.

* * * * * * *

> This man has home and child and wife
> And battle set for every day.
> This man has God and love and life;
> These stand, all else shall pass away.

And "this man's" days were long, long days: Kilmer's home, a place of boundless week-end hospitality and almost equally boundless domesticity

[46]

(guests being obliged to exercise much agility in clambering about toys with which the stairs were laden), was also year after year a place of almost unbelievable literary industry. The trying idiosyncrasies of the artistic temperament were about as discernible in Kilmer as kleptomania. He was, as you may say, social and domestic in his habits of writing to an amazing degree. Night after night he would radiantly walk up and down the floor singing a lullaby to one of his children whom he carried screaming in his arms while he dictated between vociferous sounds to his secretary or wife—his wife frequently driven by the drowsiness of two in the morning to take short naps with her head upon the typewriter while the literally tireless journalist filled and lighted his pipe.

This, however, was an atmosphere of cloistral seclusion compared with Kilmer's office at the *New York Times*. Here, where he regularly got through each week enough hard work to hold down three or four fairly capable young men, he maintained a sort of salon for a ludicrous variety of picturesque characters with nothing in particular to do and no place else to go, ranging from types of patrician leisure to stray dogs of the literary world visibly out of a job.

[47]

The latter class, indeed, apparently regarded him as a kind of a clearing house for employment. A singularly convincing commentary on the radiating humanity of this brilliant young man was one rather grotesque feature of his mail. In addition to a constant and copious stream of requests from persons but slightly known, or quite unknown to him, for advice as to how to succeed in letters, and for his personal imprimatur on their enclosed manuscripts, he was apparently constantly in receipt of innumerable epistolary stories of extraordinary distress, suffered (generally) by elderly characters defeated in the lists of literature. Though there was in Kilmer's robust nature a decided distaste, somewhat analogous to the innate aversion of the clean in spirit to moral obliquity, for what he termed "ineffectual people," there was too an amusing strain of paternal feeling toward most of those of all ages with whom he was in contact. And this feeling he did not neglect, whenever the occasion arose, to translate into practical effect.

He had a comical manner of terming his elders "young" So-and-So. I was six years his senior, which at the period of life at which we met represented a considerable difference in experience. And yet, throughout our association, in spiritual force he was the oak, I the clinging vine. And I know of cases where this was quite as much so when the other man was something like fifteen years the elder. One such instance, ludicrous in its contrast between the two men, was confessed to me with deep feeling just the other day.

"So-long" or "good-bye" was seldom Kilmer's parting word. It was rather a word he continually used which will be thought of as peculiarly his as long as his memory endures, the closing word of "Rouge Bouquet." The last time I saw him at his home, then at Larchmont Manor, New York, my companion (in marriage) and I upon leaving almost missed our car, which started a block or so from the Kilmer house. As the three of us dashed after it, Kilmer stopped this car by what seemed to me something like sheer force of his willing it to stop. Then, as he dropped away from the race, there came from him high and clear out of the night (and always shall I hear it ring) his benediction: "Farewell! Children." Yes, it is even so; as the spirit is measured and the frailties of the soul are numbered, how many who knew this wondrous boy were his "children"!

The wisdom of the maxim "A busy man is never too busy to do one thing more" was indisputable in the spectacle of Kilmer. Though this was not, so far as I recollect, a maxim he employed, he had one of his own something like it, which admirably summed up his practical philosophy. When confronted by some financial dilemma, he was fond of declaring: "The demand creates the supply. A sound economic principle." He seemed to crave serious responsibilities and insistent obligations as some men crave liquor; and he grew more rosy as these increased.

> Thank God for the mighty tide of fears
>   Against me always hurled!
> Thank God for the bitter and ceaseless strife,
>   And the sting of His chastening rod!

There was nothing incongruous to Kilmer about the incongruity expressed in a communication written in 1916 to the Reverend Edward F. Garesché, S. J.; a letter which began by saying, "I am sorry that your letter of October 11 has been so long unanswered, but this has been the busiest month of my life"; which then told of his looping the loop of the country in lecture engagements; proceeded to discuss a matter which had made a strong appeal to his heart, the founding of an Academy of Catholic Letters to be called the Marian Institute; and con-

[50]

cluded with the remark, "I will gladly take on the work of acting secretary until the members make their own selection."

IV

In 1913, Kilmer's daughter Rose, nine months of age, was stricken with infantile paralysis. It was then, upon his bringing his family to town to give his daughter the treatment of a specialist, when he came to my house to tell me of this, that I first distinctly realised that this young man was remarkable —in a manner far beyond mere talent. The idea which he kept firmly before his mind was that it had been declared there was no occasion to fear her death as a result of her affliction. During the course of his stay with me that day he said several times, "Well, there are lots of people worse off than I am." This idea, too, it was apparent, he felt he must hold before him. And then, with his amazing and unconquerable *flair* for life, he launched upon the theme that this was a "very interesting disease," and he elaborated the thought that an infirmity of the body frequently resulted in an increased vitality of the mind.

"I like to feel that I have always been a Cath-

olic," was a sentiment frequently expressed by Kilmer. It has repeatedly been declared by friends
very close to him that his minute knowledge of pious
customs and practices of which a life-long Catholic
might easily be ignorant was a constant surprise to
them, but that with respect to religion as particular-
ised in himself he kept silent, would never discuss
the steps that led to his conversion, and it was only
by chance they discovered he was a daily communi-
cant. It was late in 1913 that Kilmer astonished
the little world that then comprised his family, his
friends and acquaintances by entering, with his
wife, the Roman Catholic Church. One afternoon
not long after this occurrence he not so much invited as directed me over the telephone to meet him
that night for dinner at the Columbia Club. His
purpose soon became clear. This was the only
solemn hour I ever spent with Kilmer. I think it
well to record here what he deeply impressed upon
me: that it was this searing test of his spirit which
had come upon him in the affliction of his daughter
that fixed his religion.

Kilmer did not become a great patriot when his
country entered the world war. He was, of course,
the same in fibre then as before. Only then was
known to him and visible to others what was latent
[52]

in his heart. And in this sense it was, I think, that it was clear to him that he did not become, but had always been a Catholic, though he had not earlier realised it. He tried all things and held fast to that which he found good. He was inwardly driven to seek until his spirit found its home. That only the time of his conversion was, in a sense, accidental, and that the conversion itself was inevitable, must be evident in the fact that he was never really himself before he became, as we say, a convert. Then his fluid spirituality, his yearning sense of religion, was stabilized. What is the "secret," as we say, of all that has been told of his ability? His courage, his mental and physical energy, were, manifestly, unusual. But his character, in the faith that he embraced, found its tempered spring. His talent was a wingéd seed which in the rich soil which had mothered so much art found fructification.

It is not an unsupported assertion to say that he was in his time and place the laureate of the Catholic Church. His sentiments as to the function of a Catholic poet he has expressed very positively in his essays and lectures. He joyed in the new proof given by Helen Parry Eden "that piety and mirth may comfortably dwell together." "A convert to Catholicism," he wrote of Mr. Yeats on Lionel

Johnson, "is not a person who wanders about weeping over autumn winds and dead leaves, mumbling Latin and sniffing incense." Nor is it necessary to lay æsthetic hands on the church's treasures, "and decorate rhymes with rich ecclesiastical imagery and the fragrant names of the saints." But in Faith one may find "that purity and strength which are the guarantees of immortality."

And, once a Catholic, there never was any possibility of mistaking Kilmer's point of view: in all matters of religion, art, economics and politics, as well as in all matters of faith and morals, his point of view was obviously and unhesitatingly Catholic. Considerable as were his gifts and skill as a politician in the business of his career, the veriest zealot could not say that he did not do the most unpolitic things in the service of his faith. A very positive figure, he laboured tirelessly, alternating from one field to another, for the Catholic Church.

As a brilliant interpretative critic of Catholic writers, such as Crashaw, Patmore, Francis Thompson, Lionel Johnson and Belloc, he brought, I think I may venture to say, an altogether new touch into Catholic journalism in America, a striking and distinguished blend of "piety and mirth," which had the rare and highly effective quality of

[54]

being both engaging and highly illuminating even to, as Kilmer would amiably have said, the Pagan. Impetus, of course, was given to his style in this by his admiration for the brilliant school of English Catholic journalists, an impetus doubtless accelerated by the personal acquaintance with Belloc, the Chestertons and the Meynells he gained in a flying visit to England in 1914 to rescue his mother from war difficulties in London; when, during a few odd moments before his return, he established a lively connection with the Northcliffe papers and *T. P.'s Weekly.* Even so, Kilmer almost, or quite, alone transplanted this particular spark; and his note of witty common sense and spiritual sensibility was particularly Kilmerian, too.

One day about four years ago the village Post Office at Mahwah did a totally unprecedented and most extraordinary business in outgoing mail, and Kilmer was again multiplied manifold. The neat circulars which he had printed and with which he stuffed the mail box announced that the author of "Trees," a member of the staff of the *New York Times*, etc., etc., "offered the following lectures for the coming season." The result may best be epitomised in the parable of the gentleman who cast his bread upon the waters to have it come back to him in the form of sardine sandwiches. The rapid development of Kilmer's lecture business, which soon assumed the proportions of no mean career in itself, immensely extended his force as a quickening influence in the Catholic world. Before societies and educational institutions in many places, frequently travelling as far as Notre Dame, Indiana, and Prairie du Chien, Wisconsin, he flung his bright portraits of "seekers after that real but elusive thing called beauty, a thing which they found in their submission to her who is the mother of all learning, all culture, and all the arts, the Catholic Church."

V

As a literary lecturer and a reader of his own poems before secular audiences his success was no less abundant. In "the only combination of its kind since Bill Nye and James Whitcomb Riley," as the circular of the J. B. Pond Lyceum Bureau stated it, "the young American Poet" and the author of "Pigs is Pigs" contributed considerably to the lightening of the rigours of existence by an extended repetition of "a joint evening of readings from their works." Ellis Parker Butler, in a letter before me, writes of his partner on the programme:

MEMOIR

He was a most charming travelling companion and an ideal team-mate for the purpose we had in mind. I would not have thought of going "on tour" if I had not met Kilmer. My idea was never to "go on tour" but, after I had met Kilmer, to "go on tour with Kilmer." He was altogether lovable and loved.

It would be a decidedly false estimate of Kilmer which failed to note, even with some emphasis, that he was an excellent man of business. He "played the game," in the exceedingly difficult job of earning a thoroughly competent living at the literary profession, with a dexterity which, it was frequently apparent, was at once an inspiration and a despair to those who sought to rival him. The Kilmer cult which grew apace was considerably accelerated by a rich Kilmerian strategy. And he delivered to the little world of intensely intense literary societies and blue-nosed salons which hung upon his lips the pure milk of the word with a strongly humorous consciousness of the feat as a part of the immense sport of living.

Kilmer's "act" as it was observed from behind the scenes is excellently presented by an associate in the office of the *New York Times*. This writer says in the *Philadelphia Press:*

MEMOIR

Our editor analysed him into three distinct manners: Kilmer, the literary man; Kilmer, the lecturer; and Kilmer, himself. His first appearance in the office would give you the cue to him for the day. If he came in grinning with his pipe drawing well, we would know that nothing was to be feared; he was himself. When he got his "literary" manner on, the symptom was a tapping of his eyeglass, with his right hand on the fingers of his left. When he appeared in his cutaway coat and a particularly pastoral necktie, we knew that on that day the elderly ladies of This Literary Club or the young ladies of That Academy were to be treated to a discourse on certain aspects of Victorian verse.

One day he came in, obviously decked out for a lecture. Without his having said a word about it, the assistant Sunday editor spoke up: "Let's cut out work this afternoon and hear Kilmer lecture." A look of horror overspread his face. "For heaven's sake, don't," he said. "I couldn't go through with it." I don't believe any of us ever did hear him.

A thing which I found very singular was that, in manner Kilmer was apt, in the two or three later years of his life, to give strangers on their first meeting the impression of being somewhat too dignified for so young a man, of being, as his office associate John Bunker in an admirable, even a remarkable, portrait of him at this period published in *America*, says, "in fact just a trifle pompous." Mr. Bunker continues: "This was due partly to his physical appearance, and also, insofar as it had any basis in reality, to that protective instinct which quickly teaches a sensitive and imaginative spirit to cast a veil between itself and the outer world."

I myself think this effect had its origin in the same perverse instinct which causes you, immediately after talking with a deaf person, to speak very loud to your next auditor whom you very well know can hear perfectly; that is, it was the result of being keyed up to appearing on an elevated platform before a curious throng. He one time astonished me by the declaration that it was only by, quite early in his life, drastically schooling himself to the task, one then exceedingly trying and hateful to him, that he became able to rise and "speak" at all. The most entertaining recollection, by the way, that I have of the Kilmerian pontifical manner is of a time when he generously invited me to have my shoes polished with him, thrust his hand deep into his pocket to pay the boy, paused, and with a very large gesture directed him to call in again later in the day.

There is first-rate perspicacity in the remark of one of Kilmer's friends, Laurence J. Gomme, that at one score and ten he was, in the amount that he had lived, about seventy years old. Something of the force and sharpness of Mr. Bunker's evocation of the man as he was at last resides, I think, in the circumstance that here is no blending in the mind of the flower and the bud. He says: "When I first met Kilmer he had just passed his thirtieth year, but he gave me the impression of being somewhat older. I afterwards spoke of this to him, and it was his theory that newspaper work had served to age him. The truth was that it was due not merely to his newspaper work, but generally to the incessant and intense mental activity, the extraordinary and flaming energy, whereby he crowded into ten years the experiences of several ordinary lifetimes." And this touch of the slight Bunker portrait is, I feel, essential to any fuller picture:

As to his physical aspect, he was stockily built and about medium height, and his habit of body was what I should call plump, though later, under the stress of military drill, he changed somewhat in this last respect. I noted at once that he had a remarkable head—well rounded, with broad and high forehead and a very pronounced bulge at the back, covered thickly with dark, reddish-brown hair. But his eyes were his most remarkable feature. They were of the unusual colour of red, and they had a most peculiar quality which I can only inadequately suggest by saying that they literally glowed. It actually seemed as if there were a fire behind them, not a leaping and blazing fire, but a steady and unquenchable flame which appeared to suffuse the whole eyeball with a brooding light. This characteristic was so striking that I cannot help dilating on it. And I observed later on that this glow, this brooding and somewhat sombre light, never left his eyes even in his most weary or most care-free moments, so that they gave the impression of what I believe was the fact—the impression of a brain behind them which was working intensely and perhaps even feverishly every hour of the waking day.

The better poet Kilmer became, as his friend Richardson Wright says in his admirable "Appreciation" in *The Bellman,* the less like a poet he acted. And after he grew up, he would about as soon have æstheticised, off the platform, as he would have forged a check. Whenever he did refer to poetry as related to himself he, as the slang term has it, took it smiling. One of Kilmer's most pronounced pet aversions was the phrase, utterly mawkish to him, about "prostituting" one's talent. He one time explained to me, with considerable apparent pride, that he used every idea three times: in a poem, in an article, and in a lecture.

MEMOIR

Charles Willis Thompson, an editorial writer of the *New York Times,* and to whom belongs the credit of first taking, as editor of the *Sunday Magazine* and *Book Review,* Kilmer's "stuff" in any amount, inspired, so to say, the poem "Delicatessen," in this way. Mr. Thompson happened to remark to Kilmer that of course there were a lot of things which couldn't be treated in poetry. Kilmer declared he would like to know what they were. Mr. Thompson cast about in his mind for the most ridiculous theme for a poem he could think of, and finally proclaimed that no one could possibly write a poem about such a thing as a delicatessen shop. "I'll write a poem about a delicatessen shop," Kilmer promptly replied. "It will be a long poem. I'll sell it to a high-brow magazine. It will be much admired. And it will be a good poem." He insisted on betting on this the sum of several dollars.

The origin of "The Twelve-Forty-Five" I do not exactly know. But I remember shortly before that poem was written, sitting disgusted and miserable with Kilmer in that horrible "Jersey City shed" waiting for the midnight train. Taking out of his mouth that villainously large, fifty-cent pipe (mentioned in all genuine appreciations) Kilmer, with a fervour almost violent, suddenly exclaimed: "I

[62]

certainly do like railroad stations! They are fine
places!" The very famous poem "The White
Ships and The Red" (a poem so wonderfully effective that it was at once reprinted all over the country and in Europe) was a newspaper assignment.
He rather liked the poem when he saw it in the
paper; though, with his feet cocked up on his desk,
he spoke apologetically of what he felt to be the failure of the latter stanzas to link up perfectly with the
first, explaining that a luncheon appointment, at
which he chatted for an hour or two, had split the
writing of it into two sittings. That the author of
this "Lusitania" poem thoroughly felt and meant
what he said, is, I fancy, sufficiently proven by the
event to permit of this being told.

The point is, that Kilmer was a poet, an artist of
a high order, a perfectly conscious master of what
he was doing. The febrile gush of emotion he
loathed. He knew finely that:

It is stern work, it is perilous work, to thrust your
    hand in the sun
  And pull out a spark of immortal flame to warm
    the hearts of men.

There was nothing accidental about the effect of his
own verse, any more than there was "luck" in his

[63]

worldly success. He achieved the one as he did the other by a masculine heart and mind. And while all things were necessary and joyous, it was impossible not to feel that, after all, throughout his day "the rhymer's honest trade" was his primary concern.

He was sufficiently grounded in literature to feel, as Mr. Le Gallienne says, no "weariness with those literary methods which had sufficed for Chaucer and Shakespeare and Milton, or Catullus or Bion, or François Villon—content, with reverent ambition, to tread that immortal path."

In his religious mysticism a trace, and more than a trace, has been found of Crashaw, of Vaughan, of Herbert, and of Belloc and Chesterton. And there is no difficulty at all about finding in Kilmer hints of Patmore, and there may be easily recognised something of the accents of A. E. Housman and of Edwin Arlington Robinson. He did, indeed, to put it in a racy phrase, have the drop on those who do not know that all art that endures must have its roots in a constant interrogation of the "unimpeachable testimony" of the ages. His song was as old as the hills, and as fresh as the morning. Precisely in this, in fact, is his remarkableness, his originality, as a contemporary poet; and in this will be, I think,

[64]

his abiding quality. "Simple and direct, yet not without subtle magic," wrote Father James J. Daly, S.J., in a review of "Trees and Other Poems," printed in *America,* his verse "seems artlessly naïve, yet it possesses deep undercurrents of masculine and forceful thought; it is ethical in its seriousness, and yet as playful and light-hearted as sunlight and shadows under summer oaks." And this admirable summing up of Kilmer's talent leaves little more in the way of direct criticism to be said.

Mr. Le Gallienne with felicitous tact of phrase has touched upon this, that "no young poet of our time has so reverently, on so many pages, in so many different ways, so playfully at times, as in that masterpiece of playful reverence, 'A Blue Valentine,' woven through the texture of his song the love of his lady—that lady 'Aline,' whose name will be gently twined about his as long as the printed word endures." A misquotation in the *Ladies' Home Journal* led to an interesting tribute to the author of "Trees." Many readers of the *Journal* were somewhat startled to find the editor attributing to John Masefield the lines:

A tree that looks at God all day
And lifts her leafy arms to pray.

MEMOIR

The following issue of the magazine contained this correction and acknowledgment by Mr. Bok:

I am free to confess that I did not know the correct author. I had been reading John Masefield that morning and unconsciously wrote his name as the author of these lines. A number of friends have pointed to the error and supplied the knowledge. The author is Joyce Kilmer, and to him I owe, and here express, my sense of deep apology. The exquisite lines were worthy of John Masefield, but that does not make them less worthy of their rightful author, as all will agree who read his beautiful work in his book "Trees and Other Poems."

As one, somewhat effusive commentator has remarked, "Trees" just could not be confined within the covers of a book. At once reprinted in newspapers throughout the United States (and still being so reprinted) it was crowned in that warmest of all ways in which a work of literature can be honoured, by being cut out by the world and pasted in its hat. In one version it reads, in part, in this way:

Cuando contemplo un arbol pienso: nunca vere un poema tan bello y tan intenso.
Un arbol silencioso que con ansia se aferra a la dulce y jugosa entrans de la tierra.

[66]

MEMOIR

Un arbol que mirando los cielos se extansia y en
oracion levanta los brazos noche y dia.

Many of Kilmer's poems have been translated into
Spanish by Salomon de la Selva, Enriquez Urenia
and others, and have appeared in a number of prominent South American papers.

In a letter from France to Edward W. Cook,
who in quest of material for a book on contemporary poets had written Kilmer asking several questions, Kilmer commented, among other things, on
his "earlier efforts in poetry" (as the questionnaire
apparently had put it), in a manner which is evidence again of how perfectly well he knew what he
was about. "If what I nowadays write is considered poetry," he announced, "then I became a poet
in November, 1913." Admirable for hard-headed-
ness, directness and precision, it is a statement
which leaves the critic no point upon which to take
issue. His early poems "were only the exercises of
an amateur, imitations, useful only as technical
training." The peculiar thing about these highly
skilful experiments in various forms of craftsman-
ship is that they were so very much better as poems
than the derivative efforts usually written at this
period of apprenticeship, "so free," as Mr. Le Gal-

lienne notes, "from those artistic immaturities which have made many old great poets angrily denounce unlicensed reprinters of their 'first editions.' " And in this fact they have a decided, and a perfectly legitimate, interest for the observer of the development of his talent—though Kilmer declared "they were worthless, that is, all of them which preceded a poem called 'Pennies,' which you will find in my book 'Trees and Other Poems.' " He added, "I want all of my poems written before that to be forgotten."

He was writing, one remembers, to a gentleman with whom he was so slightly acquainted that he addressed him as "Dear Mr. Cook," with the measure of whose sympathy and critical acumen, it is to be inferred, he was not conversant, and who presumably was about to estimate (with what perspective he could not perceive) his earliest productions. It were better to head off any uncertainty in the matter. Also, we all know, one's hot impatience with one's strivings of yesterday is mellowed by time into an amiable and appreciative tolerance of one's earnest efforts of twenty years ago. It is difficult to think that Kilmer at fifty would have had an unjust scorn of those charming exercises on the poetic scales he wrote at twenty-one.

[68]

MEMOIR

Anyhow, no man can, by decree or otherwise, obliterate his past; both the good and the bad that he has done continue to pursue him. Ten times thrice happy is he, rarest of men, who, like Kilmer, never penned a line or said a word or did a deed that can arise to bring confusion to those that love him. The world does not willingly let die those verses on which glistens the dew of his tender youth. They are brought forth for praise by no mean critics in tribute to his memory. And in conformity with the wishes of those most jealous of his good name as a poet a representative selection of his early poems is reprinted in these volumes.

He that lives by the pen shall perish by the pen, saith the wisdom of James Huneker. For a sapling poet, within a few short years and by the hard business of words, to attain to a secretary and a butler and a family of, at length, four children, is a modern Arabian Nights Tale. Equally impossible is it, seemingly, to accomplish another thing, which is a remarkable part of Kilmer's distinction. From first to last, from the verses contributed to *Moods* in 1909 to the last poem he wrote, "The Peacemaker," printed in the *Saturday Evening Post* in October, 1918, Kilmer was a poet's poet. "A pretty good poet," said such a poet (shaking his head at his conviction of the truth of this) as Bliss Carman. His poems were repeatedly adjudged high places among the best poems read before the Poetry Society. Among competitive honours, under the name of "John Langdon" he won easily enough with his poem, "The Annunciation," first prize in the Marian Poetry contest conducted by *The Queen's Work,* in July, 1917, an award competed for by a great number of poets, including many in other countries. He was a poet's poet who declared (with considerable vehemence, I remember) that he certainly wished he had written "Casey At The Bat." He one time said in praise of a book of essays that it was "that kind of glorified reporting which is poetry." As a singer of the simpler annals of humanity his place will draw closer and closer, I think, to that of the most widely loved poet of our own era. Only the name of James Whitcomb Riley expresses in greater measure the rich gift of speaking with authentic song to the simplest hearts. A man who believes that churches are devices of the devil and literature a syrup for crack-brained females can enjoy, with profit to his soul, "The House With Nobody In it," "Dave Lilly" and "The Servant Girl and the Grocer's Boy" equally with "The Old Swimmin'-Hole" and "Little Orphant Annie."

[70]

MEMOIR

If Colonel Roosevelt had never done anything
other than what he has done in writing, he would
undoubtedly be highly esteemed as an American
man of letters. And people have made very cred-
itable reputations as humourists who never wrote
anything like as humorous essays as those of Joyce
Kilmer. They fairly reek with the joy of life.
They explode with intellectual robustness. They
are fragrant in fancy, richly erudite in substance,
touch-and-go in manner, poetic in feeling, rocking
with mirth, and display an extraordinary *flair* for
style. If it should seem that I am not here meas-
uring my words I suggest a reference to a piece of
documentary evidence called "The Gentle Art of
Christmas Giving," a "Sunday story" in the *New
York Times,* here reprinted. Writing at top-notch
speed, never looking again at what he had written,
intentionally producing a readily marketable commodity, from which profit must be realised quickly,
Kilmer was an exceedingly rare bird in America;
that is, a belletristic journalist. There is always the
touch to his work of a man of letters. Decidedly
Bellocian, Chestertonian, certainly his humorous
essays are. But that it was a good deal more an
affinity of mind with, than an imitation of, those
splendidly humorous English philosophers is borne

out by this: Joyce Kilmer did not talk poetry, but he did talk exactly like his essays, which admirably present the brave humorous wisdom of the man as his intimate friends knew him.

Official critical authority did not dampen his verve. As a contributing editor of "Warner's Library of the World's Best Literature," he supplied the articles on Madison Cawein, John Masefield, William Vaughn Moody and Francis Thompson. He contributed prefaces to various volumes of standard authors. Excellent examples of this department of his activity are his Introduction to Thomas Hardy's "The Mayor of Casterbridge" in the Modern Library, his introduction to the American edition of the "Verses" of Hilaire Belloc, and the introduction to the volume "Dreams and Images," his anthology of Catholic poets. The Introduction to this Anthology is dated 165th Regiment, Camp Mills, Mineola, N. Y., August, 1917, just a year before Sergeant Kilmer's death in battle. Doubtless few know that at one time Kilmer had drawn a contract to write a "Life" of Father Tabb. Because of peculiar complications in the situation this enterprise, most unfortunately, fell through. In 1916 Kilmer was called to the faculty of the School of Journalism of New York University, in

[72]

succession to Arthur Guiterman, to lecture on
"Magazine and Newspaper Verse." The object of
the course, which was open to outsiders as well as
to those enrolled in the School of Journalism, was
to familiarise the students with the practical side of
writing verse for publication.

VI

It seems rather a misnomer, and something of
an absurdity, to say that Kilmer was ever neutral
in anything. But in the political sense he was a
neutral, and, if it may be put that way, neutral to
a pronounced degree, preceding the entrance of the
United States into the war. His keen feeling for
the sturdy virtues and robust customs of Old England, Merrie England, was of course, patent. His
delight in London, and the English countryside,
which he knew from a child, was manifest. The
pillars of his fairly large literature were, of course,
English. His profound sense of integrity was violently jolted by the violation of Belgium. As the
war went on, however, he developed an attitude
which was quite capable of being interpreted as
Pro-German, by anyone interested in so interpreting it. The explanation of this attitude is simple
enough. Instinctively a combative character intel-

lectually, his humorous essays, which expressed him
so intimately, almost without exception found their
spring in his running counter to some current idea.
As he one time remarked, he was "bored by feminism, futurism, free love;" and, too, he was invari-
ably for the under dog. It may seem rather grotesque to present Germany by implication as an
under dog in the early years of the war; the point is,
the force of the argument was so overwhelmingly
against Germany that Kilmer reacted to this in a
characteristic fashion, stood boldly against the current, and was, in fact, a neutral—until the sinking
of the Lusitania. All reports agree, including even
reports from sources of strong anti-English feeling
where Kilmer's inclination to see what could be said
for Germany was coveted, that from this point on
his manner was altogether hostile to Germany.
Outside of his Lusitania poem he did not, so far as
I know, denounce the deed; but the unanimity and
the precision with which the change in him is fixed
by all who observed him is striking.

Kilmer's successive literary passions were a curi.
ous medley. He seemed to have been born with a
great love for Scott, and he held stoutly to Sir
Walter throughout the years. In his burly days he
found a humorous sport in defending, with jovial

[74]

emphasis, the old-fashioned chivalrous romance against the scientific modern novel. In his æsthetic period he had a touch, hardly more, of Oscar Wilde, though early in his literary career he experienced a rather severe case of Swinburneitus. Some time shortly after this he was very much intrigued by the Celtic revival. Shaemas O'Sheel, a friend dating back to Columbia days, bears testimony that an early boast of Kilmer's was that an ancestor of his had been hanged for taking a rebel's part in 'ninety-eight. And though as we know, Kilmer's immediate ancestry was not Irish, a Gaelic enthusiast who has made a specialty of the Irish language, suggests in his ardour, that the name Kilmer is a derivation of Mac Gilla Mor. At any rate, an affection for Ireland—her literature, her lore, her traditions, and her people—was indeed natural with him.

In his Yeats period Kilmer had about chosen "Nine Bean Rows" as the name of his house then in the course of construction, though it was not altogether "of clay and wattles made." The thing which deterred him from this decision was that persons unacquainted with the poem "Innisfree," to whom he spoke of the matter, conceived his address as Number Nine Beanrose Avenue. What a funny street, they said, that is. Literary merely, of course, that; and though a part of the whole, remote from later, deeper and graver things. Something inherently Irish in Kilmer undoubtedly was felt by many, Irish themselves and very much so, who, in some cases, are "quite certain" that the fact of their being Irish was the reason why he regarded them and their work as writers with friendship. He did, indeed, like all manner of Irish. He liked the Irish fairies, he liked Lady Gregory, he liked most decidedly the poor Irish people who went to the Catholic church, and (as he later showed), of all soldiers, Irish soldiers he liked best.

> Romantic Ireland is not old;
> For years untold her youth will shine,
> Her heart is fed on Heavenly bread,
> The blood of martyrs is her wine.

Everything chivalrous and sacrificial appealing to his deepest instincts, he felt noble "delight in hopes that were vain." It is not at all improbable that had he been an Irishman born and resident in Ireland he would have been among the martyrs of Easter Week. In certain qualities of his soul a kinship with these spirits may readily be traced. Some of them, I have been told, he knew personally; and his reverence for Plunkett he has written.

[76]

MEMOIR

There is no rope can strangle song,
    And not for long death takes his toll;
No prison bars can dim the stars,
    Nor quicklime eat the living soul.

And all that Kilmer wrote, every line of it, he wrote in two ways; he wrote it in words, and he wrote it in his acts. When the idea of the Poets' Meeting to express the sympathy of American poets with the three Irish martyred poets of Easter Week, Pearse, MacDonough and Plunkett, first occurred to Eleanor Rogers Cox, she asked Kilmer's advice about it over the telephone. And he said, "Go ahead, I'll back you up," with the result that the meeting, a success, took place in Central Park, with Edwin Markham presiding, Kilmer, Margaret Widdemer, Miss Cox, Louis Untermeyer, and many other representative poets taking part.

When you say of the making of ballads and songs
    that it is a woman's work,
You forget all the fighting poets that have been in
    every land.
There was Byron, who left all his lady-loves, to
    fight against the Turk,
And David, the singing king of the Jews, who was
    born with a sword in his hand.

[77]

MEMOIR

It was yesterday that Rupert Brooke went out to
    the Wars and died,
And Sir Philip Sidney's lyric voice was as sweet as
    his arm was strong;
And Sir Walter Raleigh met the axe as a lover
    meets his bride,
Because he carried in his soul the courage of his
    song.

Indeed, in the logical scheme of things (or, at any
rate, in Joyce Kilmer's scheme of things) the poet
is a soldier, an idealist with the courage of his song;
and, in a manner of speaking, all soldiers are poets,
whether or not they ever pen a line, for they give
supreme expression to the conviction of their soul.
And then, as Christopher Morley has finely written
in his tribute to Kilmer, "the poet must go where
the greatest songs are singing." To anyone who
knew Kilmer it would have been perfectly dum-
founding if, when war was declared between his
country and Germany, he had *not* done exactly as
he did. It is inconceivable—to picture him moving
about here, from restaurant to office, in this hour.
Flatly, the thing can't be done. With him, when
he joined the army, it was only one fight more, the
best, and as it proved, the last.

He hated many things, but I believe that of all

things he hated most a pacifist—a pacifist in anything. He was a fighter. He fought for his home,
stone by stone; he fought for his renown. His conception of the church was the Church Militant. His
thoughts dwelt continually on warrior-saints. He
believed in the nobility of war and the warrior's calling, so long as the cause was holy, or believed to be
holy. As he saw it, there was no question as to his
duty. This I know, you might as well have asked
Niagara Falls why it pours over its ledge, as have
discussed with Kilmer the matter of his going to
war. That was, in its way, just such another force
of nature. As to what might happen to him, it is
hardly necessary to remark that his faith told him
that that would be all right, too. John Bunker was
among the last to bid him farewell. There is the
Kilmerian splendour in what he wrote:

You didn't pose, self-conscious of your lot,
  Or speak of what might be or might have been;
You always thought heroics simply rot,
  And so you merely wore your old-time grin.

Kilmer had first joined the Officers' Reserve
Training corps. He soon resigned from this. In
less than three weeks after the United States entered the war he enlisted as a private in the Seventh

Regiment, National Guard, New York. His own statement was: "I haven't time for Plattsburg: had too much work to finish, but I had to get in." The Regiment was mustered into the Federal Service on July 15, 1917; and Kilmer expected to go to training camp somewhere in the South for a couple of months, then to be sent to "France, or Russia, or Cuba, or Mexico or somewhere else." He had a great distaste for going to Russia, because he disliked cold climates. He one time expressed a decided aversion to a book commonly held to be quite good. When asked what was the matter with it, he denounced it as being about "one of those cold countries." It would not, of course, have been Kilmer had he not found elation in the distinguished and picturesque character of the crack regiment to which he belonged. "We are the oldest outfit in the Guard—Lafayette reviewed us in 1824 and Joffre two weeks ago." If you had not seen the dress uniform of "the Seventh" you heard all about it at lunch. And "hard newspaper man" as he was, he became even "harder" now. "Can't hurt my feelings," he wrote requesting a friend to be quite frank with him. "Hard military character, seriously considering acquisition of habit of chewing tobacco."

Shortly before the Seventh left New York for

Spartanburg, South Carolina, Kilmer was transferred, at his own request, to the 165th Infantry,
U. S. A., formerly the famous old "Fighting Sixty-
ninth," New York, a unit of the Rainbow Division,
assembled at Camp Mills, Mineola, Long Island.
He was most particular to impress upon his friends
the point that he had been transferred at his own
volition. I do not know that he ever said so, in so
many words, but I gathered from him the impression that a considerable part of his motive in having
himself transferred was occasioned by his belief that
the 165th would go sooner than the Seventh to the
battlefield. Then, too, as we know, he was "half
Irish"; and an Irish-American regiment doubtless
was a powerful magnet to him. In the 165th the
people he liked best of all were "the wild Irish boys
who left Ireland a few years ago, some of them to
escape threatened conscription, and travelled about
the country in gangs, generally working on the railroads. They have delightful songs that have never
been written down, but sung in vagabonds' camps
and country jails. I have got some of the songs
down and hope to get more—'The Boston Burglar'
—'Sitting in My Cell All Alone'—they are a fine,
a veritable Irish-American folk-lore."

Kilmer at this time was the father of four children, named respectively Kenton Sinclair, Rose, Deborah Clanton and Michael Barry. One day he appeared in my office on an errand of business relating to the handling of his literary property. He was, in outward effect, perfectly composed, an admirable picture of a young soldier. It was then, in what followed, that he displayed the most extraordinary, the most amazing, measure of spiritual stature that I ever observed in any man or ever read of in any human book. Settled, with his customary air, in my chair, he demanded some pipe tobacco. I had none. And for this he heartily damned me out. Then he said: "Bob, my affairs are somewhat in disarray." Thinking that perhaps he wanted to borrow two dollars, or something like that, I asked: "What's the matter, Joyce?" "Well," he answered, quite in his ordinary way, "several days ago Rose died; yesterday my son, Christopher, was born; Kenton is with my wife at her mother's; my family is, in fact, very much scattered; I'm expecting to go to France within a few days—and I have many other difficulties." That was all he said as to this. He then talked excellent business. I went to the elevator with him. We shook hands more quietly than usual; he said, "Good-bye, Bob;" and the door of the car closed upon him, standing erect in his mil-

[82]

itary overcoat, looking somewhat serious. That was all.

From Company H. Kilmer was transferred, within a short time, to Headquarters Company, and exchanged his eight hours a day of violent physical exercise ("most deadening to the brain, a useful anodyne for one, coming as it did after my grief," he wrote in an intimate letter) for exacting but "interesting" statistical work. Though called Senior Regimental Statistician he continued to rank as a private. His work was under the direction of the Regimental Chaplain, Father Francis Patrick Duffy. He was thankful, he wrote from Mineola in a letter at this time, that he was not with the Seventh at Spartanburg, as from Mineola he could telephone to his wife every night, and he said: 'I'll be an accomplished cuss when I get back from the wars—I'll know how to typewrite and to serve Mass and to sing the 'Boston Burglar.' "

VII

It was "the pleasantest war he had ever attended," so he wrote back from France. "Nice war, nice people, nice country, nice everything," he said on the back of a postcard. To the Reverend James

[83]

MEMOIR

J. Daly he wrote, "When I next visit Campion,
I'll teach you (in addition to 'The Boston Burglar')
an admirable song called 'Down in the Heart of
the Gas-House District.' I sing it beautifully."
And "as a common soldier, I have the privilege of
intimacy with the French peasants—and I find
them edifyingly good Catholics." But his pleasures in war he has told, as none but the author of
"Trees" and "Main Street" could tell them, in his
letters. What he never told must be read between
the lines. When the war was over, he said, he never
wanted again to go far away from Browne's Chop
House and Shanley's Bar. Though it is firmly held
in the background, there is in all that he wrote from
France, it seems to me, a reflection that his life was,
so to say, somewhat in disarray. And clearly
enough, though proudly, too, in the few poems
that he sent back he spoke his body's pain:

Upon his will he binds a radiant chain,
    For Freedom's sake he is no longer free.
    It is his task, the slave of liberty,
With his own blood to wipe away a stain.
That pain may cease, he yields his flesh to pain,
    To banish war, he must a warrior be;
    He dwells in Night, eternal Dawn to see,
And gladly dies, abundant life to gain.

[84]

MEMOIR

And:

My shoulders ache beneath my pack
(Lie easier, Cross, upon His back).

I march with feet that burn and smart
(Tread, Holy feet, upon my heart).

Men shout at me who may not speak
(They scourged Thy back and smote Thy cheek).

I may not lift a hand to clear
My eyes of salty drops that sear.

(Then shall my fickle soul forget
Thy Agony of Bloody Sweat?)

My rifle hand is stiff and numb
(From Thy pierced palm red rivers come).

And in the closing lines of this poem certainly is
given, as fully as anything can be told in this world,
the answer to the question, How did the war most
affect Joyce Kilmer?—

> Lord, Thou didst suffer more for me
> Than all the hosts of land and sea.
>
> So let me render back again
> This millionth of Thy gift. Amen.

MEMOIR

Though he said, "I have very little chance to read contemporary poetry out here," he did read, as he says, "what do you suppose? The 'Oxford Book of English Verse.'" And he hoped that contemporary poetry was

reflecting the virtues which are blossoming on the blood-soaked soil of this land—courage, and self-abnegation, and love, and faith—this last not faith in some abstract goodness, but faith which God Himself founded and still rules. France has turned to her ancient faith with more passionate devotion than she has shown for centuries. I believe that America is learning the same lesson from war, and is cleansing herself of cynicism and pessimism and materialism and the lust for novelty which has hampered our national development. I hope that our poets already see this tendency and rejoice in it—if they do not they are unworthy of their craft.

"Just what effect the war would have had on Kilmer had he been spared is of course an entirely elusive topic," has said one very able and on the whole most valuable commentator, speaking from the testimony then in hand, and voicing, I fancy, an idea still rather general. It is not now, I think, an elusive topic at all, but a matter as plain as a pikestaff. And the matter is, by the way, the second of

[86]

the two most indispensable pages in Kilmer's story.
It is a page in which his character underwent another metamorphosis as consequential in its effect
on his talent even, if that could be possible, as his
conversion to the Catholic faith.

Kilmer left the United States a professional
writer from his twenty-third year, and one of the
most accomplished, prolific and industrious journalists of his day. Writing with him had become a
habit almost as natural as speech. It was his inten-
tion when he left New York to write a war book.
He discussed this project with his publishers even
so definitely as to have settled upon a title: "Here
and There With the Fighting Sixty-Ninth." As
time passed it became puzzling why no "copy" of
any kind came from him. And as still more time
passed this matter assumed for me an element of
more than considerable mystery. It was incomprehensible because none of the reasons which would
ordinarily apply in such a situation explained Kilmer's case to me. If it had been anyone else I
should have concluded that he was unable to find
time to write anything. But precisely the point
about Kilmer was that he did the impossible: it was
quite his habit to, in the racy phrase, "get away
with" situations which would have floored anyone

else. It was to my mind an illogical hypothesis that he could be frustrated by obstacles. And I felt that, inexplicable as it was for Kilmer to fail in anything or to neglect any opportunity, he was here failing in justice to his career. How was it in fact? As it had always been. He was receiving the light opened to him. There could not be, I submit, any more telling proof that he had genius, the capacity to become an absolutely great writer, than this: that in this war which has prompted more people to write, and has produced more "copy" than nearly all the other events of history put together, he ceased altogether to be a journalist of any kind; that is, even the instinct of the journalist dropped from him, when he touched it.

He had had no thought, he says, of attempting to report the war: "If I had, I'd have come over as a correspondent instead of as a soldier." All his days he had been trying to get closer and closer to the heart of life. In the war his profound instinct for humanity found fulfilment. Of his close comrades he writes: "Say a prayer for them all, they're brave men and good, and splendid company. Danger shared together and hardships mutually borne develops in us a sort of friendship I never knew in civilian life, a friendship clean of jealousy and

[88]

gossip and envy and suspicion—a fine, hearty, roaring, mirthful sort of thing, like an open fire of whole pine-trees in a giant's castle."

He was at present "a poet trying to be a soldier." "To tell the truth, I am not at all interested in writing nowadays, except in so far as writing is the expression of something beautiful. And I see daily and nightly the expression of beauty in action instead of words, and I find it more satisfactory."

"My days of hack writing are over, for a time at least." Upon his return to civilian life his civilian work "may be straight reporting." As for "that mob of war writers (thank God—let me pharisaically say—that I am not one of them)." The book? "The only sort of book I care to write about the war is the sort people will read after the war is over—a century after it is over!"

Kilmer's "Holy Ireland," a sketch of a lodging for the night enjoyed by a little group of Irish-American soldiers at a farmhouse in France, is the only piece of prose writing of any extent at all that came from him overseas. He himself wrote of it to his publishers: "I sent you a prose sketch 'Holy Ireland,' which represents the best prose writing I can do nowadays." It is unmistakably a piece of literature, that is to say, though slight enough in

[89]

substance, a work of firm and exquisite and endur-
ing art.

In a letter to the Reverend Edward F. Garesché,
S.J., one of the last he wrote, the following para-
graphs occur:

I have written very little—two prose sketches and
two poems—since I left the States, but I have a
rich store of memories. Not that what I write
matters—I have discovered, since some unforgettable experiences, that writing is not the tremendously important thing I once considered it. You
will find me less a bookman when you next see me,
and more, I hope, a man.

And he ends with these words: "Pray for me, my
dear Father, that I may love God more and that I
may be unceasingly conscious of Him—that is the
greatest desire I have."

Though he gloried in being a private soldier, it is
quite evident, too, that he was charmed with his pro-
motion. "I am now a sergeant," appears on the
back of every copy of the well-known "tin-hat"
post-card, and in every letter near this date. In
more than one intimate letter he says: "I'll never be
anything higher. To get a commission I'd have to
go away for three months to school, and then

[90]

whether or not I was made an officer—I'd be sent to some outfit other than this, and I don't want to leave this crowd. I'd rather be a sergeant in the 69th than a lieutenant in any other regiment in the world." "A volunteer regiment, the bravest and best regiment in the army." "I have a new stripe —an inverted chevron of bright gold on the left cuff for six months' service . . . let my children be proud of it." And, "a long moustache I have."

For a while he had worked in the Adjutant's Office, having special charge of recording and reporting statistics. Then he was no longer ("thank God!") doing statistics. Someone over here had said that he had "a bullet-proof job." "I had one, but succeeded, after two months intriguing, in getting rid of it." "At that time I was just an office hack—now I am a soldier, in the most fascinating branch of the service there is—sheer romance, night and day—especially night." He had become attached to the Regimental Intelligence Section, working as an observer—"very amusing work," "wonderful life!"—"the finest job in the army!" But "I don't know what I'll be able to do in civilian life—unless I become a fireman!" "I am having a delightful time, but it won't break my heart for the war to end."

"Rouge Bouquet" was his "first attempt at versification in a dug-out." He had lived in "billets,
dug-outs, trenches, observatories and all sorts of
queer places." And at length, he was "(after a
most violent and amusing month) resting (six hours
out of every twenty-four!) in a beautiful place,
among the firs and pines on a lovely mountain top,
from which I can see strange things." "I sleep on a
couch made soft with deftly laid young spruce
boughs and eat at a table set under good, kind
trees." And with that inimitable, irrepressible and
incomparable Kilmerian pleasure he contemplated
what he called "my senility":

I picture myself at sixty, with a long white
moustache, a pale gray tweed suit, a very large
panama hat, I can see my gnarled but beautifully
groomed hands as they tremblingly pour out the
glass of dry sherry which belongs to every old man's
breakfast. I cannot think of myself at seventy or
eighty—I grow hysterical with applause—I am
lost in a delirium of massive ebony canes, golden
snuff-boxes, and dainty silk hats.

"When we first met over here," wrote Kilmer's
friend Charles L. O'Donnell, Chaplain 332d Infantry, in a letter to Thomas Walsh which should be
written into the record, "he was in the personnel

department of his regiment, having had his time
of service in the field and done some particularly
good work in the intelligence line. He was then
about to go into the intelligence permanently and so
avid of it was he as to be ready to relinquish his
hard-earned sergeant's chevrons. In the event,
however, that sacrifice was not demanded. After
this change in his work he was much more agreeably
placed, in particular he had more freedom and more
time to see his friends. He was worshipped by the
men about him. I have heard them speak with awe
of his coolness and his nerve in scouting patrols in
No Man's Land. As an intelligence man he made
personally a few very valuable discoveries: this was
when I was with him in our comparatively quiet
sector. I can only conceive that he distinguished
himself later in the larger opportunities that came
his way." The letter continues:

We were both in the army but he was also of it.
I was amazed to find him so quickly become a soldier with the soldier's point of view. But he had
seen so much more than I, even then, and each day
in this war is equivalent to long campaigns of other
times. I felt, and was a rookie beside him. He had
got a perspective on his life at home that made him
smile with indulgent pity on some literary aspects

of it. I spoke of what must have been his earlier
views, the good he was doing and the need of doing
it. But he was not ready to relinquish a position he
had bought at the price of suffering, cold, hunger,
fatigue, with the hourly self denials that military
discipline means. Not that he spoke of these things
in this way, but I knew they had gone into the creation of his new stand and I knew in my heart it *was*
higher ground.

A closer witness is Sergeant-Major Lemist
Esler, who served side by side with Kilmer in the
Marne advance. Shortly afterward returned to the
United States for service as an instructor at an
army cantonment, he said in an interview in the
New York Times: "The front was his goal and no
sooner had the regiment reached France than he
made every possible effort to be transferred."

He finally had himself moved to the Intelligence
Department. It was in that department that he
was elevated to the rank of Sergeant. I was supply
sergeant at the time and Joyce Kilmer was a perfect trial to me. He would always be doing more
than his orders called for—that is, getting much
nearer to the enemy's positions than any officer
would ever be inclined to send him. Night after
night he would lie out in No Man's Land, crawling
through barbed wires, in an effort to locate enemy

[94]

positions, and enemy guns, and tearing his clothes to shreds. On the following day he would come to me for a new uniform.

"There was something of what the Scots call 'fey' about him as a soldier," is the testimony of the chaplain of the 165th Infantry, Father Duffy. "He was absolutely the coolest and most indifferent man in the face of danger I have ever seen. It was not for lack of love of life, for he enjoyed his life as a soldier—his only cross was distance from home. It was partly from his inborn courage and devotion —he would not stint his sacrifice—partly his deep and real belief that what God wills is best."

Once Marshal Foch's advance began, Kilmer seems to have been constantly in the thick of the fighting. In the *New York Evening Sun* of August 8 a correspondent told how a party composed of Major Donovan, Joyce Kilmer and John Kayes advanced to the edge of a wood and captured a German dressed in an American uniform.

"Joyce was one of those soldiers who had a romantic love of death in battle," Father Duffy has added, "and it could not have missed him in time." No, the stars move in their appointed courses; and there are certain things written aforetime. While he had life there was a defiant hope among us who knew his great gift for triumph that somehow this would see him through, that even over the inevitable he would prevail. But Destiny would not have been her immemorial self had she stayed her tragic hand from this shining figure, type and symbol in his taking of her unscrutable ways with man. And, somehow, in his death his life was all of a piece, and one cannot but admire the poetic justice of his end.

> Never fear but in the skies
> Saints and angels stand
> Smiling with their holy eyes
> On this new-come band
>
> .   .   .   .   .   .
>
> .   .   .   .   .   .
>
> Your souls shall be where the heroes are
> And your memory shine like the morning-star.

Sergeant Kilmer was killed in action near the Ourcq, July 30, 1918. "He had," runs the report in *The Stars and Stripes,* the newspaper of the American Expeditionary Force, "volunteered his services to the major of the foremost battalion because his own battalion would not be in the lead that day." From the report of Sergeant Esler and a letter (printed in the *New York Times*) to a friend in New York by Alexander Woollcott, dramatic

[96]

critic of the *Times* before his service abroad, the facts are established.

At the dawn of a misty Sunday, July 28, the 165th had made a gallant and irresistible charge across the river and up the hill. In the height of the great five days battle for the mastery of the heights which followed Kilmer was killed. It so happened that he was close to the Major when the battalion adjutant fell and, in the emergency of the battle, without commission or appointment, he was serving as a sort of aid to the battalion commander. Discovering that the woods ahead harboured some machine guns, he had reported this fact, and was sent in the lead of a patrol to establish their exact location. When a couple of hours later the battalion advanced into the woods to clear the spot of the enemy, several of Kilmer's comrades caught sight of him lying, as if still scouting, with his eyes bent over a little ridge. So like his living self he was, they called to him, then ran up—to find him dead with a bullet through his brain. He lies buried, we read, beside Lieutenant Oliver Ames at the edge of a little copse that is known as the Wood of the Burned Bridge, so close to the purling Ourcq that, standing by the graveside, one could throw a pebble into its waters. Perhaps ten minutes walk to the

north lies the half obliterated village Seringes, captured by American troops the night before Kilmer
was killed. Eloquent of affection in the making of
it, the grave is of course, marked by a wooden cross,
on which is written, "Sergeant Joyce Kilmer."
Then, after the inscription of his company and regiment, is the line: "Killed in Action—July 30, 1918."

It is not a rule to bury enlisted men with officers,
but Kilmer had won so much admiration and respect not only from the enlisted men in his company
but also from the officers, that the commander of
the regiment authorised that his grave be dug on the
spot and that he be buried next to the grave of the
heroic Lieutenant who had just lost his life.

Sergeant Woollcott was with the regiment in the
woods the day they came out of the line to catch
their breaths, and the news of Kilmer's death, he
says, "greeted me on every turn. The Captain
under whom he had been serving for several months,
the Major at whose side he fell, stray cooks, dough-
boys, runners—all shook their heads sorrowfully
and talked among themselves of what a good soldier
he had been and what an infinite pity it was that the
bullet had had to single him out. And in such days
as these, there are no platitudes of polite regret.
When men, good men and close pals, are falling

about you by hundreds, when every man in the regiment has come out of the fight the poorer for the loss of not one but many friends, there is no time to say pretty things about a man just because he exists no longer. Death is too common to distinguish anyone. So the glowing praise and admiration I heard for Joyce was real—every word of it."

It is, I think, fitting to preserve in a form more durable than its newspaper publication more of this letter. It continues:

I gathered that his stock among men of all ranks had been climbing steadily from the first days when many of them, including myself, felt that he was out of his own element in a rip-roaring regiment. As the regiment's laureate, they all knew him and they knew, too, that he was at work on a history of the regiment. He had become quite an institution, with his arms full of maps as they used to be full of minor poetry, and his mouth full of that imperishable pipe. They all knew his verse. I found any number of men who had only to fish around in their tattered blouses to bring out the copy of a poem Kilmer wrote in memory of some of their number who were killed by a shell in March. You see that there is a refrain which calls for bugle notes, and I am told that at the funeral services, where the lines were first read, the desperately sad notes of "Taps" sounded faintly from a distant grave when the refrain in-

voked them. The lines were read by Joyce's own
beloved Father Duffy, and those who were there
told me the tears streamed down the face of every
boy in the regiment. They just blubbered.

VIII

Indeed, such was the power of his spirit over
other men that even now he has become a legend,
his excellence a popular heritage, benefiting and
enriching human life. Writing with the pen of all
those who knew him in his overcoat of glory and
debonair hat, his friend Charles Willis Thompson
says: "I had a great affection and a deep admiration and respect for him, different from that which
I had for anybody else I knew." And expressing,
I think, the heart of innumerable ones who did not
chance his way, Booth Tarkington says: "But I had
a sense of him as of something fine and of fine
promise. I haven't read much that he wrote; but
it was like knowing that there was a good picture
somewhere in a gallery that I hadn't visited, but
might, some day."

The full beauty of his life is known only to God.
As religion was the first thing in his life let it be the
last thing said of him. In one of his last letters,
he wrote to Sister M. Emerentia of St. Joseph's

[100]

MEMOIR

College, Toronto, Ontario: "Pray that I may love
God more. It seems to me that if I can learn to love
God more passionately, more constantly, without
distractions, that absolutely nothing else can matter.
Except while we are in the trenches I receive Holy
Communion every morning, so it ought to be all the
easier for me to attain this object of my prayers.
I got Faith, you know, by praying for it. I hope to
get Love the same way."

POEMS FROM FRANCE

ROUGE BOUQUET

IN a wood they call the Rouge Bouquet
    There is a new-made grave to-day,
Built by never a spade nor pick
Yet covered with earth ten metres thick.
There lie many fighting men,
    Dead in their youthful prime,
Never to laugh nor love again
    Nor taste the Summertime.
For Death came flying through the air
And stopped his flight at the dugout stair,
Touched his prey and left them there,
    Clay to clay.
He hid their bodies stealthily
In the soil of the land they fought to free
    And fled away.
Now over the grave abrupt and clear
    Three volleys ring;
And perhaps their brave young spirits hear
    The bugle sing:
"Go to sleep!
Go to sleep!
Slumber well where the shell screamed and fell.

Let your rifles rest on the muddy floor,
You will not need them any more.
Danger's past;
Now at last,
Go to sleep!"

There is on earth no worthier grave
To hold the bodies of the brave
Than this place of pain and pride
Where they nobly fought and nobly died.
Never fear but in the skies
Saints and angels stand
Smiling with their holy eyes
   On this new-come band.
St. Michael's sword darts through the air
And touches the aureole on his hair
As he sees them stand saluting there,
   His stalwart sons;
And Patrick, Brigid, Columkill
Rejoice that in veins of warriors still
   The Gael's blood runs.
And up to Heaven's doorway floats,
   From the wood called Rouge Bouquet,
A delicate cloud of buglenotes
   That softly say:
"Farewell!

ROUGE BOUQUET

Farewell!
Comrades true, born anew, peace to you!
Your souls shall be where the heroes are
And your memory shine like the morning-star.
Brave and dear,
Shield us here.
Farewell!'

THE PEACEMAKER

UPON his will he binds a radiant chain,
   For Freedom's sake he is no longer free.
 It is his task, the slave of Liberty,
With his own blood to wipe away a stain.
That pain may cease, he yields his flesh to pain.
   To banish war, he must a warrior be.
   He dwells in Night, eternal Dawn to see,
And gladly dies, abundant life to gain.

What matters Death, if Freedom be not dead?
   No flags are fair, if Freedom's flag be furled.
Who fights for Freedom, goes with joyful tread
   To meet the fires of Hell against him hurled,
And has for captain Him whose thorn-wreathed
      head
   Smiles from the Cross upon a conquered world.

The Peacemak[er]

Upon his will he binds a rad[iant]
For Freedom's sake he is [...]
It is his task, the sla[ve]
With his own blood to w[...]
That pain may cease, he y[...]
To banish war, he m[...]
He dwells in night, e[...]
And gladly dies, abunda[...]

What matters death, if Fr[eedom]
No flags are fair, if [...]
Who fights for Freedom, go[es]
To meet the fires of Hell
And has for Captain Him
Smiles from the Cros[s]

165th Inf. (69th N.Y.N.G
A. E. F., France, June 14, 191[...]

t chain,
o longer free.
of Liberty,
e away a 'stain
lds his flesh to pain.
st a warrior be.
nal dawn to see,
o life to gain.

dom be not dead?
reedom's flag be furled.
with joyful tread
gainst him hurled.
whose thorn - wreathed head
upon a conquered world,

Joyce Kilmer.

PRAYER OF A SOLDIER IN FRANCE

MY shoulders ache beneath my pack
(Lie easier, Cross, upon His back).

I march with feet that burn and smart
(Tread, Holy Feet, upon my heart).

Men shout at me who may not speak
(They scourged Thy back and smote Thy cheek).

I may not lift a hand to clear
My eyes of salty drops that sear.

(Then shall my fickle soul forget
Thy Agony of Bloody Sweat?)

My rifle hand is stiff and numb
(From Thy pierced palm red rivers come).

Lord, Thou didst suffer more for me
Than all the hosts of land and sea.

So let me render back again
This millionth of Thy gift. Amen.

WHEN THE SIXTY-NINTH COMES
BACK

THE Sixty-ninth is on its way—France heard
    it long ago,
And the Germans know we're coming, to give them
    blow for blow.
We've taken on the contract, and when the job is
    through
We'll let them hear a Yankee cheer and an Irish
    ballad too.

The Harp that once through Tara's Halls shall
    fill the air with song,
And the Shamrock be cheered as the port is
    neared by our triumphant throng.
With the Potsdam Palace on a truck and the
    Kaiser in a sack,
New York will be seen one Irish green when the
    Sixty-ninth comes back.

We brought back from the Border our Flag—'twas
    never lost;
We left behind the land we love, the stormy sea we
    crossed.

THE SIXTY-NINTH COMES BACK

We heard the cry of Belgium, and France the free
    and fair,
For where there's work for fighting-men, the Sixty-
    ninth is there.

    The Harp that once through Tara's Halls shall
        fill the air with song,
    And the Shamrock be cheered as the port is
        neared by our triumphant throng.
    With the Potsdam Palace on a truck and the
        Kaiser in a sack,
    New York will be seen one Irish green when the
        Sixty-ninth comes back.

The men who fought at Marye's Heights will aid us
    from the sky,
They showed the world at Fredericksburg how Irish
    soldiers die.
At Blackburn Ford they think of us, Atlanta and
    Bull Run;
There are many silver rings on the old flagstaff but
    there's room for another one.

    The Harp that once through Tara's Halls shall
        fill the air with song,
    And the Shamrock be cheered as the port is
        neared by our triumphant throng.

With the Potsdam Palace on a truck and the
    Kaiser in a sack,
New York will be seen one Irish green when the
    Sixty-ninth comes back.

God rest our valiant leaders dead, whom we cannot
    forget;
They'll see the Fighting Irish are the Fighting
    Irish yet.
While Ryan, Roe, and Corcoran on History's pages
    shine,
A wreath of laurel and shamrock waits the head of
    Colonel Hine.

The Harp that once through Tara's Halls shall
    fill the air with song,
And the Shamrock be cheered as the port is
    neared by our triumphant throng.
With the Potsdam Palace on a truck and the
    Kaiser in a sack,
New York will be seen one Irish green when the
    Sixty-ninth comes back.

MIRAGE DU CANTONMENT

MANY laughing ladies, leisurely and wise,
　　Low rich voice, delicate gay cries,
Tea in fragile china cups, ices, macaroons,
Sheraton and Heppelwhite and old thin spoons,
Rather dim paintings on very high walls,
Windows showing lawns whereon the sunlight falls,
Pink and silver gardens and broad kind trees,
And fountains scattering rainbows at the whim of
　　a breeze,
Fragrance, mirth and gentleness, a Summer day
In a world that has forgotten everything but play.

POEMS AT HOME

WARTIME CHRISTMAS

LED by a star, a golden star,
　　The youngest star, an olden star,
Here the kings and the shepherds are,
Akneeling on the ground.
What did they come to the inn to see?
God in the Highest, and this is He,
A baby asleep on His mother's knee
And with her kisses crowned.

Now is the earth a dreary place,
A troubled place, a weary place.
Peace has hidden her lovely face
And turned in tears away.
Yet the sun, through the war-cloud, sees
Babies asleep on their mother's knees.
While there are love and home—and these—
There shall be Christmas Day.

MAIN STREET
(For S. M. L.)

I LIKE to look at the blossomy track of the moon
    upon the sea,
But it isn't half so fine a sight as Main Street used
    to be
When it all was covered over with a couple of feet
    of snow,
And over the crisp and radiant road the ringing
    sleighs would go.

Now, Main Street bordered with autumn leaves, it
    was a pleasant thing,
And its gutters were gay with dandelions early in
    the Spring;
I like to think of it white with frost or dusty in the
    heat,
Because I think it is humaner than any other street.

A city street that is busy and wide is ground by a
    thousand wheels,
And a burden of traffic on its breast is all it ever
    feels:
It is dully conscious of weight and speed and of
    work that never ends,
But it cannot be human like Main Street, and recog-
    nise its friends.

[118]

MAIN STREET

There were only about a hundred teams on Main
    Street in a day,
And twenty or thirty people, I guess, and some chil-
    dren out to play.
And there wasn't a wagon or buggy, or a man or a
    girl or a boy
That Main Street didn't remember, and somehow
    seem to enjoy.

The truck and the motor and trolley car and the
    elevated train
They make the weary city street reverberate with
    pain:
But there is yet an echo left deep down within my
    heart
Of the music the Main Street cobblestones made be-
    neath a butcher's cart.

God be thanked for the Milky Way that runs across
    the sky,
That's the path that my feet would tread whenever
    I have to die.
Some folks call it a Silver Sword, and some a Pearly
    Crown,
But the only thing I think it is, is Main Street,
    Heaventown.

ROOFS

(For Amelia Josephine Burr)

THE road is wide and the stars are out and the
 breath of the night is sweet,
And this is the time when wanderlust should seize
 upon my feet.
But I'm glad to turn from the open road and the
 starlight on my face,
And to leave the splendour of out-of-doors for a
 human dwelling place.

I never have seen a vagabond who really liked to
 roam
All up and down the streets of the world and not to
 have a home:
The tramp who slept in your barn last night and
 left at break of day
Will wander only until he finds another place to
 stay.

A gypsy-man will sleep in his cart with canvas over-
 head;
Or else he'll go into his tent when it is time for bed.
[120]

ROOFS

He'll sit on the grass and take his ease so long as
    the sun is high,
But when it is dark he wants a roof to keep away
    the sky.

If you call a gypsy a vagabond, I think you do him
    wrong,
For he never goes a-travelling but he takes his home
    along.
And the only reason a road is good, as every wan-
    derer knows,
Is just because of the homes, the homes, the homes
    to which it goes.

They say that life is a highway and its milestones
    are the years,
And now and then there's a toll-gate where you
    buy your way with tears.
It's a rough road and a steep road and it stretches
    broad and far,
But at last it leads to a golden Town where golden
    Houses are.

THE SNOWMAN IN THE YARD
(For Thomas Augustine Daly)

THE Judge's house has a splendid porch, with
    pillars and steps of stone,
  And the Judge has a lovely flowering hedge that
    came from across the seas;
In the Hales' garage you could put my house and
    everything I own,
  And the Hales have a lawn like an emerald and a
    row of poplar trees.

Now I have only a little house, and only a little lot,
  And only a few square yards of lawn, with dande-
    lions starred;
But when Winter comes, I have something there
    that the Judge and the Hales have not,
  And it's better worth having than all their wealth
    —it's a snowman in the yard.

The Judge's money brings architects to make his
    mansion fair;
  The Hales have seven gardeners to make their
    roses grow;
The Judge can get his trees from Spain and France
    and everywhere,
  And raise his orchids under glass in the midst of
    all the snow.

[122]

THE SNOWMAN IN THE YARD

But I have something no architect or gardener ever
    made,
  A thing that is shaped by the busy touch of little
    mittened hands:
And the Judge would give up his lonely estate,
    where the level snow is laid
  For the tiny house with the trampled yard, the
    yard where the snowman stands.

They say that after Adam and Eve were driven
    away in tears
  To toil and suffer their life-time through, be-
    cause of the sin they sinned,
The Lord made Winter to punish them for half
    their exiled years,
  To chill their blood with the snow, and pierce
    their flesh with the icy wind.

But we who inherit the primal curse, and labour
    for our bread,
  Have yet, thank God, the gift of Home, though
    Eden's gate is barred:
And through the Winter's crystal veil, Love's roses
    blossom red,
  For him who lives in a house that has a snowman
    in the yard.

A BLUE VALENTINE

(For Aline)

MONSIGNORE,
    Right Reverend Bishop Valentinus,
Sometime of Interamna, which is called Ferni,
Now of the delightful Court of Heaven,
I respectfully salute you,
I genuflect
And I kiss your episcopal ring.

It is not, Monsignore,
The fragrant memory of your holy life,
Nor that of your shining and joyous martyrdom,
Which causes me now to address you.
But since this is your august festival, Monsignore,
It seems appropriate to me to state
According to a venerable and agreeable custom,
That I love a beautiful lady.
Her eyes, Monsignore,
Are so blue that they put lovely little blue reflec-
    tions
On everything that she looks at,
Such as a wall
Or the moon
Or my heart.

[124]

A BLUE VALENTINE

It is like the light coming through blue stained glass,
Yet not quite like it,
For the blueness is not transparent,
Only translucent.
Her soul's light shines through,
But her soul cannot be seen.
It is something elusive, whimsical, tender, wanton,
    infantile, wise
And noble.
She wears, Monsignore, a blue garment,
Made in the manner of the Japanese.
It is very blue—
I think that her eyes have made it more blue,
Sweetly staining it
As the pressure of her body has graciously given it
    form.
Loving her, Monsignore,
I love all her attributes;
But I believe
That even if I did not love her
I would love the blueness of her eyes,
And her blue garment, made in the manner of the
    Japanese.

Monsignore,
I have never before troubled you with a request.

The saints whose ears I chiefly worry with my pleas
    are the most exquisite and maternal Brigid,
Gallant Saint Stephen, who puts fire in my blood,
And your brother bishop, my patron,
The generous and jovial Saint Nicholas of Bari.
But, of your courtesy, Monsignore,
Do me this favour:
When you this morning make your way
To the Ivory Throne that bursts into bloom with
    roses because of her who sits upon it,
When you come to pay your devoir to Our Lady,
I beg you, say to her:
"Madame, a poor poet, one of your singing servants
    yet on earth,
Has asked me to say that at this moment he is espe-
    cially grateful to you
For wearing a blue gown."

HOUSES

(For Aline)

WHEN you shall die and to the sky
    Serenely, delicately go,
Saint Peter, when he sees you there,
    Will clash his keys and say:
"Now talk to her, Sir Christopher!
    And hurry, Michelangelo!
She wants to play at building,
    And you've got to help her play!"

Every architect will help erect
    A palace on a lawn of cloud,
With rainbow beams and a sunset roof,
    And a level star-tiled floor;
And at your will you may use the skill
    Of this gay angelic crowd,
When a house is made you will throw it down,
    And they'll build you twenty more.

For Christopher Wren and these other men
    Who used to build on earth
Will love to go to work again
    If they may work for you.

"This porch," you'll say, "should go this way!"
  And they'll work for all they're worth,
And they'll come to your palace every morning,
  And ask you what to do.

And when night comes down on Heaven-town
  (If there should be night up there)
You will choose the house you like the best
  Of all that you can see:
And its walls will glow as you drowsily go
  To the bed up the golden stair,
And I hope you'll be gentle enough to keep
  A room in your house for me.

IN MEMORY

I

SERENE and beautiful and very wise,
　　Most erudite in curious Grecian lore,
　　You lay and read your learned books, and bore
A weight of unshed tears and silent sighs.
The song within your heart could never rise
　　Until love bade it spread its wings and soar.
　　Nor could you look on Beauty's face before
A poet's burning mouth had touched your eyes.
Love is made out of ecstasy and wonder;
　　Love is a poignant and accustomed pain.
It is a burst of Heaven-shaking thunder;
　　It is a linnet's fluting after rain.
Love's voice is through your song; above and under
　　And in each note to echo and remain.

II

Because Mankind is glad and brave and young,
　　Full of gay flames that white and scarlet glow,
　　All joys and passions that Mankind may know
By you were nobly felt and nobly sung.
Because Mankind's heart every day is wrung
　　By Fate's wild hands that twist and tear it so,
　　Therefore you echoed Man's undying woe,
A harp Aeolian on Life's branches hung.

So did the ghosts of toiling children hover
   About the piteous portals of your mind;
Your eyes, that looked on glory, could discover
   The angry scar to which the world was blind:
And it was grief that made Mankind your lover,
   And it was grief that made you love Mankind.

III

Before Christ left the Citadel of Light,
   To tread the dreadful way of human birth,
   His shadow sometimes fell upon the earth
And those who saw it wept with joy and fright.
"Thou art Apollo, than the sun more bright!"
   They cried. "Our music is of little worth,
   But thrill our blood with thy creative mirth,
Thou god of song, thou lord of lyric might!"

O singing pilgrim! who could love and follow
   Your lover Christ, through even love's despair,
You knew within the cypress-darkened hollow
   The feet that on the mountain are so fair.
For it was Christ that was your own Apollo,
   And thorns were in the laurel on your hair.

APOLOGY

(For Eleanor Rogers Cox)

FOR blows on the fort of evil
    That never shows a breach,
For terrible life-long races
    To a goal no foot can reach,
For reckless leaps into darkness
    With hands outstretched to a star,
There is jubilation in Heaven
    Where the great dead poets are.

There is joy over disappointment
    And delight in hopes that were vain.
Each poet is glad there was no cure
    To stop his lonely pain.
For nothing keeps a poet
    In his high singing mood
Like unappeasable hunger
    For unattainable food.

So fools are glad of the folly
    That made them weep and sing,
And Keats is thankful for Fanny Brawne
    And Drummond for his king.

They know that on flinty sorrow
And failure and desire
The steel of their souls was hammered
To bring forth the lyric fire.

Lord Byron and Shelley and Plunkett,
McDonough and Hunt and Pearse
See now why their hatred of tyrants
Was so insistently fierce.
Is Freedom only a Will-o'-the-wisp
To cheat a poet's eye?
Be it phantom or fact, it's a noble cause
In which to sing and to die!

So not for the Rainbow taken
And the magical White Bird snared
The poets sing grateful carols
In the place to which they have fared;
But for their lifetime's passion,
The quest that was fruitless and long,
They chorus their loud thanksgiving
To the thorn-crowned Master of Song.

THE PROUD POET

(For Shaemas O'Sheel)

ONE winter night a Devil came and sat upon
    my bed,
His eyes were full of laughter for his heart was
    full of crime.
"Why don't you take up fancy work, or embroi-
    dery?" he said,
  "For a needle is as manly a tool as a pen that
    makes a rhyme!"
"You little ugly Devil," said I, "go back to
    Hell,
For the idea you express I will not listen
    to:
I have trouble enough with poetry and poverty as
    well,
  Without having to pay attention to orators like
    you.

"When you say of the making of ballads and songs
    that it is woman's work
You forget all the fighting poets that have been
    in every land.
There was Byron, who left all his lady-loves to fight
    against the Turk,

And David, the Singing King of the Jews, who
    was born with a sword in his hand.
It was yesterday that Rupert Brooke went out to
    the Wars and died,
    And Sir Philip Sidney's lyric voice was as sweet
        as his arm was strong;
And Sir Walter Raleigh met the axe as a lover
    meets his bride,
    Because he carried in his soul the courage of his
        song.

"And there is no consolation so quickening to the
    heart
    As the warmth and whiteness that come from the
        lines of noble poetry.
It is strong joy to read it when the wounds of the
    spirit smart,
    It puts the flame in a lonely breast where only
        ashes be.
It is strong joy to read it, and to make it is a thing
    That exalts a man with a sacreder pride than any
        pride on earth.
For it makes him kneel to a broken slave and set his
    foot on a king,
    And it shakes the walls of his little soul with the
        echo of God's mirth.

[134]

THE PROUD POET

"There was the poet Homer had the sorrow to be
  blind,
  Yet a hundred people with good eyes would listen
    to him all night;
For they took great enjoyment in the heaven of his
  mind,
  And were glad when the old blind poet let them
    share his powers of sight.
And there was Heine lying on his mattress all day
  long,
  He had no wealth, he had no friends, he had no
    joy at all,
Except to pour his sorrow into little cups of song,
  And the world finds in them the magic wine that
    his broken heart let fall.

"And these are only a couple of names from a list of
  a thousand score
  Who have put their glory on the world in poverty
    and pain.
And the title of poet's a noble thing, worth living
  and dying for,
  Though all the devils on earth and in Hell spit
    at me their disdain.
It is stern work, it is perilous work, to thrust your
  hand in the sun

And pull out a spark of immortal flame to warm
 the hearts of men:
But Prometheus, torn by the claws and beaks whose
 task is never done,
Would be tortured another eternity to go stealing
 fire again."

LIONEL JOHNSON

(For the Rev. John J. Burke, C.S.P.)

THERE was a murkier tinge in London's air
    As if the honest fog blushed black for shame.
Fools sang of sin, for other fools' acclaim,
And Milton's wreath was tossed to Baudelaire.
The flowers of evil blossomed everywhere,
    But in their midst a radiant lily came,
    Candescent, pure, a cup of living flame,
Bloomed for a day, and left the earth more fair.

And was it Charles, thy "fair and fatal King,"
    Who bade thee welcome to the lovely land?
Or did Lord David cease to harp and sing
    To take in his thine emulative hand?
Or did Our Lady's smile shine forth, to bring
    Her lyric Knight within her choir to stand?

FATHER GERARD HOPKINS, S.J.

WHY didst thou carve thy speech laboriously,
    And match and blend thy words with
      curious art?
For Song, one saith, is but a human heart
Speaking aloud, undisciplined and free.
Nay, God be praised, Who fixed thy task for thee!
    Austere, ecstatic craftsman, set apart
    From all who traffic in Apollo's mart,
On thy phrased paten shall the Splendour be!

Now, carelessly we throw a rhyme to God,
    Singing His praise when other songs are done.
But thou, who knewest paths Teresa trod,
    Losing thyself, what is it thou hast won?
O bleeding feet, with peace and glory shod!
    O happy moth, that flew into the Sun!

GATES AND DOORS

GATES AND DOORS

(For Richardson Little Wright)

THERE was a gentle hostler
    (And blessèd be his name!)
He opened up the stable
    The night Our Lady came.
Our Lady and Saint Joseph,
    He gave them food and bed,
And Jesus Christ has given him
    A glory round his head.

So let the gate swing open
    However poor the yard,
Lest weary people visit you
    And find their passage barred;
Unlatch the door at midnight
    And let your lantern's glow
Shine out to guide the traveller's feet
    To you across the snow.

There was a courteous hostler
    (He is in Heaven to-night)
He held Our Lady's bridle
    And helped her to alight;

He spread clean straw before her
  Whereon she might lie down,
And Jesus Christ has given him
  An everlasting crown.

Unlock the door this evening
  And let your gate swing wide,
Let all who ask for shelter
  Come speedily inside.
What if your yard be narrow?
  What if your house be small?
There is a Guest is coming
  Will glorify it all.

There was a joyous hostler
  Who knelt on Christmas morn
Beside the radiant manger
  Wherein his Lord was born.
His heart was full of laughter,
  His soul was full of bliss
When Jesus, on His Mother's lap,
  Gave him His hand to kiss.

Unbar your heart this evening
  And keep no stranger out,
Take from your soul's great portal
  The barrier of doubt.

GATES AND DOORS

To humble folk and weary
Give hearty welcoming,
Your breast shall be to-morrow
The cradle of a King.

THE ROBE OF CHRIST

(For Cecil Chesterton)

At the foot of the Cross on Calvary
  Three soldiers sat and diced,
And one of them was the Devil
  And he won the Robe of Christ.

When the Devil comes in his proper form
  To the chamber where I dwell,
I know him and make the Sign of the Cross
  Which drives him back to Hell.

And when he comes like a friendly man
  And puts his hand in mine,
The fervour in his voice is not
  From love or joy or wine.

And when he comes like a woman,
  With lovely, smiling eyes,
Black dreams float over his golden head
  Like a swarm of carrion flies.

Now many a million tortured souls
  In his red halls there be:
Why does he spend his subtle craft
  In hunting after me?

THE ROBE OF CHRIST

Kings, queens and crested warriors
  Whose memory rings through time,
These are his prey, and what to him
  Is this poor man of rhyme,

That he, with such laborious skill,
  Should change from rôle to rôle,
Should daily act so many a part
  To get my little soul?

Oh, he can be the forest,
  And he can be the sun,
Or a buttercup, or an hour of rest
  When the weary day is done.

I saw him through a thousand veils,
  And has not this sufficed?
Now, must I look on the Devil robed
  In the radiant Robe of Christ?

He comes, and his face is sad and mild,
  With thorns his head is crowned;
There are great bleeding wounds in his feet,
  And in each hand a wound.

How can I tell, who am a fool,
  If this be Christ or no?
Those bleeding hands outstretched to me!
  Those eyes that love me so!

I see the Robe—I look—I hope—
  I fear—but there is one
Who will direct my troubled mind;
  Christ's Mother knows her Son.

O Mother of Good Counsel, lend
  Intelligence to me!
Encompass me with wisdom,
  Thou Tower of Ivory!

"This is the Man of Lies," she says,
  "Disguised with fearful art:
He has the wounded hands and feet,
  But not the wounded heart."

Beside the Cross on Calvary
  She watched them as they diced.
She saw the Devil join the game
  And win the Robe of Christ.

THE SINGING GIRL

(For the Rev. Edward F. Garesché, S.J.)

THERE was a little maiden
  In blue and silver drest,
She sang to God in Heaven
  And God within her breast.

It flooded me with pleasure,
  It pierced me like a sword,
When this young maiden sang: "My soul
  Doth magnify the Lord."

The stars sing all together
  And hear the angels sing,
But they said they had never heard
  So beautiful a thing.

Saint Mary and Saint Joseph,
  And Saint Elizabeth,
Pray for us poets now
  And at the hour of death.

THE ANNUNCIATION

(For Helen Parry Eden)

"HAIL Mary, full of grace," the Angel saith.
Our Lady bows her head, and is ashamed;
She has a Bridegroom Who may not be named,
Her mortal flesh bears Him Who conquers death.
Now in the dust her spirit grovelleth;
Too bright a Sun before her eyes has flamed,
Too fair a herald joy too high proclaimed,
And human lips have trembled in God's breath.

O Mother-Maid, thou art ashamed to cover
With thy white self, whereon no stain can be,
Thy God, Who came from Heaven to be thy Lover,
Thy God, Who came from Heaven to dwell in
thee.
About thy head celestial legions hover,
Chanting the praise of thy humility.

ROSES

(For Katherine Brègy)

I WENT to gather roses and twine them in a
ring,
For I would make a posy, a posy for the King.
I got an hundred roses, the loveliest there be,
From the white rose vine and the pink rose bush and
from the red rose tree.

But when I took my posy and laid it at His feet
I found He had His roses a million times more
sweet.
There was a scarlet blossom upon each foot and
hand,
And a great pink rose bloomed from His side for
the healing of the land.

Now of this fair and awful King there is this marvel
told,
That He wears a crown of linkèd thorns instead
of one of gold.
Where there are thorns are roses, and I saw a line
of red,
A little wreath of roses around His radiant head.

[147]

A red rose is His Sacred Heart, a white rose is His
    face,
And His breath has turned the barren world to a
    rich and flowery place.
He is the Rose of Sharon, His gardener am I,
And I shall drink His fragrance in Heaven when
    I die.

THE VISITATION

(For Louise Imogen Guiney)

THERE is a wall of flesh before the eyes
    Of John, who yet perceives and hails his
        King.
  It is Our Lady's painful bliss to bring
Before mankind the Glory of the skies.
Her cousin feels her womb's sweet burden rise
    And leap with joy, and she comes forth to sing,
    With trembling mouth, her words of welcoming.
She knows her hidden God, and prophesies.

Saint John, pray for us, weary souls that tarry
    Where life is withered by sin's deadly breath.
Pray for us, whom the dogs of Satan harry,
    Saint John, Saint Anne, and Saint Elizabeth.
And, Mother Mary, give us Christ to carry
    Within our hearts, that we may conquer death.

MULTIPLICATION
(For S. M. E.)

I TAKE my leave, with sorrow, of Him I love so
 well;
I look my last upon His small and radiant prison-
 cell;
O happy lamp! to serve Him with never ceasing
 light!
O happy flame! to tremble forever in His sight!

I leave the holy quiet for the loudly human train,
And my heart that He has breathed upon is filled
 with lonely pain.
O King, O Friend, O Lover! What sorer grief
 can be
In all the reddest depths of Hell than banishment
 from Thee?

But from my window as I speed across the sleeping
 land
I see the towns and villages wherein His houses
 stand.
Above the roofs I see a cross outlined against the
 night,
And I know that there my Lover dwells in His
 sacramental might.

[150]

MULTIPLICATION

Dominions kneel before Him, and Powers kiss
    His feet,
Yet for me He keeps His weary watch in the tur-
    moil of the street:
The King of Kings awaits me, wherever I may go,
O who am I that He should deign to love and serve
    me so?

THANKSGIVING

(For John Bunker)

THE roar of the world is in my ears.
    Thank God for the roar of the world!
Thank God for the mighty tide of fears
    Against me always hurled!

Thank God for the bitter and ceaseless strife,
    And the sting of His chastening rod!
Thank God for the stress and the pain of life,
    And Oh, thank God for God!

THE THORN

(For the Rev. Charles L. O'Donnell, C.S.C.)

THE garden of God is a radiant place,
   And every flower has a holy face:
Our Lady like a lily bends above the cloudy sod,
But Saint Michael is the thorn on the rose-bush of
   God.
David is the song upon God's lips,
And Our Lady is the goblet that He sips:
And Gabriel's the breath of His command,
But Saint Michael is the sword in God's right hand.

The Ivory Tower is fair to see,
And may her walls encompass me!
But when the Devil comes with the thunder of his
   might,
Saint Michael, show me how to fight!

[153]

THE BIG TOP

THE boom and blare of the big brass band is
cheering to my heart
And I like the smell of the trampled grass and
elephants and hay.
I take off my hat to the acrobat with his delicate,
strong art,
And the motley mirth of the chalk-faced clown
drives all my care away.

I wish I could feel as they must feel, these players
brave and fair,
Who nonchalantly juggle death before a staring
throng.
It must be fine to walk a line of silver in the air
And to cleave a hundred feet of space with a
gesture like a song.

Sir Henry Irving never knew a keener, sweeter
thrill
Than that which stirs the breast of him who
turns his painted face
To the circling crowd who laugh aloud and clap
hands with a will
As a tribute to the clown who won the great
wheel-barrow race.

[154]

THE BIG TOP

Now, one shall work in the living rock with a mallet
    and a knife,
    And another shall dance on a big white horse that
        canters round a ring,
By another's hand shall colours stand in similitude
    of life;
    And the hearts of the three shall be moved by one
        mysterious high thing.

For the sculptor and the acrobat and the painter
    are the same.
    They know one hope, one fear, one pride, one
        sorrow and one mirth,
And they take delight in the endless fight for the
    fickle world's acclaim;
    For they worship art above the clouds and serve
        her on the earth.

But you, who can build of the stubborn rock no
    form of loveliness,
    Who can never mingle the radiant hues to make
        a wonder live,
Who can only show your little woe to the world in a
    rhythmic dress—
    What kind of a counterpart of you does the three-
        ring circus give?

POEMS AT HOME

Well—here in a little side-show tent to-day some
    people stand,
  One is a giant, one a dwarf, and one has a figured
    skin,
And each is scarred and seared and marred by
    Fate's relentless hand,
  And each one shows his grief for pay, with a sort
    of pride therein.

You put your sorrow into rhyme and want the
    world to look;
  You sing the news of your ruined hope and want
    the world to hear;
Their woe is pent in a canvas tent and yours in a
    printed book.
  O, poet of the broken heart, salute your brothers
    here!

MID-OCEAN IN WAR-TIME

(For My Mother)

THE fragile splendour of the level sea,
  The moon's serene and silver-veilèd face,
 Make of this vessel an enchanted place
Full of white mirth and golden sorcery.
Now, for a time, shall careless laughter be
 Blended with song, to lend song sweeter grace,
 And the old stars, in their unending race,
Shall heed and envy young humanity.

And yet to-night, a hundred leagues away,
 These waters blush a strange and awful red.
Before the moon, a cloud obscenely grey
 Rises from decks that crash with flying lead.
And these stars smile their immemorial way
 On waves that shroud a thousand newly dead!

QUEEN ELIZABETH SPEAKS

MY hands were stained with blood, my heart
    was proud and cold,
My soul is black with shame . . . but I gave
    Shakespeare gold.
So after æons of flame, I may, by grace of God,
Rise up to kiss the dust that Shakespeare's feet have
    trod.

IN MEMORY OF RUPERT BROOKE

IN alien earth, across a troubled sea,
  His body lies that was so fair and young.
His mouth is stopped, with half his songs unsung;
His arm is still, that struck to make men free.
But let no cloud of lamentation be
  Where, on a warrior's grave, a lyre is hung.
  We keep the echoes of his golden tongue,
We keep the vision of his chivalry.

So Israel's joy, the loveliest of kings,
  Smote now his harp, and now the hostile horde.
To-day the starry roof of Heaven rings
  With psalms a soldier made to praise his Lord;
And David rests beneath Eternal wings,
  Song on his lips, and in his hand a sword.

THE NEW SCHOOL

(For My Mother)

THE halls that were loud with the merry tread
    of young and careless feet
  Are still with a stillness that is too drear to seem
    like holiday,
And never a gust of laughter breaks the calm of the
    dreaming street
  Or rises to shake the ivied walls and frighten the
    doves away.

The dust is on book and on empty desk, and the
    tennis-racquet and balls
  Lie still in their lonely locker and wait for a game
    that is never played,
And over the study and lecture-room and the river
    and meadow falls
  A stern peace, a strange peace, a peace that War
    has made.

For many a youthful shoulder now is gay with an
    epaulet,
  And the hand that was deft with a cricket-bat is
    defter with a sword,

[160]

THE NEW SCHOOL

And some of the lads will laugh to-day where the
    trench is red and wet,
  And some will win on the bloody field the ac-
    colade of the Lord.

They have taken their youth and mirth away from
    the study and playing-ground
  To a new school in an alien land beneath an alien
    sky;
Out in the smoke and roar of the fight their lessons
    and games are found,
  And they who were learning how to live are learn-
    ing how to die.

And after the golden day has come and the war is
    at an end,
  A slab of bronze on the chapel wall will tell of
    the noble dead.
And every name on that radiant list will be the
    name of a friend,
  A name that shall through the centuries in grate-
    ful prayers be said.

And there will be ghosts in the old school, brave
    ghosts with laughing eyes,
  On the field with a ghostly cricket-bat, by the
    stream with a ghostly rod;

They will touch the hearts of the living with a flame
  that sanctifies,
A flame that they took with strong young hands
  from the altar-fires of God.

EASTER WEEK

(In memory of Joseph Mary Plunkett)

(*"Romantic Ireland's dead and gone,
It's with O'Leary in the grave."*)

WILLIAM BUTLER YEATS.

"ROMANTIC Ireland's dead and gone,
It's with O'Leary in the grave."
Then, Yeats, what gave that Easter dawn
A hue so radiantly brave?

There was a rain of blood that day,
Red rain in gay blue April weather.
It blessed the earth till it gave birth
To valour thick as blooms of heather.

Romantic Ireland never dies!
O'Leary lies in fertile ground,
And songs and spears throughout the years
Rise up where patriot graves are found.

Immortal patriots newly dead
And ye that bled in bygone years,
What banners rise before your eyes?
What is the tune that greets your ears?

[163]

POEMS AT HOME

The young Republic's banners smile
    For many a mile where troops convene.
O'Connell Street is loudly sweet
    With strains of Wearing of the Green.

The soil of Ireland throbs and glows
    With life that knows the hour is here
To strike again like Irishmen
    For that which Irishmen hold dear.

Lord Edward leaves his resting place
    And Sarsfield's face is glad and fierce.
See Emmet leap from troubled sleep
    To grasp the hand of Padraic Pearse!

There is no rope can strangle song
    And not for long death takes his toll.
No prison bars can dim the stars
    Nor quicklime eat the living soul.

Romantic Ireland is not old.
    For years untold her youth will shine.
Her heart is fed on Heavenly bread,
    The blood of martyrs is her wine.

THE CATHEDRAL OF RHEIMS

THE CATHEDRAL OF RHEIMS

(From the French of Émile Verhaeren)

HE who walks through the meadows of Cham-
    pagne
  At noon in Fall, when leaves like gold appear,
  Sees it draw near
Like some great mountain set upon the plain,
From radiant dawn until the close of day,
    Nearer it grows
    To him who goes
Across the country. When tall towers lay
    Their shadowy pall
    Upon his way,
    He enters, where
The solid stone is hollowed deep by all
Its centuries of beauty and of prayer.

Ancient French temple! thou whose hundred kings
Watch over thee, emblazoned on thy walls,
Tell me, within thy memory-hallowed halls
What chant of triumph, or what war-song rings?
Thou hast known Clovis and his Frankish train,
Whose mighty hand Saint Remy's hand did keep
And in thy spacious vault perhaps may sleep
An echo of the voice of Charlemagne.

[165]

For God thou hast known fear, when from His side
Men wandered, seeking alien shrines and new,
But still the sky was bountiful and blue
And thou wast crowned with France's love and
    pride.
Sacred thou art, from pinnacle to base;
And in thy panes of gold and scarlet glass
The setting sun sees thousandfold his face;
Sorrow and joy, in stately silence pass
Across thy walls, the shadow and the light;
Around thy lofty pillars, tapers white
Illuminate, with delicate sharp flames,
The brows of saints with venerable names,
And in the night erect a fiery wall.
A great but silent fervour burns in all
Those simple folk who kneel, pathetic, dumb,
And know that down below, beside the Rhine—
Cannon, horses, soldiers, flags in line—
With blare of trumpets, mighty armies come.

Suddenly, each knows fear;
Swift rumours pass, that every one must hear,
The hostile banners blaze against the sky
And by the embassies mobs rage and cry.
Now war has come, and peace is at an end.
On Paris town the German troops descend.

THE CATHEDRAL OF RHEIMS

They are turned back, and driven to Champagne.
And now, as to so many weary men,
The glorious temple gives them welcome, when
It meets them at the bottom of the plain.

At once, they set their cannon in its way.
    There is no gable now, nor wall
That does not suffer, night and day,
    As shot and shell in crushing torrents fall.
The stricken tocsin quivers through the tower;
    The triple nave, the apse, the lonely choir
Are circled, hour by hour,
    With thundering bands of fire
And Death is scattered broadcast among men.

And then
That which was splendid with baptismal grace;
The stately arches soaring into space,
The transepts, columns, windows gray and gold,
The organ, in whose tones the ocean rolled,
The crypts, of mighty shades the dwelling places,
The Virgin's gentle hands, the Saints' pure faces,
All, even the pardoning hands of Christ the Lord
Were struck and broken by the wanton sword
Of sacrilegious lust.
O beauty slain, O glory in the dust!

POEMS AT HOME

Strong walls of faith, most basely overthrown!
The crawling flames, like adders glistening
Ate the white fabric of this lovely thing.
Now from its soul arose a piteous moan,
The soul that always loved the just and fair.
Granite and marble loud their woe confessed,
The silver monstrances that Popes had blessed,
The chalices and lamps and crosiers rare
Were seared and twisted by a flaming breath;
The horror everywhere did range and swell,
The guardian Saints into this furnace fell,
Their bitter tears and screams were stilled in death.

Around the flames armed hosts are skirmishing,
The burning sun reflects the lurid scene;
The German army, fighting for its life,
Rallies its torn and terrified left wing;
  And, as they near this place
  The imperial eagles see
  Before them in their flight,
Here, in the solemn night,
The old cathedral, to the years to be
  Showing, with wounded arms, their own disgrace.

KINGS

(For the Rev. James B. Dollard)

THE Kings of the earth are men of might,
  And cities are burned for their delight,
And the skies rain death in the silent night,
  And the hills belch death all day!

But the King of Heaven, Who made them all,
Is fair and gentle, and very small;
He lies in the straw, by the oxen's stall—
  Let them think of Him to-day!

THE WHITE SHIPS AND THE RED

(For Alden March)

WITH drooping sail and pennant
That never a wind may reach,
They float in sunless waters
Beside a sunless beach.
Their mighty masts and funnels
Are white as driven snow,
And with a pallid radiance
Their ghostly bulwarks glow.

Here is a Spanish galleon
That once with gold was gay,
Here is a Roman trireme
Whose hues outshone the day.
But Tyrian dyes have faded,
And prows that once were bright
With rainbow stains wear only
Death's livid, dreadful white.

White as the ice that clove her
That unforgotten day,
Among her pallid sisters
The grim *Titanic* lay.

[170]

THE WHITE SHIPS AND THE RED

And through the leagues above her
    She looked aghast, and said:
"What is this living ship that comes
    Where every ship is dead?"

The ghostly vessels trembled
    From ruined stern to prow;
What was this thing of terror
    That broke their vigil now?
Down through the startled ocean
    A mighty vessel came,
Not white, as all dead ships must be,
    But red, like living flame!

The pale green waves about her
    Were swiftly, strangely dyed,
By the great scarlet stream that flowed
    From out her wounded side.
And all her decks were scarlet
    And all her shattered crew.
She sank among the white ghost ships
    And stained them through and through.

The grim *Titanic* greeted her.
    "And who art thou?" she said;
"Why dost thou join our ghostly fleet
    Arrayed in living red?

We are the ships of sorrow
  Who spend the weary night,
Until the dawn of Judgment Day,
  Obscure and still and white."

"Nay," said the scarlet visitor,
  "Though I sink through the sea,
A ruined thing that was a ship,
  I sink not as did ye.
For ye met with your destiny
  By storm or rock or fight,
So through the lagging centuries
  Ye wear your robes of white.

"But never crashing iceberg
  Nor honest shot of foe,
Nor hidden reef has sent me
  The way that I must go.
My wound that stains the waters,
  My blood that is like flame,
Bear witness to a loathly deed,
  A deed without a name.

"I went not forth to battle,
  I carried friendly men,
The children played about my decks,
  The women sang—and then—

THE WHITE SHIPS AND THE RED

And then—the sun blushed scarlet
   And Heaven hid its face,
The world that God created
   Became a shameful place!

"My wrong cries out for vengeance,
   The blow that sent me here
Was aimed in Hell. My dying scream
   Has reached Jehovah's ear.
Not all the seven oceans
   Shall wash away that stain;
Upon a brow that wears a crown
   I am the brand of Cain."

When God's great voice assembles
   The fleet on Judgment Day,
The ghosts of ruined ships will rise
   In sea and strait and bay.
Though they have lain for ages
   Beneath the changeless flood,
They shall be white as silver,
   But one—shall be like blood.

THE TWELVE-FORTY-FIVE

(For Edward J. Wheeler)

WITHIN the Jersey City shed
    The engine coughs and shakes its head.
The smoke, a plume of red and white,
Waves madly in the face of night.
And now the grave incurious stars
Gleam on the groaning hurrying cars.
Against the kind and awful reign
Of darkness, this our angry train,
A noisy little rebel, pouts
Its brief defiance, flames and shouts—
And passes on, and leaves no trace.
For darkness holds its ancient place,
Serene and absolute, the king
Unchanged, of every living thing.
The houses lie obscure and still
In Rutherford and Carlton Hill.
Our lamps intensify the dark
Of slumbering Passaic Park.
And quiet holds the weary feet
That daily tramp through Prospect Street.
What though we clang and clank and roar
Through all Passaic's streets? No door

THE TWELVE-FORTY-FIVE

Will open, not an eye will see
Who this loud vagabond may be.
Upon my crimson cushioned seat,
In manufactured light and heat,
I feel unnatural and mean.
Outside the towns are cool and clean;
Curtained awhile from sound and sight
They take God's gracious gift of night.
The stars are watchful over them.
On Clifton as on Bethlehem
The angels, leaning down the sky,
Shed peace and gentle dreams.   And I—
I ride, I blasphemously ride
Through all the silent countryside.
The engine's shriek, the headlight's glare,
Pollute the still nocturnal air.
The cottages of Lake View sigh
And sleeping, frown as we pass by.
Why, even strident Paterson
Rests quietly as any nun.
Her foolish warring children keep
The grateful armistice of sleep.
For what tremendous errand's sake
Are we so blatantly awake?
What precious secret is our freight?
What king must be abroad so late?

POEMS AT HOME

Perhaps Death roams the hills to-night
And we rush forth to give him fight.
Or else, perhaps, we speed his way
To some remote unthinking prey.
Perhaps a woman writhes in pain
And listens—listens for the train!
The train, that like an angel sings,
The train, with healing on its wings.
Now "Hawthorne!" the conductor cries.
My neighbor starts and rubs his eyes.
He hurries yawning through the car
And steps out where the houses are.
This is the reason of our quest!
Not wantonly we break the rest
Of town and village, nor do we
Lightly profane night's sanctity.
What Love commands the train fulfills,
And beautiful upon the hills
Are these our feet of burnished steel.
Subtly and certainly I feel
That Glen Rock welcomes us to her
And silent Ridgewood seems to stir
And smile, because she knows the train
Has brought her children back again.
We carry people home—and so
God speeds us, wheresoe'er we go.

THE TWELVE-FORTY-FIVE

Hohokus, Waldwick, Allendale
Lift sleepy heads to give us hail.
In Ramsey, Mahwah, Suffern stand
Houses that wistfully demand
A father—son—some human thing
That this, the midnight train, may bring.
The trains that travel in the day
They hurry folks to work or play.
The midnight train is slow and old,
But of it let this thing be told,
To its high honor be it said,
It carries people home to bed.
My cottage lamp shines white and clear.
God bless the train that brought me here.

PENNIES

A FEW long-hoarded pennies in his hand,
    Behold him stand;
A kilted Hedonist, perplexed and sad.
The joy that once he had,
The first delight of ownership is fled.
He bows his little head.
Ah, cruel Time, to kill
That splendid thrill!

Then in his tear-dimmed eyes
New lights arise.
He drops his treasured pennies on the ground,
They roll and bound
And scattered, rest.
Now with what zest
He runs to find his errant wealth again!

So unto men
Doth God, depriving that He may bestow.
Fame, health and money go,
But that they may, new found, be newly sweet.
Yea, at His feet
Sit, waiting us, to their concealment bid,
All they, our lovers, whom His Love hath hid.

[178]

PENNIES

Lo, comfort blooms on pain, and peace on strife,
  And gain on loss.
What is the key to Everlasting Life?
  A blood-stained Cross.

TREES

(For Mrs. Henry Mills Alden)

I THINK that I shall never see
A poem lovely as a tree.

A tree whose hungry mouth is prest
Against the earth's sweet flowing breast;

A tree that looks at God all day,
And lifts her leafy arms to pray;

A tree that may in Summer wear
A nest of robins in her hair;

Upon whose bosom snow has lain;
Who intimately lives with rain.

Poems are made by fools like me,
But only God can make a tree.

STARS

(For the Rev. James J. Daly, S.J.)

BRIGHT stars, yellow stars, flashing through
the air,
Are you errant strands of Lady Mary's hair?
As she slits the cloudy veil and bends down through,
Do you fall across her cheeks and over heaven too?

Gay stars, little stars, you are little eyes,
Eyes of baby angels playing in the skies.
Now and then a wingéd child turns his merry face
Down toward the spinning world—what a funny
place!

Jesus Christ came from the Cross (Christ receive
my soul!)
In each perfect hand and foot there was a bloody
hole.
Four great iron spikes there were, red and never
dry,
Michael plucked them from the Cross and set them
in the sky.

[181]

Christ's Troop, Mary's Guard, God's own men,
Draw your swords and strike at Hell and strike
    again.
Every steel-born spark that flies where God's battles
    are,
Flashes past the face of God, and is a star.

OLD POETS

(For Robert Cortes Holliday)

IF I should live in a forest
    And sleep underneath a tree,
No grove of impudent saplings
    Would make a home for me.

I'd go where the old oaks gather,
    Serene and good and strong,
And they would not sigh and tremble
    And vex me with a song.

The pleasantest sort of poet
    Is the poet who's old and wise,
With an old white beard and wrinkles
    About his kind old eyes.

For these young flippertigibbets
    A-rhyming their hours away
They won't be still like honest men
    And listen to what you say.

The young poet screams forever
    About his sex and his soul;
But the old man listens, and smokes his pipe,
    And polishes its bowl.

[183]

POEMS AT HOME

There should be a club for poets
    Who have come to seventy year.
They should sit in a great hall drinking
    Red wine and golden beer.

They would shuffle in of an evening,
    Each one to his cushioned seat,
And there would be mellow talking
    And silence rich and sweet.

There is no peace to be taken
    With poets who are young,
For they worry about the wars to be fought
    And the songs that must be sung.

But the old man knows that he's in his chair
    And that God's on His throne in the sky.
So he sits by the fire in comfort
    And he lets the world spin by.

DELICATESSEN

WHY is that wanton gossip Fame
So dumb about this man's affairs!
Why do we twitter at his name
Who come to buy his curious wares?

Here is a shop of wonderment.
From every land has come a prize;
Rich spices from the Orient,
And fruit that knew Italian skies,

And figs that ripened by the sea
In Smyrna, nuts from hot Brazil,
Strange pungent meats from Germany,
And currants from a Grecian hill.

He is the lord of goodly things
That make the poor man's table gay,
Yet of his worth no minstrel sings
And on his tomb there is no bay.

Perhaps he lives and dies unpraised,
This trafficker in humble sweets,
Because his little shops are raised
By thousands in the city streets.

Yet stars in greater numbers shine,
    And violets in millions grow,
And they in many a golden line
    Are sung, as every child must know.

Perhaps Fame thinks his worried eyes,
    His wrinkled, shrewd, pathetic face,
His shop, and all he sells and buys
    Are desperately commonplace.

Well, it is true he has no sword
    To dangle at his booted knees.
He leans across a slab of board,
    And draws his knife and slices cheese.

He never heard of chivalry,
    He longs for no heroic times;
He thinks of pickles, olives, tea,
    And dollars, nickels, cents and dimes.

His world has narrow walls, it seems;
    By counters is his soul confined;
His wares are all his hopes and dreams,
    They are the fabric of his mind.

DELICATESSEN

Yet—in a room above the store
   There is a woman—and a child
Pattered just now across the floor;
   The shopman looked at him and smiled.

For, once he thrilled with high romance
   And turned to love his eager voice.
Like any cavalier of France
   He wooed the maiden of his choice.

And now deep in his weary heart
   Are sacred flames that whitely burn.
He has of Heaven's grace a part
   Who loves, who is beloved in turn.

And when the long day's work is done,
   (How slow the leaden minutes ran!)
Home, with his wife and little son,
   He is no huckster, but a man!

And there are those who grasp his hand,
   Who drink with him and wish him well.
O in no drear and lonely land
   Shall he who honours friendship dwell.

And in his little shop, who knows
What bitter games of war are played?
Why, daily on each corner grows
A foe to rob him of his trade.

He fights, and for his fireside's sake;
He fights for clothing and for bread:
The lances of his foemen make
A steely halo round his head.

He decks his window artfully,
He haggles over paltry sums.
In this strange field his war must be
And by such blows his triumph comes.

What if no trumpet sounds to call
His arméd legions to his side?
What if to no ancestral hall
He comes in all a victor's pride?

The scene shall never fit the deed.
Grotesquely wonders come to pass.
The fool shall mount an Arab steed
And Jesus ride upon an ass.

DELICATESSEN

This man has home and child and wife
    And battle set for every day.
This man has God and love and life;
    These stand, all else shall pass away.

O Carpenter of Nazareth,
    Whose mother was a village maid,
Shall we, Thy children, blow our breath
    In scorn on any humble trade?

Have pity on our foolishness
    And give us eyes, that we may see
Beneath the shopman's clumsy dress
    The splendour of humanity!

SERVANT GIRL AND GROCER'S BOY

HER lips' remark was: "Oh, you kid!"
Her soul spoke thus (I know it did):

"O king of realms of endless joy,
My own, my golden grocer's boy,

I am a princess forced to dwell
Within a lonely kitchen cell,

While you go dashing through the land
With loveliness on every hand.

Your whistle strikes my eager ears
Like music of the choiring spheres.

The mighty earth grows faint and reels
Beneath your thundering wagon wheels.

How keenly, perilously sweet
To cling upon that swaying seat!

How happy she who by your side
May share the splendours of that ride!

Ah, if you will not take my hand
And bear me off across the land,

SERVANT GIRL AND GROCER'S BOY

Then, traveller from Arcady,
Remain awhile and comfort me.

What other maiden can you find
So young and delicate and kind?"

Her lips' remark was: "Oh, you kid!"
Her soul spoke thus (I know it did).

WEALTH

(For Aline)

FROM what old ballad, or from what rich frame
  Did you descend to glorify the earth?
Was it from Chaucer's singing book you came?
  Or did Watteau's small brushes give you birth?

Nothing so exquisite as that slight hand
  Could Raphael or Leonardo trace.
Nor could the poets know in Fairyland
  The changing wonder of your lyric face.

I would possess a host of lovely things,
  But I am poor and such joys may not be.
So God who lifts the poor and humbles kings
  Sent loveliness itself to dwell with me.

MARTIN

WHEN I am tired of earnest men,
  Intense and keen and sharp and clever,
Pursuing fame with brush or pen,
  Or counting metal disks forever,
Then from the halls of Shadowland,
  Beyond the trackless purple sea,
Old Martin's ghost comes back to stand
  Beside my desk and talk to me.

Still on his delicate pale face
  A quizzical thin smile is showing,
His cheeks are wrinkled like fine lace,
  His kind blue eyes are gay and glowing.
He wears a brilliant-hued cravat,
  A suit to match his soft grey hair,
A rakish stick, a knowing hat,
  A manner blithe and debonair.

How good that he who always knew
  That being lovely was a duty,
Should have gold halls to wander through
  And should himself inhabit beauty.

[193]

How like his old unselfish way
  To leave those halls of splendid mirth
And comfort those condemned to stay
  Upon the dull and sombre earth.

Some people ask: "What cruel chance
  Made Martin's life so sad a story?"
Martin? Why, he exhaled romance,
  And wore an overcoat of glory.
A fleck of sunlight in the street,
  A horse, a book, a girl who smiled,
Such visions made each moment sweet
  For this receptive ancient child.

Because it was old Martin's lot
  To be, not make, a decoration,
Shall we then scorn him, having not
  His genius of appreciation?
Rich joy and love he got and gave;
  His heart was merry as his dress;
Pile laurel wreaths upon his grave
  Who did not gain, but was, success!

THE APARTMENT HOUSE

SEVERE against the pleasant arc of sky
  The great stone box is cruelly displayed.
The street becomes more dreary from its shade,
And vagrant breezes touch its walls and die.
Here sullen convicts in their chains might lie,
  Or slaves toil dumbly at some dreary trade.
  How worse than folly is their labour made
Who cleft the rocks that this might rise on high!

Yet, as I look, I see a woman's face
  Gleam from a window far above the street.
This is a house of homes, a sacred place,
  By human passion made divinely sweet.
How all the building thrills with sudden grace
  Beneath the magic of Love's golden feet!

[195]

AS WINDS THAT BLOW AGAINST A STAR

(For Aline)

NOW by what whim of wanton chance
    Do radiant eyes know sombre days?
And feet that shod in light should dance
    Walk weary and laborious ways?

But rays from Heaven, white and whole,
    May penetrate the gloom of earth;
And tears but nourish, in your soul,
    The glory of celestial mirth.

The darts of toil and sorrow, sent
    Against your peaceful beauty, are
As foolish and as impotent
    As winds that blow against a star.

ST. LAURENCE

WITHIN the broken Vatican
    The murdered Pope is lying dead.
The soldiers of Valerian
    Their evil hands are wet and red.

Unarmed, unmoved, St. Laurence waits,
    His cassock is his only mail.
The troops of Hell have burst the gates,
    But Christ is Lord, He shall prevail.

They have encompassed him with steel,
    They spit upon his gentle face,
He smiles and bleeds, nor will reveal
    The Church's hidden treasure-place.

Ah, faithful steward, worthy knight,
    Well hast thou done.   Behold thy fee!
Since thou hast fought the goodly fight
    A martyr's death is fixed for thee.

St. Laurence, pray for us to bear
    The faith which glorifies thy name.
St. Laurence, pray for us to share
    The wounds of Love's consuming flame.

[197]

TO A YOUNG POET WHO KILLED HIMSELF

WHEN you had played with life a space
  And made it drink and lust and sing,
You flung it back into God's face
  And thought you did a noble thing.
"Lo, I have lived and loved," you said,
  "And sung to fools too dull to hear me.
Now for a cool and grassy bed
  With violets in blossom near me."

Well, rest is good for weary feet,
  Although they ran for no great prize;
And violets are very sweet,
  Although their roots are in your eyes.
But hark to what the earthworms say
  Who share with you your muddy haven:
"The fight was on—you ran away.
  You are a coward and a craven.

"The rug is ruined where you bled;
  It was a dirty way to die!
To put a bullet through your head
  And make a silly woman cry!

TO A YOUNG POET

You could not vex the merry stars
   Nor make them heed you, dead or living.
Not all your puny anger mars
   God's irresistible forgiving.

"Yes, God forgives and men forget,
   And you're forgiven and forgotten.
You might be gaily sinning yet
   And quick and fresh instead of rotten.
And when you think of love and fame
   And all that might have come to pass,
Then don't you feel a little shame?
   And don't you think you were an ass?"

MEMORIAL DAY

"Dulce et decorum est"

THE bugle echoes shrill and sweet,
But not of war it sings to-day.
The road is rhythmic with the feet
Of men-at-arms who come to pray.

The roses blossom white and red
On tombs where weary soldiers lie;
Flags wave above the honoured dead
And martial music cleaves the sky.

Above their wreath-strewn graves we kneel,
They kept the faith and fought the fight.
Through flying lead and crimson steel
They plunged for Freedom and the Right.

May we, their grateful children, learn
Their strength, who lie beneath this sod,
Who went through fire and death to earn
At last the accolade of God.

In shining rank on rank arrayed
They march, the legions of the Lord;
He is their Captain unafraid,
The Prince of Peace . . . Who brought a
sword.

THE ROSARY

NOT on the lute, or harp of many strings
　　Shall all men praise the Master of all song.
Our life is brief, one saith, and art is long;
And skilled must be the laureates of kings.
Silent, O lips that utter foolish things!
　　Rest, awkward fingers striking all notes wrong!
　　How from your toil shall issue, white and strong,
Music like that God's chosen poet sings?

There is one harp that any hand can play,
　　And from its strings what harmonies arise!
There is one song that any mouth can say,—
　　A song that lingers when all singing dies.
When on their beads our Mother's children pray,
　　Immortal music charms the grateful skies.

VISION

(For Aline)

HOMER, they tell us, was blind and could not
    see the beautiful faces
  Looking up into his own and reflecting the joy of
    his dream,
    Yet did he seem
Gifted with eyes that could follow the gods to their
    holiest places.

I have no vision of gods, not of Eros with love-
    arrows laden,
  Jupiter thundering death or of Juno his white-
    breasted queen,
    Yet have I seen
All of the joy of the world in the innocent heart of
    a maiden.

TO CERTAIN POETS

NOW is the rhymer's honest trade
A thing for scornful laughter made.

The merchant's sneer, the clerk's disdain,
These are the burden of our pain.

Because of you did this befall,
You brought this shame upon us all.

You little poets mincing there
With women's hearts and women's hair!

How sick Dan Chaucer's ghost must be
To hear you lisp of "Poesie"!

A heavy-handed blow, I think,
Would make your veins drip scented ink.

You strut and smirk your little while
So mildly, delicately vile!

Your tiny voices mock God's wrath,
You snails that crawl along His path!

Why, what has God or man to do
With wet, amorphous things like you?

[203]

POEMS AT HOME

This thing alone you have achieved:
Because of you, it is believed

That all who earn their bread by rhyme
Are like yourselves, exuding slime.

Oh, cease to write, for very shame,
Ere all men spit upon our name!

Take up your needles, drop your pen,
And leave the poet's craft to men!

LOVE'S LANTERN

(For Aline)

BECAUSE the road was steep and long
    And through the dark and lonely land,
God set upon my lips a song
    And put a lantern in my hand.

Through miles on weary miles of night
    That stretch relentless in my way
My lantern burns serene and white,
    An unexhausted cup of day.

O golden lights and lights like wine,
    How dim your boasted splendours are.
Behold this little lamp of mine;
    It is more starlike than a star!

POEMS AT HOME

ST. ALEXIS

Patron of Beggars

WE who beg for bread as we daily tread
    Country lane and city street,
Let us kneel and pray on the broad highway
    To the saint with the vagrant feet.
Our altar light is a buttercup bright,
    And our shrine is a bank of sod,
But still we share St. Alexis' care,
    The Vagabond of God.

They gave him a home in purple Rome
    And a princess for his bride,
But he rowed away on his wedding day
    Down the Tiber's rushing tide.
And he came to land on the Asian strand
    Where the heathen people dwell;
As a beggar he strayed and he preached and prayed
    And he saved their souls from hell.

Bowed with years and pain he came back again
    To his father's dwelling place.
There was none to see who this tramp might be,
    For they knew not his bearded face.

[206]

ST. ALEXIS

But his father said, "Give him drink and bread
  And a couch underneath the stair."
So Alexis crept to his hole and slept.
  But he might not linger there.

For when night came down on the seven-hilled
      town,
  And the emperor hurried in,
Saying, "Lo, I hear that a saint is near
  Who will cleanse us of our sin,"
Then they looked in vain where the saint had lain.
  For his soul had fled afar,
From his fleshly home he had gone to roam
  Where the gold-paved highways are.

We who beg for bread as we daily tread
  Country lane and city street,
Let us kneel and pray on the broad highway
  To the saint with the vagrant feet.
Our altar light is a buttercup bright,
  And our shrine is a bank of sod,
But still we share St. Alexis' care,
  The Vagabond of God!

FOLLY

(For A. K. K.)

WHAT distant mountains thrill and glow
    Beneath our Lady Folly's tread?
Why has she left us, wise in woe,
    Shrewd, practical, uncomforted?
We cannot love or dream or sing,
    We are too cynical to pray,
There is no joy in anything
    Since Lady Folly went away.

Many a knight and gentle maid,
    Whose glory shines from years gone by,
Through ignorance was unafraid
    And as a fool knew how to die.
Saint Folly rode beside Jehanne
    And broke the ranks of Hell with her,
And Folly's smile shone brightly on
    Christ's plaything, Brother Juniper.

Our minds are troubled and defiled
    By study in a weary school.
O for the folly of the child!
    The ready courage of the fool!

FOLLY

Lord, crush our knowledge utterly
  And make us humble, simple men;
And cleansed of wisdom, let us see
  Our Lady Folly's face again.

MADNESS

(For Sara Teasdale)

THE lonely farm, the crowded street,
The palace and the slum,
Give welcome to my silent feet
As, bearing gifts, I come.

Last night a beggar crouched alone,
A ragged helpless thing;
I set him on a moonbeam throne—
To-day he is a king.

Last night a king in orb and crown
Held court with splendid cheer;
To-day he tears his purple gown
And moans and shrieks in fear.

Not iron bars, nor flashing spears,
Not land, nor sky, nor sea,
Nor love's artillery of tears
Can keep mine own from me.

Serene, unchanging, ever fair,
I smile with secret mirth
And in a net of mine own hair
I swing the captive earth.

POETS

VAIN is the chiming of forgotten bells
     That the wind sways above a ruined shrine.
Vainer his voice in whom no longer dwells
     Hunger that craves immortal Bread and Wine.

Light songs we breathe that perish with our breath
     Out of our lips that have not kissed the rod.
They shall not live who have not tasted death.
     They only sing who are struck dumb by God.

CITIZEN OF THE WORLD

NO longer of Him be it said,
    "He hath no place to lay His head."

In every land a constant lamp
Flames by His small and mighty camp.

There is no strange and distant place
That is not gladdened by His face.

And every nation kneels to hail
The Splendour shining through Its veil.

Cloistered beside the shouting street,
Silent, He calls me to His feet.

Imprisoned for His love of me,
He makes my spirit greatly free.

And through my lips that uttered sin
The King of Glory enters in.

TO A BLACKBIRD AND HIS MATE

TO A BLACKBIRD AND HIS MATE WHO DIED IN THE SPRING

(For Kenton)

AN iron hand has stilled the throats
    That throbbed with loud and rhythmic glee
And dammed the flood of silver notes
    That drenched the world in melody.
The blosmy apple boughs are yearning
For their wild choristers' returning,
    But no swift wings flash through the tree.

Ye that were glad and fleet and strong,
    Shall Silence take you in her net?
And shall Death quell that radiant song
    Whose echo thrills the meadow yet?
Burst the frail web about you clinging
And charm Death's cruel heart with singing
    Till with strange tears his eyes are wet.

The scented morning of the year
    Is old and stale now ye are gone.
No friendly songs the children hear
    Among the bushes on the lawn.
When babies wander out a-Maying
Will ye, their bards, afar be straying?
    Unhymned by you, what is the dawn?

Nay, since ye loved ye cannot die.
  Above the stars is set your nest.
Through Heaven's fields ye sing and fly
  And in the trees of Heaven rest.
And little children in their dreaming
Shall see your soft black plumage gleaming
  And smile, by your clear music blest.

THE FOURTH SHEPHERD
(For Thomas Walsh)

I

ON nights like this the huddled sheep
 Are like white clouds upon the grass,
And merry herdsmen guard their sleep,
 And chat and watch the big stars pass.

It is a pleasant thing to lie
 Upon the meadow on the hill
With kindly fellowship near by
 Of sheep and men of gentle will.

I lean upon my broken crook
 And dream of sheep and grass and men—
O shameful eyes that cannot look
 On any honest thing again!

On bloody feet I clambered down
 And fled the wages of my sin,
I am the leavings of the town,
 And meanly serve its meanest inn.

I tramp the courtyard stones in grief,
 While sleep takes man and beast to her.
And every cloud is calling "Thief!"
 And every star calls "Murderer!"

POEMS AT HOME

The hand of God is sure and strong,
    Nor shall a man forever flee
The bitter punishment of wrong.
    The wrath of God is over me!

With ashen bread and wine of tears
    Shall I be solaced in my pain.
I wear through black and endless years
    Upon my brow the mark of Cain.

Poor vagabond, so old and mild,
    Will they not keep him for a night?
And She, a woman great with child,
    So frail and pitiful and white.

Good people, since the tavern door
    Is shut to you, come here instead.
See, I have cleansed my stable floor
    And piled fresh hay to make a bed.

Here is some milk and oaten cake.
    Lie down and sleep and rest you fair,
Nor fear, O simple folk, to take
    The bounty of a child of care.

On nights like this the huddled sheep—
    I never saw a night so fair.
How huge the sky is, and how deep!
    And how the planets flash and glare!

THE FOURTH SHEPHERD

At dawn beside my drowsy flock
   What wingéd music I have heard!
But now the clouds with singing rock
   As if the sky were turning bird.

O blinding Light, O blinding Light!
   Burn through my heart with sweetest pain.
O flaming Song, most loudly bright,
   Consume away my deadly stain!

The stable glows against the sky,
   And who are these that throng the way?
My three old comrades hasten by
   And shining angels kneel and pray.

The door swings wide—I cannot go—
   I must and yet I dare not see.
Lord, who am I that I should know—
   Lord, God, be merciful to me!

O Whiteness, whiter than the fleece
   Of new-washed sheep on April sod!
O Breath of Life, O Prince of Peace,
   O Lamb of God, O Lamb of God!

EASTER

THE air is like a butterfly
   With frail blue wings.
The happy earth looks at the sky
   And sings.

MOUNT HOUVENKOPF

SERENE he stands, with mist serenely crowned,
   And draws a cloak of trees about his breast.
The thunder roars but cannot break his rest
And from his rugged face the tempests bound.
He does not heed the angry lightning's wound,
   The raging blizzard is his harmless guest,
   And human life is but a passing jest
To him who sees Time spin the years around.

But fragile souls, in skyey reaches find
   High vantage-points and view him from afar.
How low he seems to the ascended mind,
   How brief he seems where all things endless are;
This little playmate of the mighty wind,
   This young companion of an ancient star.

THE HOUSE WITH NOBODY IN IT

WHENEVER I walk to Suffern along the
    Erie track
I go by a poor old farmhouse with its shingles
    broken and black.
I suppose I've passed it a hundred times, but I al-
    ways stop for a minute
And look at the house, the tragic house, the house
    with nobody in it.

I never have seen a haunted house, but I hear there
    are such things;
That they hold the talk of spirits, their mirth and
    sorrowings.
I know this house isn't haunted, and I wish it were,
    I do;
For it wouldn't be so lonely if it had a ghost or two.

This house on the road to Suffern needs a dozen
    panes of glass,
And somebody ought to weed the walk and take a
    scythe to the grass.
It needs new paint and shingles, and the vines
    should be trimmed and tied;
But what it needs the most of all is some people liv-
    ing inside.

THE HOUSE WITH NOBODY IN IT

If I had a lot of money and all my debts were paid
I'd put a gang of men to work with brush and saw
and spade.
I'd buy that place and fix it up the way it used to be
And I'd find some people who wanted a home and
give it to them free.

Now, a new house standing empty, with staring
window and door,
Looks idle, perhaps, and foolish, like a hat on its
block in the store.
But there's nothing mournful about it; it cannot be
sad and lone
For the lack of something within it that it has never
known.

But a house that has done what a house should do,
a house that has sheltered life,
That has put its loving wooden arms around a man
and his wife,
A house that has echoed a baby's laugh and held up
his stumbling feet,
Is the saddest sight, when it's left alone, that ever
your eyes could meet.

So whenever I go to Suffern along the Erie track
I never go by the empty house without stopping and
looking back,

Yet it hurts me to look at the crumbling roof and
    the shutters fallen apart,
For I can't help thinking the poor old house is a
    house with a broken heart.

DAVE LILLY

THERE'S a brook on the side of Greylock that
    used to be full of trout,
But there's nothing there now but minnows; they
    say it is all fished out.
I fished there many a Summer day some twenty
    years ago,
And I never quit without getting a mess of a dozen
    or so.

There was a man, Dave Lilly, who lived on the
    North Adams road,
And he spent all his time fishing, while his neigh-
    bors reaped and sowed.
He was the luckiest fisherman in the Berkshire hills,
    I think.
And when he didn't go fishing he'd sit in the tavern
    and drink.

Well, Dave is dead and buried and nobody cares
    very much;
They have no use in Greylock for drunkards and
    loafers and such.

But I always liked Dave Lilly, he was pleasant as
you could wish;
He was shiftless and good-for-nothing, but he certainly could fish.

The other night I was walking up the hill from
Williamstown
And I came to the brook I mentioned, and I
stopped on the bridge and sat down.
I looked at the blackened water with its little flecks
of white
And I heard it ripple and whisper in the still of the
Summer night.

And after I'd been there a minute it seemed to me
I could feel
The presence of someone near me, and I heard the
hum of a reel.
And the water was churned and broken, and some-
thing was brought to land
By a twist and flirt of a shadowy rod in a deft and
shadowy hand.

I scrambled down to the brookside and hunted all
about;
There wasn't a sign of a fisherman; there wasn't
a sign of a trout.

DAVE LILLY

But I heard somebody chuckle behind the hollow
    oak
And I got a whiff of tobacco like Lilly used to
    smoke.

It's fifteen years, they tell me, since anyone fished
    that brook;
And there's nothing in it but minnows that nibble
    the bait off your hook.
But before the sun has risen and after the moon has
    set
I know that it's full of ghostly trout for Lilly's
    ghost to get.

I guess I'll go to the tavern and get a bottle of rye
And leave it down by the hollow oak, where Lilly's
    ghost went by.
I meant to go up on the hillside and try to find his
    grave
And put some flowers on it—but this will be better
    for Dave.

ALARM CLOCKS

WHEN Dawn strides out to wake a dewy
      farm
  Across green fields and yellow hills of hay
  The little twittering birds laugh in his way
And poise triumphant on his shining arm.
He bears a sword of flame but not to harm
  The wakened life that feels his quickening sway
  And barnyard voices shrilling "It is day!"
Take by his grace a new and alien charm.

But in the city, like a wounded thing
  That limps to cover from the angry chase,
He steals down streets where sickly arc-lights sing,
  And wanly mock his young and shameful face;
And tiny gongs with cruel fervour ring
  In many a high and dreary sleeping place.

WAVERLEY

1814-1914

WHEN on a novel's newly printed page
   We find a maudlin eulogy of sin,
  And read of ways that harlots wander in,
 And of sick souls that writhe in helpless rage;
Or when Romance, bespectacled and sage,
   Taps on her desk and bids the class begin
   To con the problems that have always been
Perplexed mankind's unhappy heritage;

Then in what robes of honour habited
   The laureled wizard of the North appears!
Who raised Prince Charlie's cohorts from the dead,
   Made Rose's mirth and Flora's noble tears,
And formed that shining legion at whose head
   Rides Waverley, triumphant o'er the years!

EARLY POEMS

IN A BOOK-SHOP

ALL day I serve among the volumes telling
   Old tales of love and war and high romance;
Good company, God wot, is in them dwelling,
   Brave knights who dared to scorn untoward
      chance.

King Arthur—Sidney—Copperfield—the daring
   And friendly souls of Meredith's bright page—
The Pilgrim on his darksome journey faring,
   And Shakespeare's heroes, great in love and rage.

Fair ladies, too—here Beatricè smiling
   Through hell leads Dante to the happy stars;
And Heloise, the cruel guards beguiling,
   With Abelard makes mock of convent bars.

Yet when night comes I leave these folks with
      pleasure
   To open Love's great summer-scented tome
Within whose pages—precious beyond measure—
   My own White Flower Lady hath her home.

SLENDER YOUR HANDS

SLENDER your hands and soft and
white
  As petals of moon-kissed roses;
Yet the grasp of your fingers slight
  My passionate heart encloses.

Innocent eyes like delicate spheres
  That are born when day is dying;
Yet the wisdom of all the years
  Is in their lovelight lying.

SLEEP SONG

The Lady World
Is sleeping on her white and cloudy bed.
Like petals furled
Her eyelids close.   Beside her dream-filled head
Her lover stands in silver cloak and shoon,
The faithful Moon.

So Love, my Love,
Sleep on, my Love, my Life, be not afraid.
The Moon above
Shall guard the World, and I my little maid.
Your life, your love, your dreams are mine to
keep,
So sleep, so sleep.

WHITE BIRD OF LOVE

LITTLE white bird of the summer sky,
    Silver against the golden sun,
Over the green of the hills you fly,
    You and the sweet, wild air are one.

Glorious sights are in that far place
    Reached by your daisy-petal wing,
Rose-coloured meteors dive through space,
    Stars made of molten music sing.

Still, though your quivering eager flight
    Reaches the groves by Heaven town,
Where all the angels cry out, "Alight!
    Stop, little bird, come down, come down!"

Careless you speed over fields of stars,
    Darting through Heaven swift and free;
Nothing your arrowy passage bars
    Back to the earth and back to me.

Here in the orchard of dream-fruit fair
    Out of my dreams is built your nest.
Blossoming dreams all the branches bear,
    Fit for my silver dream-bird's rest.

WHITE BIRD OF LOVE

Here, since they love you, the young stars shine,
    Through the white petals come their beams.
Little white love-laden bird of mine,
    Let them shine on you through my dreams.

TRANSFIGURATION

IF it should be my task, I being God,
　From whirling atoms to evolve your mate,
　With hands omnipotent I should create
A great-souled hero, with the starlight shod.
The subject worlds should tremble at his nod
　And all the angel host upon him wait,
　Yet he should leave his pomp and splendid state
And kneel to kiss the ground whereon you trod.

But God, who like a little child is wise,
　Made me, a common thing of earthly clay;
Then bade me go and see within your eyes
　The flame of love that burns more bright than
　　day,
And as I looked I knew with wild surprise
　I was transformed—your heart in my heart lay.

BALLADE OF MY LADY'S BEAUTY

BALLADE OF MY LADY'S BEAUTY

SQUIRE ADAM had two wives, they say,
   Two wives had he, for his delight,
He kissed and clypt them all the day
   And clypt and kissed them all the night.
   Now Eve like ocean foam was white
And Lilith roses dipped in wine,
   But though they were a goodly sight
No lady is so fair as mine.

To Venus some folk tribute pay
   And Queen of Beauty she is hight,
And Sainte Marie the world doth sway
   In cerule napery bedight.
   My wonderment these twain invite,
Their comeliness it is divine,
   And yet I say in their despite,
No lady is so fair as mine.

Dame Helen caused a grievous fray,
   For love of her brave men did fight,
The eyes of her made sages fey
   And put their hearts in woful plight.

To her no rhymes will I indite,
For her no garlands will I twine,
    Though she be made of flowers and light
No lady is so fair as mine.

L'ENVOI

Prince Eros, Lord of lovely might
    Who on Olympus dost recline,
Do I not tell the truth aright?
    No lady is so fair as mine.

FOR A BIRTHDAY

APRIL with her violets,
　　May and June with roses,
　　　Young July with all her flowers, crimson, gold
　　　　and white,
Each in place her tribute sets,
　　Each her wreath composes,
　　　Making glad the roadway for the Lady of
　　　　Delight.

Birds with many colours gay,
　　Through the branches flitting,
　　　Sing, to greet my Lady Love, a lusty welcome
　　　　song.
Even bees make holiday,
　　Hive and honey quitting,
　　　Tremulous and jubilant they join the eager
　　　　throng.

Now the road is flower-paved;
　　Timid fawns are peering
　　　From their pleasant vantage in the roadside's
　　　　leafy green.

All the world in sunlight laved,
  Knows the hour is nearing
    That shall bring the golden presence of the
      well-loved Queen.

Hark! at last the silver trill
  Of a lute is sounding—
    Happy August, purple-clad, appears with all
      her train.
Sudden sweet the branches fill;
  Every heart is bounding;
    August comes, the kindly nurse of her who is
      to reign!

And now, with proud and valiant gait,
  An hundred centaurs come.
Pan rides the foremost one in state;
  The waiting crowd grows dumb.
Each centaur wears a jewelled thong
  And harness bright of sheen;
They draw through surging floods of song
  The carriage of the Queen!

"Hail! Hail! Hail! to the Queen in her moonstone
    car!
Hail! Hail! Hail! to the Lady whose slaves we are!
[240]

JOYCE KILMER, AGE 21

TAKEN IN ACADEMIC GOWN,
IMMEDIATELY AFTER HIS
GRADUATION, AND DIRECTLY
PRECEDING HIS MARRIAGE

FOR A BIRTHDAY

We of the meadows, the rocks and the hills,
Dwellers in oceans and rivers and rills,
Beasts of the forests and birds of the air,
Linnet and butterfly, lion and bear,
Daisy and daffodill, spruce-tree and fir,
Yield to our Queen and do homage to her!
Hail! Hail! Hail! we welcome thy royal sway!
Hail! Hail! Hail! O Queen, on this festal day!"

So all the world kneels down to you,
    And all things are your own;
Now let a humble rhymer sue
    Before your crystal throne.
Fair Queen, at your rose-petal feet
    Bid me to live and die!
Not all your world of lovers, Sweet,
    Can love so much as I.

WAYFARERS

UNDERNEATH the orchard trees lies a
  gypsy sleeping,
  Tattered cloak and swarthy face and shaggy
    moonlit hair;
One brown hand his crazy fiddle in its grasp is keep-
    ing,
  Through the Land of Dreams he strolls and sings
    his love songs there.

Up above the apple blossoms where the stars are
    shining,
  Free and careless wandering among the clouds
    he goes,
Singing of his lady-love and for her pleasure twin-
    ing
  Wreaths of Heaven flowers, violet and golden
    rose.

In his sleep he stirs, and wakes to find his love be-
    side him,
  Pours his load of Dreamland blooms before her
    silver feet,

WAYFARERS

Takes her in his arms and as her soft brown tresses
  hide him
Both together fare to Dreamland up the star-
  paved street.

PRINCESS BALLADE

NEVER a horn sounds in Sherwood to-night,
    Friar Tuck's drinking Olympian ale,
Little John's wandered away from our sight,
    Robin Hood's bow hangs unused on its nail.
    Even the moon has grown weary and pale
Sick for the glint of Maid Marian's hair,
    But there is one joy on mountain and dale,
Fairies abound all the time, everywhere!

Saints have attacked them with sacredest might,
    They could not shatter their gossamer mail;
Steam-driven engines can never affright
    Fairies who dance in their spark-sprinkled trail.
    Still for a warning the sad Banshees wail,
Still are the Leprechauns ready to bear
    Purses of gold to their captors for bail;
Fairies abound all the time, everywhere!

Oberon, king of the realms of delight,
    May your domain over us never fail.
Mab, as a rainbow-hued butterfly bright,
    Yours is the glory that age cannot stale.

PRINCESS BALLADE

When we are planted down under the shale,
Fairy-folk, drop a few daffodils there,
  Comfort our souls in the Stygian vale;
Fairies abound all the time, everywhere.

L'ENVOI

White Flower Princess, though sophisters rail,
  Let us be glad in faith that we share.
None shall the Good People safely assail;
  Fairies abound all the time, everywhere!

LULLABY FOR A BABY FAIRY

NIGHT is over; through the clover globes of
      crystal shine;
Birds are calling; sunlight falling on the wet green
      vine.
  Little wings must folded lie, little lips be still
  While the sun is in the sky, over Fairy Hill.
    Sleep, sleep, sleep,
      Baby with buttercup hair,
        Golden rays
    Into the violet creep.
    Dream, dream deep;
      Dream of the night-revels fair.
        Daylight stays;
    Sleep, little fairy child, sleep.

Rest in daytime; night is playtime, all good fairies
      know.
Under sighing grasses lying, off to slumber go.
  Night will come with stars agleam, lilies in her
      hand,
  Calling you from Hills of Dream back to Fairy-
      land.

LULLABY FOR A BABY FAIRY

Sleep, sleep, sleep,
    Baby with buttercup hair;
      Golden rays
  Into the violet creep.
Dream, dream deep;
    Dream of the night-revels fair.
      Daylight stays;
  Sleep, little fairy child, sleep.

A DEAD POET

FAIR Death, kind Death, it was a gracious deed
　　To take that weary vagrant to thy breast.
Love, Song and Wine had he, and but one need—
　　Rest.

THE MAD FIDDLER

I SLEEP beneath a bracken sheet
   In sunlight or in rain,
The road dust burns my naked feet,
   The sunrays sear my brain;
But children love my fiddle's sound
   And if a lad be straying,
His mother knows he may be found
   Where old Mad Larry's playing.

O fiddle, let us follow, follow,
   Till we see my Eileen's face,
Through the moonlight like a swallow
   Off she flew to some far place.

O, did you ever love a lass?
   I loved a lass one day,
And she would lie upon the grass
   And sing while I would play.
She was a cruel, lovely thing,
   Nor heart nor soul have I,
For Eileen took them that soft spring
   When she flew to the sky.

So fiddle, let us follow, follow,
　　Till we see my Eileen's face,
Through the moonlight like a swallow
　　Off she flew to some far place.

THE GRASS IN MADISON SQUARE

THE pleasant turf is dried and marred and
    seared,
    The grass is dead.
No soft green shoot, by rain and sunshine reared,
    Lifts up its head.

I think the grass that made the park so gay
    In early spring
Now decks the lawns of Heaven where babies play
    And dance and sing.

And poor old vagabonds who now have left
    The dusty street,
Find fields of which they were in life bereft,
    Beneath their feet.

SAID THE ROSE

NO flower hath so fair a face as this pale love of
    mine;
When he bends down to kiss my heart, my petals
    try to twine
About his lips to hold them fast. He is so very fair,
My lover with the pale, sad face and forest-fragrant
    hair.

I think it is a pleasant place, this garden where I
    grow,
With gravel walks and grassy mounds and crosses
    in a row.
There is no toil nor worry here, nor clatter of the
    street,
And here each night my lover comes, pale, sad and
    very sweet.

He never heeds the violets or lilies tall and white;
I am his love, his only love, his Flower of Delight;
And often when the cold moonbeams are lying all
    around
My lover kneels the whole night through beside me
    on the ground.

[252]

SAID THE ROSE

How can I miss the sunshine-laden breezes of the
south
When all my heart is burning with the kisses of his
mouth?
How can I miss the coming of the comfort-bringing
rain
When his hot tears are filling me with heaven-sweet
love-pain?

There is a jealous little bird that envies me my love,
He sings this bitter, bitter song from his brown nest
above:
"Was ever yet a mortal man who wed a flower wife?
He loves the girl down in your roots whose dead
breast gives you life."

O little bird, O jealous bird, fly off and cease your
chatter!
My lover is my lover, and what can a dead girl
matter?
In his hot kisses and sweet tears I shall my petals
steep;
I am his love, his only love, I have his heart to keep.

METAMORPHOSIS

HE was an evil thing to see—
 Of joy his mouth was desolate;
His body was a stunted tree,
 His eyes were pools of lust and hate.

Now silverly the linnet sings
 On leaves that from his temples start,
And gay the yellow crocus springs
 From the rich clod that was his heart.

FOR A CHILD

FOR A CHILD

HIS mind has neither need nor power to know
  The foolish things that men call right and
    wrong.
For him the streams of pleasant love-wind flow,
  For him the mystic, sleep-compelling song.
Through love he rules his love-made universe,
  And sees with eyes by ignorance made keen
The fauns and elves whom older eyes disperse,
  Great Pan and all the fairies with their queen.
King gods, I pray, bestow on him this dole,
  Not wisdom, wealth, nor mighty deeds to do,
But let him keep his happy pagan soul,
  The poet-vision, simple, free and true,
To hunt the rainbow-gold and phantom lights,
And meet with dryads on the wooded heights.

THE CLOUDED SUN
(To A. S.)

IT is not good for poets to grow old,
  For they serve Death that loves and Love that
    kills;
  And Love and Death, enthroned above the hills,
Call back their faithful servants to the fold
Before Age makes them passionless and cold.

Therefore it is that no more sorry thing
  Can shut the sunlight from the thirsty grass
  Than some grey head through which no longer
    pass
Wild dreams more lively than the scent of Spring
To fire the blood and make the glad mouth sing.

Far happier he, who, young and full of pride
  And radiant with the glory of the sun,
  Leaves earth before his singing time is done.
All wounds of Time the graveyard flowers hide,
His beauty lives, as fresh as when he died.

Then through the words wherein his spirit dwells
  The world may see his young impetuous face
  Unmarred by Time, with undiminished grace;
While memory no piteous story tells
Of barren days, stale loves and broken spells.
[256]

THE CLOUDED SUN

* * * * * * *

Brother and Master, we are wed with woe.
 Yea, Grief's funereal cloud it is that hovers
 About the head of us, thy mournful lovers.
Uncomforted and sick with pain we go,
Dust on our brows and at our hearts the snow.

The London lights flare on the chattering street,
 Young men and maidens love and dance and die;
 Wine flows, and the perfumes float up to the sky.
Once thou couldst feel that this was very sweet,
Now thou art still—mouth, hands and weary feet.

O subtle mouth, whereon the Sphinx has placed
 The smile of those she kisses at their birth,
 Sing once again, for Spring has thrilled the earth.
Nay, thou art dumb. Not even April's taste
Is sweet to thee in thy live coffin cased.

There is no harsher tragedy than this—
 That thou, who feltest as no man before
 Scent, colour, taste and sound and didst outpour
For us rich draughts of thine enchanted bliss
Shouldst be plunged down this cruel black abyss.

[257]

Brother and Master, if our love could free
   Thy flameborne spirit from its leaden chain,
   Thou shouldst rise up from this sad house of **pain,**
Be young and fair as thou wast wont to be,
And strong with joy as is the boundless sea.

Brother and Master, at thy feet we lay
   These roses, red as lips that thou hast sung,
To mingle with the green and fragrant bay,
   And cypress wreaths above thy head are hung.
We kneel awhile, then turn in tears away.

THE POET'S EPITAPH

DREAMS fade with morning light;
   Never a morn for thee,
Dreamer of dreams, good-night.

Over our earthly sight
   Shadows of woe must be;
Dreams fade with morning light.

Soldiers awake to fight—
   Thou art from strife set free,
Dreamer of dreams, good-night.

Day breaketh, cruel, white,
   Lovely the forms that flee;
Dreams fade with morning light.

Thine is the sure delight,
   Sleep-visions still to see,
Dreamer of dreams, good-night.

Pity us from thy height,
   Dawn-haunted slaves are we;
Dreams fade with morning light,
Dreamer of dreams, good-night.

[259]

BEAUTY'S HAIR

A GLEAM of light across the night,
    I know that you are there;
The heavens show the lovely glow
    Of your transcendent hair,
    Your luminous, miraculous, and morning-
    coloured hair.

I'll take my silver javelin
    And point it with a star,
For I have vowed to climb a cloud
    And reach to where you are.
My javelin's barb shall pierce your hair
    And pin it to the sky,
And I will run to the island sun
    Where captive you will lie,
And then I shall dare to touch your hair,
To steal a tress of your magic hair,
And bring to the world a tress of hair
    And win the world thereby.

Or shall I put on a green-sea cloak
    With sunset laces trimmed,
And shine so gay that the dawn will say
    That her radiance is dimmed?
There never was a lover could shine more fair
    Than I in my cloak will shine;

[260]

BEAUTY'S HAIR

And all for the sake of your merry hair,
Your whimsical, perilous, golden hair,
Your lovely, terrible, golden hair,
  More sweet than love or wine.

A twisted bit of silver
  Fell down and bruised my face.
What was it broke my broidered cloak
  And tore the sunset lace?
I must be clad in sorrow
  Because you are so gay,
And close my eyes if I would see
  A whiter light than day.
So lofty is your golden hair,
I cannot climb to touch your hair,
I must kneel down to find your hair
  Upon the trampled way.

THE WAY OF LOVE

(An Old Legend)

WHEN darkness hovers over earth
  And day gives place to night,
Then lovers see the Milky Way
  Gleam mystically bright,
And calling it the Way of Love
  They hail it with delight.

She was a lady wondrous fair,
  A right brave lover he,
And sooth they suffered grievous pain
  And sorrowed mightily,
For they were parted during life
  By leagues of land and sea.

She died. Then Death came to the man.
  He met him joyfully,
And said, "Thou Angel Death, well met!
  Quick, do thy will with me,
That I may haste to greet my love
  In Heaven's company."

[262]

THE WAY OF LOVE

Now on one side of Heaven he dwelt
    And on the other, she;
And broad between them stretched sheer space
    Whereon no way might be,
The empty, yawning, awful depth,
    Unplumbed infinity.

The deathless spheric melody
    Came gently to his ear,
And dulcet notes, the harmonies
    Of Seraphs chanting near.
He heeded not for listening
    His lady's voice to hear.

The Saints and Martyrs round him ranged
    A goodly company,
The Virgin, robed in radiance,
    The Holy Trinity.
He heeded not, but strained his eyes
    His lady's face to see.

At last from far across the void
    Her voice came, faint and sweet.
The bright-hued walls of Paradise
    Did the glad sound repeat;
The distant stars on which she stood
    Shone bright beneath her feet.

"Dear Love," she said, "Oh, come to me!
  I cannot see your face.
O will not Lord Christ grant to us
  To cross this sea of space?"
Then thrilled his heart with Love's own might.
  He answered, by Love's grace.

"The world is wide, and Heaven is wide,
  From me to thee is far,
Alas! across Infinity
  No passageways there are.
Sweetheart, I'll make my way to thee,
  I'll build it, star by star!"

Through all the curving vault of sky
  His lusty blows rang out.
He smote the jewel-studded walls
  And with a mighty shout
He tore the gleaming masonry
  And posts that stood about.

He strove to build a massive bridge
  That should the chasm span.
With heart upheld by hope and love
  His great task he began,
And toiled and laboured doughtily
  To work his God-like plan.

THE WAY OF LOVE

He took the heavy beams of gold
   That round him he did see;
The beryl, jacinth, sardius,
   That shone so brilliantly,
And no fair jewel would he spare
   So zealously worked he.

He stole the gorgeous tinted stuffs
   Whereof are sunsets made,
And his rude, grasping, eager hands
   On little stars he laid;
To rob God's sacred treasure-house
   He was no whit afraid.

And so for centuries he worked.
   Across the void at last
A bridge of precious mold did stand
   Completed, strong and fast.
So now the faithful lovers met
   And all their woe was past.

But soon a shining angel guard
   Sped to the throne of gold
And said, "Lord, see yon new-made bridge,
   A mortal, overbold,
Has built it, scorning thy desire!"
   Straightway the tale he told.

Then said: "Now, Master, Thou mayst see
  The thing that has been wrought.
Speak, then, the word, stretch forth Thine hand
  That with the speed of thought
This poor presumptuous work may fall
  And crumble into naught."

God looked upon the angel then
  And on the bridge below.
Then with His smile of majesty
  He said: "Let all things know,
This bridge, which has by Love been built,
  I will not overthrow."

When darkness hovers over earth
  And day gives place to night,
Then lovers see the Milky Way
  Gleam mystically bright,
And calling it the Way of Love,
  They hail it with delight.

CHEVELY CROSSING

THERE two roads cross by Chevely town
  A man is lying dead.
The rumbling wains of scented hay
  Roll over his fair head;
A stake is driven through his heart,
  For his own blood he shed.

*   *   *   *   *   *   *

Among the pleasant flower-stars
  By God's own garden gate,
A little maid fresh come from earth
  One summer night did wait;
Her poppy mouth dropped down with fear,
  With fear her eyes were great.

The angels saw her sinless face,
  The gate was opened wide.
She only shook her dawn-crowned head
  And would not come inside.
She was alone, and so afraid—
  She hid her face and cried.

Her tears dropped down like sun-filled rain
  Through stars and starless space,
Until at last in Chevely town
  Where in a moonlit place
Her lover knelt upon her grave,
  They fell upon his face.

Said he, "My love, my only love,
  My Elena, my Sweet!
Through what wild ways of mystery
  Have strayed your little feet?
Alone, alone this lonely night
  Where only spirits meet!

"It is not my bleak desert life
  That turns my heart to lead,
Not for my empty arms I mourn,
  Nor for my loveless bed;
But that you wander forth alone
  On heights I may not tread.

"If I could stand beside you now,
  Sin-burdened though I be,
I'd bear you through the trackless ways
  From fear and danger free,
Not God himself could daunt the strong
  Undying love of me!

[268]

CHEVELY CROSSING

"Though Heaven is a pleasant place,
    What joy for you is there?
Who tread the jewelled streets alone
    Without my heart to share
Each throb of your heart, and my arm
    Around you, O my Fair!

"I hear your sobbing in the wind,
    And in the summer rain
I feel your tears. My heart is pierced
    With your sad, lonely pain.
My Love! My only Love! I come!
    You shall not call in vain!"

*   *   *   *   *   *   *

Where two roads cross by Chevely town
    A man is lying dead.
The rumbling wains of scented hay
    Roll over his fair head;
A stake is driven through his heart,
    For his own blood he shed.

THE OTHER LOVER

I'M home from off the stormy sea,
    And down the street
The folk come out to welcome me
    On eager feet.
O neighbours, God be with you all,
But for my true love I must call;
She lingers in her father's hall
    So shy, so sweet!

Here is a string of milky pearls
    For her to wear,
An amber comb to match the curls
    Of her bright hair.
O neighbours, do not crowd me so!
Stand by! stand by! for I must go
To put on my love's hand of snow
    This gold ring fair.

Good dame, why do you block the way
    And shake your head?
Must all the things you have to say
    Just now be said?
O neighbours, let me pass—but why—
My God, what makes you women cry?
Come tell me that I too may die!
    Is my love dead?

THE OTHER LOVER

"Nay, Marjorie's a living thing,
　　And fair and strong.
Yet did you wait to give your ring
　　A year too long.
To seek her love there came the **Moon:**
Now Marjorie at night and noon
Is chained and sits alone to **croon**
　　The Moon's love-song."

JOYCE KILMER
Poems, Essays and Letters

TWO VOLUMES IN ONE
Volume Two: *Prose Works*

CONTENTS—VOLUME TWO

ESSAYS

LETTERS

MISCELLANEOUS PIECES

ESSAYS

SERGEANT JOYCE KILMER
165TH INFANTRY (69TH NEW YORK)
A. E. F., FRANCE, MAY, 1918

HOLY IRELAND

WE HAD hiked seventeen miles that stormy December day—the third of a four days' journey. The snow was piled high on our packs, our rifles were crusted with ice, the leather of our hob-nailed boots was frozen stiff over our lamed feet. The weary lieutenant led us to the door of a little house in a side street.

"Next twelve men," he said. A dozen of us dropped out of the ranks and dragged ourselves over the threshold. We tracked snow and mud over a spotless stone floor. Before an open fire stood Madame and the three children—a girl of eight years, a boy of five, a boy of three. They stared with round frightened eyes at *les soldats Americains,* the first they had ever seen. We were too tired to stare back. We at once climbed to the chill attic, our billet, our lodging for the night. First we lifted the packs from one another's aching shoulders; then, without spreading our blankets, we lay down on the bare boards.

For ten minutes there was silence, broken by an

occasional groan, an oath, the striking of a match. Cigarettes glowed like fireflies in a forest. Then a voice came from the corner.

"Where is Sergeant Reilly?" it said. We lazily searched. There was no Sergeant Reilly to be found.

"I'll bet the old bum has gone out after a pint," said the voice. And with the curiosity of the American and the enthusiasm of the Irish we lumbered downstairs in quest of Sergeant Reilly.

He was sitting on a low bench by the fire. His shoes were off and his bruised feet were in a pail of cold water. He was too good a soldier to expose them to the heat at once. The little girl was on his lap and the little boys stood by and envied him. And in a voice that twenty years of soldiering and oceans of whisky had failed to rob of its Celtic sweetness, he was softly singing "Ireland isn't Ireland any more." We listened respectfully.

"They cheer the King and then salute him," said Sergeant Reilly.

"A regular Irishman would shoot him," and we all joined in the chorus, "Ireland isn't Ireland any more."

"Ooh, la, la!" exclaimed Madame, and she and all the children began to talk at the top of their voices.

[12]

What they said Heaven knows, but the tones were friendly, even admiring.

"Gentlemen," said Sergeant Reilly from his post of honor, "the lady who runs this billet is a very nice lady indeed. She says yez can all take off your shoes and dry your socks by the fire. But take turns and don't crowd or I'll trun yez all upstairs."

Now Madame, a woman of some forty years, was a true *bourgeoise,* with all the thrift of her class. And by the terms of her agreement with the authorities she was required to let the soldiers have for one night the attic of her house to sleep in—nothing more; no light, no heat. Also, wood is very expensive in France—for reasons that are engraven in letters of blood on the pages of history. Nevertheless—

"Asseyez-vous, s'il vous plait," said Madame. And she brought nearer to the fire all the chairs the establishment possessed and some chests and boxes to be used as seats. And she and the little girl, whose name was Solange, went out into the snow and came back with heaping armfuls of small logs. The fire blazed merrily—more merrily than it had blazed since August, 1914, perhaps. We surrounded it, and soon the air was thick with steam from our drying socks.

[13]

Meanwhile Madame and the Sergeant had generously admitted all eleven of us into their conversation. A spirited conversation it was, too, in spite of
the fact that she knew no English and the extent of
his French was "du pain," "du vin," "cognac" and
"bon jour." Those of us who knew a little more of
the language of the country acted as interpreters
for the others. We learned the names of the children and their ages. We learned that our hostess
was a widow. Her husband had fallen in battle just
one month before our arrival in her home. She
showed us with simple pride and affection and re-
strained grief his picture. Then she showed us
those of her two brothers—one now fighting at
Salonica, the other a prisoner of war—of her
mother and father, of herself dressed for First Communion.

This last picture she showed somewhat shyly, as
if doubting that we would understand it. But when
one of us asked in halting French if Solange, her
little daughter, had yet made her First Communion,
then Madame's face cleared.

"Mais oui!" she exclaimed. "Et vous, ma foi,
vous etes Catholiques, n'est-ce pas?"

At once rosary beads were flourished to prove our
right to answer this question affirmatively. Tat-

tered prayer-books and somewhat dingy scapulars were brought to light. Madame and the children chattered their surprise and delight to each other, and every exhibit called for a new outburst.

"Ah, la bon S. Benoit! Ah, voila, le Conception Immacule! Ooh la la, le Sacre Coeur!" (which last exclamation sounded in no wise as irreverent as it looks in print).

Now other treasures, too, were shown—treasures chiefly photographic. There were family groups, there were Coney Island snapshots. And Madame and the children were a gratifyingly appreciative audience. They admired and sympathized; they exclaimed appropriately at the beauty of every girl's face, the tenderness of every pictured mother. We had become the intimates of Madame. She had admitted us into her family and we her into ours.

Soldiers—American soldiers of Irish descent— have souls and hearts. These organs (if the soul may be so termed) had been satisfied. But our stomachs remained—and that they yearned was evident to us. We had made our hike on a meal of hardtack and "corned willy." Mess call would sound soon. Should we force our wet shoes on again and plod through the snowy streets to the temporary mess-shack? We knew our supply

[15]

wagons had not succeeded in climbing the last hill into town, and that therefore bread and unsweetened coffee would be our portion. A great depression settled upon us.

But Sergeant Reilly rose to the occasion.

"Boys," he said, "this here lady has got a good fire going, and I'll bet she can cook. What do you say we get her to fix us up a meal?"

The proposal was received joyously at first. Then someone said:

"But I haven't got any money." "Neither have I—not a damn sou!" said another. And again the spiritual temperature of the room fell.

Again Sergeant Reilly spoke:

"I haven't got any money to speak of, meself," he said. "But let's have a show-down. I guess we've got enough to buy somethin' to eat."

It was long after pay-day, and we were not hopeful of the results of the search. But the wealthy (that is, those who had two francs) made up for the poor (that is, those who had two sous). And among the coins on the table I noticed an American dime, an English half-crown and a Chinese piece with a square hole in the center. In negotiable tender the money came in all to eight francs.

It takes more money than that to feed twelve
[16]

hungry soldiers these days in France. But there was no harm in trying. So an ex-seminarian, an ex-bookkeeper and an ex-street-car conductor aided Sergeant Reilly in explaining in French that had both a brogue and a Yankee twang that we were hungry, that this was all the money we had in the world, and that we wanted her to cook us something to eat.

Now Madame was what they call in New England a "capable" woman. In a jiffy she had the money in Solange's hand and had that admirable child cloaked and wooden-shod for the street, and fully informed as to what she was to buy. What Madame and the children had intended to have for supper I do not know, for there was nothing in the kitchen but the fire, the stove, the table, some shelves of dishes and an enormous bed. Nothing in the way of a food cupboard could be seen. And the only other room of the house was the bare attic.

When Solange came back she carried in a basket bigger than herself these articles: 1, two loaves of war-bread; 2, five bottles of red wine; 3, three cheeses; 4, numerous potatoes; 5, a lump of fat; 6, a bag of coffee. The whole represented, as was afterward demonstrated, exactly the sum of ten francs, fifty centimes.

Well, we all set to work peeling potatoes. Then, with a veritable French trench-knife Madame cut the potatoes into long strips. Meanwhile Solange had put the lump of fat into the big black pot that hung by a chain over the fire. In the boiling grease the potatoes were placed, Madame standing by with a big ladle punched full of holes (I regret that I do not know the technical name for this instrument) and keeping the potato-strips swimming, zealously frustrating any attempt on their part to lie lazily at the bottom of the pot.

We forgot all about the hike as we sat at supper that evening. The only absentees were the two little boys, Michel and Paul. And they were really absent only from our board—they were in the room, in the great built-in bed that was later to hold also Madame and Solange. Their little bodies were covered by the three-foot thick mattress-like red silk quilt, but their tousled heads protruded and they watched us unblinkingly all the evening.

But just as we sat down, before Sergeant Reilly began his task of dishing out the potatoes and starting the bottles on their way, Madame stopped her chattering and looked at Solange. And Solange stopped her chattering and looked at Madame. And they both looked rather searchingly at us. We

[18]

didn't know what was the matter, but we felt rather embarrassed.

Then Madame began to talk, slowly and loudly, as one talks to make foreigners understand. And the gist of her remarks was that she was surprised to see that American Catholics did not say grace before eating like French Catholics.

We sprang to our feet at once. But it was not Sergeant Reilly who saved the situation. Instead, the ex-seminarian (he is only temporarily an ex-seminarian, he'll be preaching missions and giving retreats yet if a bit of shrapnel doesn't hasten his journey to Heaven) said, after we had blessed ourselves: "Benedicite: nos et quae sumus sumpturi benedicat Deus, Pater et Filius et Spiritus Sanctus. Amen."

Madame and Solange, obviously relieved, joined us in the Amen, and we sat down again to eat.

It was a memorable feast. There was not much conversation—except on the part of Madame and Solange—but there was plenty of good cheer. Also there was enough cheese and bread and wine and potatoes for all of us—half starved as we were when we sat down. Even big Considine, who drains a can of condensed milk at a gulp and has been known to eat an apple pie without stopping to take breath, was satisfied. There were toasts, also, all proposed by Sergeant Reilly—toasts to Madame, and to the children, and to France, and to the United States, and to the Old Grey Mare (this last toast having an esoteric significance apparent only to *illuminati* of Sergeant Reilly's circle).

The table cleared and the "agimus tibi gratias" duly said, we sat before the fire, most of us on the floor. We were warm and happy and full of good food and good wine. I spied a slip of paper on the floor by Solange's foot and unashamedly read it. It was an accounting for the evening's expenditures—totaling exactly ten francs and fifty centimes.

Now when soldiers are unhappy—during a long, hard hike, for instance—they sing to keep up their spirits. And when they are happy, as on the evening now under consideration, they sing to express their satisfaction with life. We sang "Sweet Rosie O'Grady." We shook the kitchen-bedroom with the echoes of "Take Me Back to New York Town." We informed Madame, Solange, Paul, Michel, in fact, the whole village, that we had never been a wanderer and that we longed for our Indiana home. We grew sentimental over "Mother Machree." And Sergeant Reilly obliged with a reel—in his

[20]

socks—to an accompaniment of whistling and hand-clapping.

Now, it was our hostess's turn to entertain. We intimated as much. She responded, first by much talk, much consultation with Solange, and finally by going to one of the shelves that held the pans and taking down some paper-covered books.

There was more consultation, whispered this time, and much turning of pages. Then, after some preliminary coughing and humming, the music began—the woman's rich alto blending with the child's shrill but sweet notes. And what they sang was "Tantum ergo Sacramentum."

Why she should have thought that an appropriate song to offer this company of rough soldiers from a distant land I do not know. And why we found it appropriate it is harder still to say. But it did seem appropriate to all of us—to Sergeant Reilly, to Jim (who used to drive a truck), to Larry (who sold cigars), to Frank (who tended a bar on Fourteenth Street). It seemed, for some reason, eminently fitting. Not one of us then or later expressed any surprise that this hymn, familiar to most of us since our mothers first led us to the Parish Church down the pavements of New York or across the Irish hills, should be sung to us in this strange land and in these strange circumstances.

Since the gracious Latin of the Church was in order and since the season was appropriate, one of us suggested "Adeste Fideles" for the next item on the evening's program. Madame and Solange and our ex-seminarian knew all the words and the rest of us came in strong with "Venite, adoremus Dominum."

Then, as if to show that piety and mirth may live together, the ladies obliged with "Au Clair de la Lune" and other simple ballads of old France. And after taps had sounded in the street outside our door, and there was yawning, and wrist-watches were being scanned, the evening's entertainment ended, by general consent, with patriotic selections. We sang—as best we could—the *Star Spangled Banner,* Solange and her mother humming the air and applauding at the conclusion. Then we attempted *La Marseillaise.* Of course we did not know the words. Solange came to our rescue with two little pamphlets containing the song, so we looked over each other's shoulders and got to work in earnest. Madame sang with us, and Solange. But during the final stanza Madame did not sing. She leaned against the great family bedstead and looked at us. She had taken one of the babies from

[22]

under the red comforter and held him to her breast.
One of her red and toil-scarred hands half covered
his fat little back. There was a gentle dignity about
that plain, hard-working woman, that soldier's
widow—we all felt it. And some of us saw the tears
in her eyes.

There are mists, faint and beautiful and unchanging, that hang over the green slopes of some mountains I know. I have seen them on the Irish hills
and I have seen them on the hills of France. I think
that they are made of the tears of good brave women.

Before I went to sleep that night I exchanged a
few words with Sergeant Reilly. We lay side by
side on the floor, now piled with straw. Blankets,
shelter-halves, slickers and overcoats insured warm
sleep. Sergeant Reilly's hard old face was wrapped
round with his muffler. The final cigarette of the
day burned lazily in a corner of his mouth.

"That was a pretty good evening, Sarge," I said.
"We sure were in luck when we struck this billet."

He grunted affirmatively, then puffed in silence
for a few minutes. Then he deftly spat the cigarette into a strawless portion of the floor, where it
glowed for a few seconds before it went out.

"You said it," he remarked. "We were in luck

is right. What do you know about that lady, anyway?"

"Why," I answered, "I thought she treated us pretty white."

"Joe," said Sergeant Reilly, "do you realize how much trouble that woman took to make this bunch of roughnecks comfortable? She didn't make a damn cent on that feed, you know. The kid spent all the money we give her. And she's out about six francs for firewood, too—I wish to God I had the money to pay her. I bet she'll go cold for a week now, and hungry, too.

"And that ain't all," he continued, after a pause broken only by an occasional snore from our blissful neighbours. "Look at the way she cooked them pomme de terres and fixed things up for us and let us sit down there with her like we was her family. And look at the way she and the little Sallie there sung for us.

"I tell you, Joe, it makes me think of old times to hear a woman sing them Church hymns to me that way. It's forty years since I heard a hymn sung in a kitchen, and it was my mother, God rest her, that sang them. I sort of realize what we're fighting for now, and I never did before. It's for women like that and their kids.

[24]

HOLY IRELAND

"It gave me a turn to see her a-sitting their singing them hymns. I remembered when I was a boy in Shangolden. I wonder if there's many women like that in France now—telling their beads and singing the old hymns and treating poor traveling men the way she's just after treating us. There used to be lots of women like that in the Old Country. And I think that's why it was called 'Holy Ireland.'"

THE GENTLE ART OF CHRISTMAS GIVING

IF A dentist stuck a bit of holly in his cap and went through the streets on Christmas morning, his buzzing drill over his shoulder and his forceps in his hand, stopping at the houses of his friends to give their jaws free treatment, meanwhile trolling out lusty Yuletide staves—if he were to do this, I say, it would be said of him, among other things, that he was celebrating Christmas in a highly original manner. Undoubtedly there would be many other adjectives applied to his manner of generosity—adjectives applied, for instance, by the children whom, around their gayly festooned tree, he surprised with his gift of expert treatment. But the adjective most generally used (not perhaps in adulation) would be "original." And the use of this adjective would be utterly wrong.

The holly bedecked dentist would not be acting in an original manner. He would not be following the suggestion of his own philanthropic heart. He would be acting in accordance with tradition, a par-

[26]

ticularly annoying tradition, the evil and absurd superstition that a gift should be representative of the giver rather than of the recipient.

Now, I am aware that there is high literary authority for the dentist's Christmas morning expedition. The dentist himself would be the first to disclaim having originated the idea; if you were to question him he would tell you, as he deftly adjusted his rubber dam in your mouth, that the credit belonged to the late Ralph Waldo Emerson.

"Emerson," the dentist would say as he sharpened the point of his drill, "said that a gift was meaningless unless it was a genuine expression of the giver; it would be unfitting, for instance, for a poet to give his friend a house and lot, and a painter, his friend, a diamond necklace. The poet should give a poem and the painter should give a painting. Therefore it naturally follows that a minister should give a sermon and a school teacher should bestow upon his expectant pupils an extra page of mathematical problems. This," the dentist would say, "is the gift most expressive of my personality." And the drill would seek its goal.

Now, there is much to be said in favour of the Emersonian theory of giving. Certainly it has the advantages of cheapness and convenience. Many a

poet could more easily give his friend a whole ode
or a sequence of sonnets or a bale of vers libre than
he could give a box of cigars, or a cigar. Many a
painter could more easily cover his children's Christmas tree with his own cubist canvases than with
peppermint canes and toy locomotives and dolls
and little trumpets. A storekeeper or a manufac-
turer of any sort can more easily select his gifts
from his own stock than he can select them elsewhere. Should a brewer, for instance, desire to help
make Mr. Bryan's Christmas happy, it would be a
simpler matter for him to put in that gentleman's
stocking a case of beer than a case of grape juice.

But cheapness and convenience are not the chief
reasons for this sort of giving. A poet who gives
a poem when he should give a pair of fur gauntlets,
a painter who gives a painting when he should give
a doll, does so, it often happens, in spite of the fact
that he has thousands of dollars in the bank and
lives within a block of a department store, which he
much enjoys visiting. He gives the gifts that he
does give because of his selfishness and conceit. He
gives his own wares because they advertise his
talent.

The poet knows that his friend will not say, to
inquiring admirers of his fur gauntlets, "These were

given me by Ezra Dusenbury, author of 'Babylonian Bleatings' and other Lyrics: Smith, Parker & Co., $1 net." The painter knows that the infant he has enriched will not say to her young companions: " 'Bettina' was given me by the illustrious Gaspar Slifestein whose incomprehensiblist canvases are now on exhibition at the Microscopic Mania Gallery, 249 Fifth Avenue, New York City." These gentlemen take a violent interest in their own work, and when they give presents of that work they are trying to force their friends to share that interest and to extend it to all the world. They are trying to force their friends to become their press agents.

Of course there are exceptions to the rule that a giver should not give his own wares. Any man who deals in wares that are universally delightful may express himself in his gifts to his heart's content and no one will criticise him. So let no brewer or cigarmaker or money-changer of my acquaintance puzzle his head long in the effort to discover in the marts of the world something appropriate to my peculiar tastes. These honest citizens may be as Emersonian in their giving as they wish.

As I said, there is much to recommend the idea that inspired the hypothetical dentist on his Yuletide denting; there is much to recommend the gift-expressing-the-giver theory. It is convenient, it is cheap, it is satisfying to the giver's conceit. It is in many respects excellent. But it does not happen to be suited to Christmas Day. It is suited to the celebration of Emerson's birthday, if any one knows the date of that festival.

You see, unselfishness is supposed to be a characteristic of Christmas giving. And unselfishness, true unselfishness, was known to the philosophy of the Transcendentalists as little as it is known to that of the Nietzscheans. He who gives really in accordance with the spirit of the feast gives not to express his own personality, to call attention to his own prowess as a painter or a poet or a candlestick-maker, but to make his friend happy. If his friend remembers him when he enjoys the gift, so much the better. But the essential thing is that he shall enjoy the gift.

James Russell Lowell represented the Founder of the Feast of Christmas as saying: "Who gives himself in his gift feeds three; himself, his suffering neighbour and me." But in Lowell's mind when he wrote this was no idea of justifying the poet who thrusts poems into his friends' Christmas stocking and tips the elevator man with a villanelle. He was

[30]

thinking of sacrificial giving, of giving which necessitates a sacrifice on the part of the giver rather than on that of the recipient. And it is no sacrifice for a poet to give his poem or his book of poems. James Russell Lowell's distinguished kinswoman, now living in Boston, knows this. If Miss Amy Lowell really loves you she will give you for Christmas an automobile or one of her Keats manuscripts, rather than an autographed copy of "Sword Blades and Poppy Seeds," or "Men, Women, and Ghosts."

Few Bishops resemble Mark Twain. But there once was a Bishop who resembled Mark Twain in this respect (and in no other)—he is known to many thousands who do not know his real name. Mark Twain has thousands of friends who never heard of Samuel Langhorne Clemens. And hundreds of thousands of children yearly are gladdened by Santa Claus, yet have no association whatever with the name of Saint Nicholas of Bari.

Yet the amiable Nicholas (who is the patron of sailors, of prisoners, and of children) is the benefactor of humanity caricatured during December in every shop window and on every eleemosynary corner. His mitre has degenerated into a hat trimmed with doubtful fur; his embroidered cope has become a red jacket. But (except when he rings a little bell and begs for alms) he has retained his extra-episcopal function of giving. Saint Nicholas was a master of the art of giving; and since we have taken him so seriously as to transmogrify him into Santa Claus, we should profit by his illustrious example and model our giving upon his.

How and what did Saint Nicholas give? Well, he gave tactfully and opportunely and appropriately. There was the nobleman of Lucia whose three daughters were starving to death. Saint Nicholas gave them marriage portions, throwing purses of gold in at the window at night. When he was in Myra he gave to the poor people all the wheat that was in the ships in the harbour, promising the owners that when they arrived at the port for which they were bound their ships would still be full of wheat; and so it came about. To a drowned sailor and to children who had been killed by a cannibal he gave the gift of life. And to innocent men accused of treason and imprisoned he gave freedom.

His first gift, you see, was money, his second life, his third freedom. And thus he set an example to all the world. Now, it may not be convenient for us to celebrate Christmas by throwing money through the windows of apartments wherein repose dowerless young women. Nor are life and freedom gifts for our bestowal. But it is at any rate possible for us to imitate Saint Nicholas's manner of giving; to give tactfully, opportunely, and appropriately. There was nothing especially characteristic of his episcopal functions in the gifts that Saint Nicholas gave. Nor did he worry about whether or not they reflected his personality. Let us make Santa Claus resemble Saint Nicholas as closely as we can.

This business of expressing one s personality by one's gifts has been carried to extraordinary lengths of late years. There are people who actually select for all their friends and relatives things that they themselves would like. If they consider themselves to be dainty—as all women do—they give dainty presents, disregarding the fact that the recipient may suffer acute physical pain at the mere thought of daintiness.

They wish their beneficiaries to say on Christmas morning, "How characteristic of Mrs. Slipslop to give me this exquisite Dresden china chewing-gum holder," instead of "How generous and discerning of Mrs. Slipslop to give me this pair of rubber boots or this jar of tobacco or this hypodermic syringe!" But what every child and every grown person wants to receive is a gift suited to his tastes and habits; it is a matter of indifference whether or not it expresses the personality of the giver. Perhaps it will in his eyes supply the giver with a new and charming personality.

You have hitherto regarded Mr. Blinker, the notorious efficiency engineer, with disfavour. You have regarded him as a prosaic theorist, a curdled mass of statistics. On Christmas morning you find that he has presented you, not with an illuminated copy of "Rules for Eliminating Leisure," or a set of household ledgers or an alarm clock, but with a cocktail set or a pool table or an angora kitten or some other inefficient object.

At once your opinion of Mr. Blinker changes for the better. He assumes a new and radiant personality. Your Sunday school teacher has always exhibited to you virtues which you respect but do not enjoy; she has seemed to you lacking in magnetism. If she gives you for Christmas a Bible or a tale of juvenile virtue, you will write her a graceful letter of thanks (at your mother's dictation), but your affection for the estimable lady will not be materially increased. But if your Sunday school teacher gives you a bowie knife or a revolver or a set of the Deadwood Dick novels! then how suddenly will

the nobility of your Sunday school teacher's nature
be revealed to you!

To elevator men, janitors, domestic servants,
newspaper deliverers, and other necessary evils we
always give something appropriate—money. And
money does not express the personalities of most
of us. We—that is, the general public, the common
people, the populace, the average man, the great
washed and the rest of us—do our duty in this
matter, following religiously the admirable tradition of the Christmas box. But our retainers—if
they will permit us thus picturesquely to address
them—do not. They serve us during the year, and
are duly paid for it, but they do nothing picturesque
and extraordinary at Christmas time to justify our
gifts to them.

As a matter of fact, they are not upholding their
part of the tradition. It is not enough for them to
bow, and say, "Thank you," while they feverishly
count the money. They should revel romantically,
as did their predecessors who established the custom by which they profit. The elevator boys should
sing West Indian carols under our windows—especially if our apartment is in the twentieth story.
The janitor and his family should enact in the basement a Christmas miracle play.

It is pleasant to think of the janitor attired as a shepherd or as a Wise Man, with his children as angels or as sheep, to picture the Yule log on the janitorial hearth, and to hear in fancy, rising up the dumbwaiter shaft, the strains of "The Carnal and the Crane," or of the excellent carol which begins:

> The shepherd upon a hill he sat;
> He had on him his tabard and his hat,
> His tarbox, his pipe and his flagat;
> His name was called Joly Joly Wat,
> For he was a gud herdes boy.
> Ut hoy!
> For in his pipe he made so much joy!

In some places the newspaper deliverers and the telegraph boys feebly support this tradition by writing, or causing to be written, a "carrier's address" and leaving printed copies of it with their customers. It would be better, of course, if they were to sing or to recite these verses, but even the printed address is better than nothing. It is a pity to see even this slight concession to tradition disappearing. In bygone days some of the most distinguished of our poets were glad to write these addresses—the late Richard Watson Gilder wrote one for the newspaper carriers of Newark.

And then there are the numerous public servants

who nowadays receive from the public no special
Christmas benefaction—How gracefully they
might obtain it by infusing into their occupations a
little Yuletide pageantry! As it is, the subway
guards celebrate the golden springtime by donning
white raiment. Let them on Christmas day be
wreathed with mingled holly and mistletoe, and let
them chant, in lusty chorus:

> God rest you, merry gentlemen!
> Let nothing you dismay.
> Please slip us some coin, you've got money to
> boin,
> And this is Christmas day.

Few subterranean voyagers could resist this appeal.

And the street cleaners, how comes it that they
are unrewarded of the public? Their predecessors,
the crossing sweepers of London fifty years ago,
exacted tribute from pedestrians not only at Christmas time, but on every day of the year. Let our
street cleaners assume holiday garb and manner,
let them expect Christmas gifts, but give in turn a
Christmas spectacle. Methods of doing this will
readily suggest themselves—an appropriate thing
would be for them to procure mediæval attire at any
theatrical costumer's, and build great bonfires at

such points of vantage as Columbus Circle, Times Square, Madison Square, and Union Square. Over these bonfires boars' heads should be roasted and great bowls of steaming punch should hang. From passersby who partook of their hospitality the street cleaners, through one of their number dressed as an almoner, should request a golden remembrance. These things may yet come to pass. They are not so archaic as seemed in nineteen-thirteen a world-wide war. And the municipal Christmas trees are a good beginning.

But to return to our muttons, or, rather, to our geese and plum puddings, the most important thing for us to remember in the selection of Christmas presents is their suitability to the person for whom they are intended. We may like books, but let us not therefore feel obliged to sustain our literary reputation by giving books to our neighbour who wants a box of cigars or a jumping-jack. We have the precedent, furnished by Saint Nicholas, and we have a higher precedent still. For the first great Christmas gift to humanity was what humanity most needed, and always needs—a child.

A BOUQUET FOR JENNY

SO FAR as I know, in no other library but mine is to be found a book illustrated by Jenny Hand. Therefore, more than much vellum and crushed levant, more than first editions and association copies bearing famous signatures, do I prize a certain fat volume, a foxed and dog-eared and battered volume, which was published by Grigg and Elliot (God rest them!) in Philadelphia at number nine North Fourth Street in 1847. This is a book of poetry, but it is no slender little pamphlet of a thing, the shelter of one bardling's lyrical ejaculations. Five full-grown poets, two of them men of noble girth, comfortably share this stately tenement. The book's solid and imposing name is "The Poetical Works of Rogers, Campbell, J. Montgomery, Lamb and Kirk White."

A detailed consideration of this volume might, to the profit of the reading public, fill all of one issue of any book-review supplement or literary, so to speak, section printed in America. But for the moment I would write, not of the excellencies of the volume in general, but of the distinguishing feature of my copy—its unique virtue, which gives me the right to pity all other bibliophiles now rejoicing in this illustrious Grigg and Elliot imprint. I refer to the illustrations by Jenny Hand.

Messrs. Grigg and Elliot illustrated, to the best of their ability, every copy of this work. They illustrated it with what they doubtless termed "elegant steel engravings." These steel engravings are indeed "elegant," also they are "appropriate," also they are "chaste." Take down from its shelf your copy of "The Poetical Works of, etc.," and you will find, facing page ninety-four, a representation of "Morning among the Alps," painted, the legend tells you, by T. Doughty, and engraved by George W. Hatch. The sun is rising, much as Mr. Belasco might direct, and upon a pleasant little pond in the foreground are three of those famous Alpine early birds known as swan. This picture is designed to accompany Samuel Rogers' "The Alps at Daybreak," lines which I may recall to your memory by saying that they begin, "The sunbeams streak the azure skies." The picture was not intended by the artists to be Alpine in character, but it is a nice picture, very harmonious with the text.

Furthermore, the generous Messrs. Grigg and Elliot, being greatly moved by those lines of the ingenious Kirke White which begin: "Behold the shepherd boy, who homeward tends, Finish'd his daily labour.—O'er his path, Deep overhung with herbage, does he stroll With pace irregular; by fits he runs, Then sudden stops with vacant countenance, And picks the pungent herb"—being greatly moved, I say, by these lines, they determined to give them a supplementary embellishment. Therefore they caused one O. Pelton to engrave on steel a picture first "Drawn by Cristall" (as who should say "Painted by Raphael"). This shows us a plump youth, with the vacant countenance celebrated by the poet, standing upon the side of Vesuvius, carrying over his shoulder a large spade, and in his left hand a basket of potatoes. In their sensational journalistic way, Messrs. Grigg and Elliot affixed to this picture the caption, "The Shepherd Boy," and forthwith the poem was illustrated.

But while you will take pleasure, if you are a worthy possessor of this volume, in these altogether admirable engravings, you will look through your copy in vain for expressions of the genius of Jenny Hand. The Jenny Hand illustrations are two in number, and they are to be found only in my copy.

One of the advantages of illustrating a book with steel engravings is that it necessitates the inclusion of blank pages. When a steel engraving occupies one side of a page, there may be nothing whatever printed on the reverse.

There may be nothing printed, I said, on the reverse. But on the reverse anything in the world may be drawn or written. Therein we see the origin of the entertaining practice of extra-illustration. To the eager pencil of Jenny Hand, these virginal white pages, oases among pages of dry verse, offered irresistible opportunities. And my library is therefore the richer.

This book never belonged to Jenny Hand, except so far as anything belongs to one who makes it more beautiful and interesting and useful. The book belonged to Jenny's sister, Esther. On the fly-leaf is written "Mifs E. C. Hand, with regards of C. F. Q." Obviously E. C. stands for Esther Conway. Obviously, also, Esther did not herself draw pictures on the beautiful volume of poesy (with gold scroll work all over the cover) which the amorous and tasteful Mr. C. F. Q. presented to her. This delightful work was done by Esther's younger sister, who in 1847 was aged perhaps thirteen, and should have been and probably was named Jenny. C. F. Q. stands for Charles Francis Quigley. This is not a random guess; it is a wholly logical deduction from the portrait of the gentleman drawn by Jenny, who knew him well.

It was one summer afternoon in 1847 that Jenny first began to improve "The Poetical Works of Rogers, Campbell, J. Mongomery, Lamb and Kirke White." At three o'clock Jenny had been out playing—keeping the porch and the front gate well in sight, for she knew that not for nothing had Esther put on her pearl necklace and her blue sash and spent three-quarters of an hour over her hair. Jenny's suspicions were justified and her vigilance rewarded. At four o'clock the front gate clicked and the gravel walk resounded under a manly tread. Charlie Quigley, in a high stock, a flowered waistcoat, a long black coat, tight blue trousers and a tall silk hat, came to call on Esther. And he brought a gift. Was it a box of candy? If so Jenny would, as a dutiful sister, help to entertain the company. She would wait—Esther was unwrapping the present. No, it was not a box of candy—it was a book. And it was not even a novel, it was a book of poetry, of all things in the world! How could that Charlie Quigley be so silly?

Well, Jenny lost interest in Charlie and his gift for a while. She rolled her hoop and played with the puppy while Esther and Charlie sat on the porch

and looked at the foolish book. When Jenny came
up on the porch, toward sunset, they had gone into
the parlour. They had left the book open face
downward on a bench, open to Thomas Campbell's
"Song," beginning "Oh, how hard it is to find The
one just suited to our mind"—certain lines of which
Charlie had roguishly underscored.

Jenny turned the pages of the book, but found
therein little entertainment. At length, however,
she came upon "Morning in the Alps," with its
blank and inviting reverse. Among the jackstones
in her pocket was the stub of a pencil, and soon that
pencil was at its predestined task of depicting the
event of the afternoon—for my edification some
threescore years later.

Jenny drew a side view of the broad stone steps,
with a little of the railings and Grecian pillars. She
drew the locust tree, and since she knew that there
was a robin's nest in it, she outlined two little birds
against the skyey background. She drew Esther,
grand in her hoopskirts, necklace, curls and blue
sash—no, it wasn't blue, it was green plaid, and the
fabric was satin, for, as I live, there is a faded corner
of it in this very book, sentimentally cut off and
placed there by Esther herself! Why was Esther
so particular about saving a fragment of that sash?

A BOUQUET FOR JENNY

Was this really a momentous afternoon? Was this the sash that Charlie's black broadcloth sleeve surrounded when Esther consented to become Mrs. Quigley? And were they married, and did Charlie's friends all make flat jokes about his claiming the hand of Hand?

And were all these things going on while the artistic Jenny was busy on the porch? Possibly. Probably. But with such conjectures the author of this serious essay in art criticism has no concern. To return to the account of the picture—Jenny drew next the renowned Charles Francis Quigley. But now her pencil was dipped in a mild solution of venom—imparted to it, I fear, when she thoughtfully placed its point between her small lips. For those same lips had desired chocolates—and the chocolates had turned out to be nothing but poesy. Therefore she sacrificed realism to satire, and made Charlie (really a very nice fellow, whom she came to like very much in later years) something of a fop. She made the cut of his coat too extreme, his hair too curly, his mustache too obviously waxed. She deliberately gave his eye a sentimental expression; she smiled derisively as she padded his pictured sleeve.

And then she gave her drawing its crowning

charm—she put in the "selbst-portrait." She drew the little cedar tree that flanked the porch, and she drew herself kneeling beside it—seeing, but not seen by, the rapt Esther and Charlie. Far from being ashamed of this act of sisterly espionage, she gloried in it, and brought all her art to the task of immortalising it.

So in my book the locust tree is forever in leaf and two little birds poise always against the summer sky. And always Charlie, hat in hand, presents to the radiant Esther "The Poetical Works of Rogers, Campbell, J. Montgomery, Lamb and Kirke White." And always the little artist, with long curls hanging over her white frock, laughs at the lovers from behind her cedar tree.

The light was fading now, but Jenny had found another blank page—that preceding the section devoted to Kirke White's verses. Supper wouldn't be ready for fifteen minutes, so she started on a picture more difficult than the simple incident just drawn. She chose for her scene Riley's Riding Academy, where she and Esther spent every Wednesday morning. There was Esther, seated with the sedateness appropriate to her eighteen years, upon the tamest of nags. And there was Jenny, in her fetching habit, perilously poised upon her

[46]

wildly careering steed. With enthusiastic pencil did Jenny depict her own brave unconcern, and Esther's timorousness. How firmly Esther clutches the reins of her mild beast, how startled is her face as she looks upon her daring and nonchalant younger sister!

Did the Quigleys and the Hands, I wonder, shed tears over Mr. Southey's "Account of the Life of Henry Kirke White"? Did they know Francis Boott, of Boston, the young American gentleman who placed, Mr. Southey tells us, a tablet to Henry's memory in All Saints Church, Cambridge? Were they moved by James Montgomery's "Prison Amusements; Written during nine months confinement in the Castle of York, in the years of 1795 and 1796"? Mr. Montgomery tells us in the prefatory advertisement, "they were the transcripts of melancholy feelings—the warm effusions of a bleeding heart." Did they read "Gertrude of Wyoming," "Theodric; a Domestic Tale," and the "Pleasures of Hope"?

Did they read the memoirs prefaced to the various selections? If so, I hope they found them as delightful as I do. There is the inexhaustibly fascinating "Memoirs of Charles Lamb," in which the anonymous critic improves the occasion by reprov-

[47]

ing sternly the Lake Poets, or the "Lakers," as he calls them. "The thousand Songs," he tells us, "of our writers in verse of past time dwell on all tongues, with the melodies of Moore. But who learns or repeats the cumbrous verses of Wordsworth, which require an initiation from their writer to comprehend?" Later this gentleman has occasion to refer to "Another School of Poetry," which "arose in opposition to that of the Lakers." "Their talents," he writes, "are before the world. To this new school belonged the late poet Shelley, whose lofty powers are unquestionable; Keats, also now deceased; and Leigh Hunt." Keats, also now deceased! What porridge fed the writer of this memoir?

Well, my concern is not with the poor hack who edited this book and wrote the memoirs. I hope Messrs. Grigg and Elliot paid him well. And as for Charlie and Esther and Jenny and the robins in the locust tree—well, Charlie Quigley's dust and his good sword's rust, and his soul is with the saints, I trust. I hope Esther married him. I'm glad he brought her "The Poetical Works of Rogers, Campbell, J. Montgomery, Lamb and Kirke White," even if Jenny was disappointed. For if she'd made her drawings on the cover of a candy box they would not now be in my library.

THE INEFFICIENT LIBRARY

THERE ARE young gentlemen whose delight it is to tell their married and established and venerable friends how to form libraries. Generally, these young gentlemen wear spectacles rimmed with tortoise shell, and the condensed milk of their alma mater is yet wet upon their lips. They peer at your laden shelves and say: "It is better to have one good book than a dozen bad ones. Of any standard work you should have the definitive edition —not necessarily a rare imprint or something in fine binding, but the most modern and comprehensive edition. It is better to have one good anthology than a shelfful of third-rate poets. Go through your shelves and throw away all the rubbish; buy sets of the classics, a volume at a time, and in this way you will gradually build up a useful and really representative library, something appropriate and coherent."

When a young gentleman talks to you in this wise, the only thing to do is to lead him gently away from the bookshelves and make him sit in a comfortable corner and talk to you about hockey or socialism or some other of his boyish sports. He knows absolutely nothing about libraries. Probably he lives in the shadow of Washington Arch, and his own library—on the bureau—consists of the "Life of General Ulysses S. Grant," inscribed "To dearest Teddy, from Aunt Mag., Xmas, 1916," and a copy of the New Republic for last August, containing a letter in which he took exception to an editorial on the relation between pragmatism and Freud's second theory of the semi-subconscious. To-morrow he will sell General Grant to a second-hand book dealer for fifteen cents, and thereby diminish his library by one half. What right has he to tell you what books you shall keep and what you shall destroy?

Now, it would not be so bad if this raving about a library was confined to young persons like him I have mentioned. But the trouble is, there are people of means and reputation for intelligence who are actually putting into practice the evil theories he advances, who are deliberately "building up libraries," instead of surrounding themselves with books they like. Against this pernicious heresy it is the duty of every honest bibliophile to protest.

We need waste no words on the purchaser of "subscription sets" and many-volumed collections of "Kings and Queens of Neo-Cymric Realism and Romance," and "The Universalest of All Libraries of Super-extraordinary Fiction," in forty-eight volumes, fifteen dollars down and five dollars a month until the purchaser is summoned to a Better Land. Either these people want books for mere shelf-furniture, or else they are the victims of voracious book agents, and deserve a tear of sympathy rather than a rebuke. Our concern, the concern of those who have at heart the good name of printed literature and the liberty of the individual householder of literary tastes, is with the person who is highly literate and possessed of an account with a bookseller, and is abusing his talent and privilege by "efficiently" building up a library.

When efficiency confined itself to the office and the factory, it was bad enough. When it (loathsome animal that it is!) crawled up a leg of the table and began to preach to us about our food, babbling obscenely of proteids and carbohydrates, we felt that the limit of endurance had been reached. But no sooner do we cuff efficiency from the dining table than it pops up in the library. And this is not to be endured. Efficiency must be plucked down, kindly, of course, but resolutely, from the bookshelves, and put in a covered basket to await the coming of the wagon which shall convey it to the lethal of the S. P. C. A.

Except for an efficient family, what could be less interesting than an efficient library? Think of the sameness of it—every study in a block of houses containing the "Oxford Dictionary" and "Roget's Thesaurus" and the "Collected Essays of Hamilton Wright Mabie" and similar works of reference, with a few standard fictions such as Arnold Bennett's "Your United States," and Owen Wister's "The Pentecost of Calamity"! There would be no adventures among books possible in such libraries. Indeed, efficiency in the library would soon reduce it, if logically developed, to a collection of anthologies and reference books, and possibly some such practical jokes as ex-President Eliot's "Five Foot Shelf."

An advocate of the efficient library, a spectacled young gentleman of the type already described, once engaged in some ignoble literary task—book-reviewing I believe it was called—while a guest at my house. The volume of which he was writing a criticism had to do with a single-tax experiment in New Zealand, and therefore he wished to include in his review a quotation from the "Life of Benvenuto Cellini." He did not find the "Life of Benvenuto

Cellini" on my shelves, and therefore reproached me, and made my library the object of his callow disapproval.

I reasoned with him. He had read Benvenuto, I said, and Benvenuto was waiting for him in the public library if he desired to renew his acquaintance with him. Here, I said, are many volumes of biography and autobiography in place of the one for which you cry. Here is a book entitled "The Life and Labours of Henry W. Grady, his Speeches, Writings, etc., Being in Addition to a Graphic Sketch of His Life, a Collection of His Most Remarkable Speeches and Such of His Writings as Best Illustrate His Character and Show the Wonderful Brilliancy of His Intellect, also Such Letters, Speeches, and Newspaper Articles in connection with His Life and Death as Will Be of General Interest." Here, I said, is "Colonel Thomas Blood, Crown Stealer," by Wilbur Cortez Abbott, a highly entertaining book. Here, I continued, as a preface to this collection of the "Essays in Prose and Verse of J. Clarence Mangan," is an illuminating biographical essay by Mr. C. P. Meehan, together with Mr. J. Wilson's "Phrenological Description of Mangan's Head," and "The Poet's Own Recipe to Make Tar Water." Here is—

But my friend rudely interrupted my well-meant remarks, and went in quest of Cellini to the southwest corner of Fifth Avenue and Forty-second Street, where he found a library more suited to his efficient tastes. In doing this he was perfectly justified. Public Libraries should be efficient. They are places to which you go to get useful but uninteresting information. But there is no more reason for your own library to resemble a public library than there is for your study to resemble your office, or for your dining-room to resemble the Automat, or for every bedroom in your house to bear on its door printed directions to ring twice for your wife to bring you hot water and three times for a clean collar.

The crowning virtue of the successful private library is inefficiency. As an example closely approaching the ideal, as a model to householders who have been allowed a closet or vault in which to keep books, I respectfully present my own library. And in order that the radiance of its inefficiency may be as penetrating as possible, I wish my library to be considered in comparison with its efficient rivals.

Let us therefore assume that the spectacled young gentleman already several times celebrated in this treatise has, without acquiring more sense, got married, and perhaps thereby acquired a sufficient competency to warrant his establishing a library. Let us begin our survey of his books with the shelves of poetry. Where is there a good basis for comparison? Ah, here we have it—here is Milton in the efficient library, and here the long-winded old gentleman is found again in my own! Is any comparison between these volumes possible? Would any real bibliophile hesitate a moment in making his choice between the two? The efficient Milton is a tall, sombre-looking volume with a long biographical preface by a man who used to be a poet before he became a college professor, a preface which proves that Milton never went blind, lived in Wales rather than in England, had only one daughter and knew no Latin. At the foot of every page there is a thick sprinkling of notes conveying unnecessary information. There is an appendix of variant readings and an exhaustive, monumental bibliography.

Could anything be more depressing? The only illustration in the book is John himself, in a black cloak, with what seems to be a baby's bib under his chin, and this picture can scarcely be called a decoration. My "Milton's Poetical Works," which was published in New York in 1857 and purchased by me from a stall on Twenty-third Street for a quarter, is more entertaining in every respect. **In the first place, it has no notes**—which alone makes it worth the price of admission. In the second place, the only biographical introduction is "The Life of Milton, by His Nephew, Edward Philips," a most estimable piece of writing, which begins, "Of all the several parts of history, that which sets forth the lives, and commemorates the most remarkable actions, sayings or writings of famous and illustrious persons, whether in war or peace—whether many together, or any one in particular—as it is not the least useful in itself, so it is in the highest vogue and esteem among the studious and reading part of mankind." Doesn't a biography of this sort promise more flavours and exciting things than one written by a college professor, and beginning, "John Milton was born in London, England, December 9th, 1608"?

Furthermore, my Milton is bound in black cloth, with stars and wreaths and baskets of flowers stamped in gold all over it. Furthermore, my Milton has all sorts of highly entertaining steel engravings, most delightfully 1857—Lycidas being shipwrecked on St. Michael's Mount, and the Warring Angels mustering for battle, and skeletons and devils and angels and "wood nymphs, deck'd with daisies trim," keeping "their merry wakes and pastimes," and Melancholy, who looks like Queen Victoria in her old age, and the "Goddess fair and free, in heaven yclep'd Euphrosyne," wearing a very becoming white frock. Furthermore, my Milton was "Presented to Mifs Ellen R. Baxter, by Her Resp't'l friend, J. Stuart, Oswego, May 4, 1859"—so the violet ink inscription on the flyleaf tells me. And some one has drawn in pencil a very attractive cat on the blank page opposite the opening of "Samson Agonistes." The efficient library's copy of Milton lacks all these amiable associations.

My efficient friend possesses a Byron, it is true. But not to be mentioned in the same breath with the volume which stands in my study between Witter Bynner and Bliss Carman. My Byron contains eight contemporary memoirs of the poet, by distinguished fellow-craftsmen, and sixteen pictures— himself, his birthplace, his Newfoundland dog, his daughter, and a dozen landscapes which the publisher happened to have on hand. Also, in the preface of my Byron I find this sentence: "Thus died Lord Byron at the early age of thirty-seven, leaving behind him a name second only to that of the renowned Emperor, Napoleon Bonaparte, and a memory which the sublime effusions of his muse

will endear to all posterity." My friend's Byron
has nothing to compare with this.

The trouble with my friend's library is that it has
no surprises. Any one who has seen his waistcoat—
the V of which is edged with heavy white cord—and
his cuff links—which are oval and bear, engraven on
their golden surfaces, his initials—could describe
his library to a volume. It is obvious; its obvious-
ness is a part of its efficiency.

I suppose Benvenuto Cellini is on a shelf of the
efficient library. He must be, since he is in the public library. Probably my efficient friend has also
Benjamin Franklin's "Autobiography" and the
"Complete Works of Mrs. Humphry Ward." He
has a limp-leather tissue-paper encyclopedia, and an
obese dictionary, and a magnificent atlas. And in a
corner of his study he has a map of the world in the
form of a great globe on a pivot.

I envy him this last possession, for one may
amuse himself by spinning a geographical globe, as
one entertains himself by spinning a piano stool.
But aside from this, there is nothing in my friend's
library that I desire. And my own triumphantly
inefficient library—what treasures it contains!

You mention French literature. Do I over-
whelm you with a sumptuous Voltaire, or sicken you

with a sentimentally illustrated "Paul et Virginie"?
I do not. I exhibit to you yellow-back volumes of
the later verse of Francis Jammes—which are supposed to be going to be bound one of these days—or
I show you a play or two of Rostand's. If you desire to have further dealings with the literature of
France, the French department of the university is,
for a consideration, at your service. You mention
Fraser's "Golden Bough"? I show you something
equally informing and more entertaining, comfortable volumes in which the mythology of Ireland is
narrated to us by Jeremiah Curtin and by Seumas
MacManus, and I show you a stray volume of
Louis Ginzberg's "The Legends of the Jews."

I should not try to make the possessors of efficient
libraries unhappy. But I do it for their own good,
in the hope that I may eventually reform them.
And when I look upon my two volumes of "The
Evergreen," a quarterly published in Edinburgh
some twenty years ago, numbering among its con-
tributors Fiona MacLeod, Nora Hopper, Douglas
Hyde, Standish O'Grady and Rosa Mulholland,
and "The Squire's Recipes," by Kendall Banning,
and "Scottish Heraldry Made Easy," and Shaemas
O'Sheel's "The Dear Old Lady of Eighty-sixth
Street," and a bound volume of The Gentleman's

Magazine for 1761 and "L. Annsei Senecae et Aliorum Tragoediae (Amsterodami, Apud Guiljel: Ians: Caesium)" and a battered edition of Scott's "Marmion," enriched by the comments of a Louise Cogswell who owned it in 1810 and wrote approvingly, "and very well told too" under the sub-title "A Tale of Flodden Field," and Joseph Forster's "Studies in Black and Red" (very ghastly), and both of Ernest Dowson's novels and his translations from the French, as well as his poems, and "The American Annual of Photography" for 1916, and "Miss Thackeray's Works," complete in one volume, and Layton Crippen's "Clay and Fire," and Bithell's "Contemporary Belgian Poetry," and Sir Francis Burnand's "More Happy Thoughts," and a volume containing "The Poetical Works of Rogers, Campbell, J. Montgomery Lamb, and Kirke White," and an inscribed copy of Palmer Cox's "The Brownies, Their Book"—when I contemplate, among the more commonplace inhabitants of my shelves, these books, then I cannot keep from feeling a sense of superiority to all those who have laboriously "built up" their libraries in accordance with the mandates of strict utility.

My library is inefficient and impractical, entertaining and unexacting. Its members have come to me by chance and by momentary inclination. For if a man's books are to be, as the old phrase has it, his friends, they must be allowed to him because of some fitness on his part subtly felt by them. A man does not deliberately select his friends; there must be a selection by them as well as by him. Unless he is applying the principles of efficiency to friendship. And in that case he has no friends at all.

THE POETRY OF HILAIRE BELLOC

FAR FROM the poets being astray in prose-writing (said Francis Thompson), it might plausibly be contended that English prose, as an art, is but a secondary stream of the Pierian fount, and owes its very origin to the poets. The first writer one remembers with whom prose became an art was Sir Philip Sidney. And Sidney was a poet.

This quotation is relevant to a consideration of Hilaire Belloc, because Belloc is a poet who happens to be known chiefly for his prose. His *Danton* and *Robespierre* have been read by every intelligent student of French history, his *Path to Rome,* that most high-spirited and engaging of travel books, has passed through many editions, his political writings are known to all lovers—and many foes—of democracy, his whimsically imaginative novels have their large and appreciative audience, and his exquisite brief essays are contemporary classics. And since the unforgetable month of August of the unforgetable year 1914, Hilaire Belloc has added to the number of his friends many thousands who care

[62]

little for *belles lettres* and less for the French Revolution—he has become certainly the most popular, and by general opinion the shrewdest and best informed, of all chroniclers and critics of the Great War.

There is nothing, it may be said, about these achievements to indicate the poet. How can this most public of publicists woo the shy and exacting Muse? His superabundant energy may now and again overflow in little lyrical rivulets, but how can he find time to turn it into the deep channels of song?

Well, what is the difference between a poet who writes prose and a prose-writer who writes verse? The difference is easy to see but hard to describe. Mr. Thomas Hardy is a prose writer. He has forsaken the novel, of which he was so distinguished a master, to make cynical little sonnet portraits and to pour the acid wine of his philosophy—a sort of perverted Presbyterianism—into the graceful amphora of poetic drama. But he is not a poet. Thackeray was a prose-writer, in spite of his delicious light verse. Every novelist writes or has written verse, but not all of them are poets.

Of course, Sir Walter Scott was first of all a poet—the greatest poet who ever wrote a novel.

And no one who has read *Love in the Valley* can hesitate to give Meredith his proper title. Was Macaulay a poet? I think so—but perhaps I am in a hopeless minority in my belief that the author of *The Battle of Naseby* and *The Lays of Ancient Rome* was the last of the great English ballad makers.

But this general truth cannot, I think, honestly be denied; there have been many great poets who have devoted most of their lives to writing prose. Some of them have died without discovering their neglected talent. I think that Walter Pater was one of these; much that is annoyingly subtle or annoyingly elaborate in his essays needs only rhyme and rhythm—the lovely accidents of poetry—to become graceful and appropriate. His famous description of the Mona Lisa is worthless if considered as a piece of serious æsthetic criticism. But it would make an admirable sonnet. And it is significant that Walter Pater's two greatest pupils—Lionel Johnson and Father Gerard Hopkins, S.J.,—found expression for their genius not in prose, the chosen medium of their "unforgetably most gracious friend," but in verse.

From Walter Pater, that exquisite of letters, to the robust Hilaire Belloc may seem a long journey. But there is, I insist, this similarity between these contrasting writers, both are poets, and both are known to fame by their prose.

For proof that Walter Pater was a poet, it is necessary only to read his *Renaissance Studies* or his interpretations—unsound but fascinating—of the soul of ancient Greece. Often his essays, too delicately accurate in phrasing or too heavily laden with golden rhetoric, seem almost to cry aloud for the relief of rhyme and rhythm.

Now, Hilaire Belloc suggests in many of his prose sketches that he is not using his true medium. I remember a brief essay on sleep which appeared in *The New Witness*—or, as it was then called, *The Eye Witness*—several years ago, which was not so much a complete work in itself as it was a draft for a poem. It had the economy of phrase, the concentration of idea, which is proper to poetry.

But it is not necessary in the case of Hilaire Belloc, as it is in that of Walter Pater, to search pages of prose for proof that their author is a poet. Now and then—all too seldom—the idea in this man's brain has insisted on its right, has scorned the proffered dress of prose, however fine of warp and woof, however stiff with rich verbal embroidery, and has demanded its rhymed and rhythmed wedding

[65]

garments. Therefore, for proof that Hilaire Belloc is a poet it is necessary only to read his poetry.

II

Hilaire Belloc is a poet. Also he is a Frenchman, an Englishman, an Oxford man, a Roman Catholic, a country gentleman, a soldier, a democrat, and a practical journalist. He is always all these things.

One sign that he is naturally a poet is that he is never deliberately a poet. No one can imagine him writing a poem to order—even to his own order. The poems knock at the door of his brain and demand to be let out. And he lets them out, carelessly enough, setting them comfortably down on paper simply because that is the treatment they desire. And this happens to be the way all real poetry is made.

Not that all verse makers work that way. There are men who come upon a waterfall or mountain or an emotion and say: "Aha! here is something out of which I can extract a poem!" And they sit down in front of that waterfall or mountain or an emotion and think up clever things to say about it. These things they put into metrical form, and the result they fondly call a poem.

There's no harm in that. It's good exercise for

the mind, and of it comes much interesting verse. But it is not the way in which the sum of the world's literature is increased.

Could anything, for example, be less studied, be more clearly marked with the stigmata of that noble spontaneity we call inspiration, than the passionate, rushing, irresistible lines "To the Balliol Men Still in Africa"? Like Gilbert K. Chesterton and many another English democrat, Hilaire Belloc deeply resented his country's war upon the Boers. Yet his heart went out to the friends of his university days who were fighting in Africa. They were fighting, he thought, in an unjust cause; but they were his friends and they were, at any rate, fighting. And so he made something that seems (like all great writing) an utterance rather than a composition; he put his love of war in general and his hatred of this war in particular, his devotion to Balliol and to the friends of his youth into one of the very few pieces of genuine poetry which the Boer War produced. Nor has any of Oxford's much-sung colleges known praise more fit than this

"House that armours a man
    With the eyes of a boy and the heart of a ranger,
And a laughing way in the teeth of the world,
    And a holy hunger and thirst for danger."

[67]

But perhaps a more typical example of Hilaire Belloc's wanton genius is to be found not among those poems which are, throughout, the beautiful expressions of beautiful impressions, but among those which are careless, whimsical, colloquial. There is that delightful, but somewhat exasperating *Dedicatory Ode*. Hilaire Belloc is talking—charmingly, as is his custom—to some of his friends, who had belonged, in their university days, to a youthful revolutionary organisation called the Republican Club. He happens to be talking in verse, for no particular reason except that it amuses him to talk in verse. He makes a number of excellent jokes, and enjoys them very much; his Pegasus is cantering down the road at a jolly gait, when suddenly, to the amazement of the spectators, it spreads out great golden wings and flashes like a meteor across the vault of heaven! We have been laughing at the droll tragedy of the opium-smoking Uncle Paul; we have been enjoying the humorous spectacle of the contemplative freshman—and suddenly we come upon a bit of astonishingly fine poetry. Who would expect, in all this whimsical and jovial writing, to find this really great stanza?

THE POETRY OF HILAIRE BELLOC

"From quiet homes and first beginning
  Out to the undiscovered ends,
There's nothing worth the wear of winning
  But laughter and the love of friends."

Who having read these four lines, can forget
them? And who but a poet could write them? But
Hilaire Belloc has not forced himself into this
high mood, nor does he bother to maintain it. He
gaily passes on to another verse of drollery, and
then, not because he wishes to bring the poem to an
effective climax, but merely because it happens to
be his mood, he ends the escapade he calls an Ode
with eight or ten stanzas of nobly beautiful poetry.

There is something almost uncanny about the
flashes of inspiration which dart out at the astonished reader of Hilaire Belloc's most frivolous
verses. Let me alter a famous epigram and call
his light verse a circus illuminated by lightning.
There is that monumental burlesque, the New-
digate Poem—*A Prize Poem Submitted by Mr.
Lambkin of Burford to the Examiners of the University of Oxford on the Prescribed Poetic Theme
Set by Them in 1893, "The Benefits of the Electric Light."* It is a tremendous joke; with every
line the reader echoes the author's laughter. But
without the slightest warning Hilaire Belloc

passes from rollicking burlesque to shrewd satire;
he has been merrily jesting with a bladder on a stick,
he suddenly draws a gleaming rapier and thrusts it
into the heart of error. He makes Mr. Lambkin
say:

"Life is a veil, its paths are dark and rough
Only because we do not know enough:
When Science has discovered something more
We shall be happier than we were before."

Here we find the directness and restraint which
belong to really great satire. This is the material-
istic theory, the religion of Science, not burlesqued,
not parodied, but merely stated nakedly, without
the verbal frills and furbelows with which our for-
ward-looking leaders of popular thought are accustomed to cover its obscene absurdity. Almost
these very words have been uttered in a dozen "ra-
tionalistic" pulpits I could mention, pulpits occu-
pied by robustuous practical gentlemen with very
large eyes, great favourites with the women's clubs.
Their pet doctrine, their only and most offensive
dogma, is not attacked, is not ridiculed; it is merely
stated for them, in all kindness and simplicity.
They cannot answer it, they cannot deny that it is
a mercilessly fair statement of the "philosophy"
[70]

that is their stock in trade. I hope that many of them will read it.

III

Hilaire Belloc was born July 27, 1870. He was educated at the Oratory School, Edgbaston, and at Balliol College, Oxford. After leaving school he served as a driver in the Eighth Regiment of French Artillery at Toul Meurthe-et-Moselle, being at that time a French citizen. Later he was naturalised as a British subject, and entered the House of Commons in 1906 as Liberal Member for South Salford. British politicians will not soon forget the motion which Hilaire Belloc introduced one day in the early Spring of 1908, the motion that the Party funds, hitherto secretly administered, be publicly audited. His vigorous and persistent campaign against the party system has placed him, with Cecil Chesterton, in the very front ranks of those to whom the democrats of Great Britain must look for leadership and inspiration. He was always a keen student of military affairs; he prophesied, long before the event, the present international conflict, describing with astonishing accuracy the details of the German invasion of Belgium and the resistance of Liège. Now he occu-

[71]

pies a unique position among the journalists who comment upon the War, having tremendously increased the circulation of *Land and Water,* the periodical for which he writes regularly, and lecturing to a huge audience once a week on the events of the War in one of the largest of London's concert halls—Queen's Hall, where the same vast crowds that listen to the War lectures used to gather to hear the works of the foremost German composers.

IV

Hilaire Belloc, as I have said, is a Frenchman, an Englishman, an Oxford man, a country gentleman, a soldier, a democrat, and a practical journalist. In all these characters he utters his poetry. As a Frenchman, he is vivacious and gallant and quick. He has the noble English frankness, and that broad irresistible English mirthfulness which is so much more inclusive than that narrow possession, a sense of humour. Democrat though he is, there is about him something of the atmosphere of the country squire of some generations ago; it is in his heartiness, his jovial dignity, his deep love of the land. The author of *The South Country* and *Courtesy* has made Sussex his inalienable possession; he owns Sussex, as Dickens owns London, and

THE POETRY OF HILAIRE BELLOC

Blackmore owns Devonshire. And he is thoroughly a soldier, a happy warrior, as brave and dexterous, no one can doubt, with a sword of steel as with a sword of words.

He has taken the most severe risk which a poet can take: he has written poems about childhood. What happened when the late Algernon Charles Swinburne bent his energies to the task of celebrating this theme? As the result of his solemn meditation on the mystery of childhood, he arrived at two conclusions, which he melodiously announced to the world. They were, first, that the face of a baby wearing a plush cap looks like a moss-rose bud in its soft sheath, and, second, that "astrolabe" rhymes with "babe." Very charming, of course, but certainly unworthy of a great poet. And upon this the obvious comment is that Swinburne was not a great poet. He took a theme terribly great and terribly simple, and about it he wrote . . . something rather pretty.

Now, when a really great poet—Francis Thompson, for example—has before him such a theme as childhood, he does not spend his time making far-fetched comparisons with moss-rose buds, or hunting for words that rhyme with "babe." Childhood suggests Him Who made childhood sacred, so the poet writes *Ex Ore Infantium,* or such a poem as that which ends with the line:

"Look for me in the nurseries of Heaven."

A poet may write pleasingly about mountains, and cyclones and battles, and the love of woman, but if he is at all timid about the verdict of posterity he should avoid the theme of childhood as he would avoid the plague. For only great poets can write about childhood poems worthy to be printed.

Hilaire Belloc has written poems about children, and they are worthy to be printed. He is never ironic when he thinks about childhood; he is gay, whimsical, with a slight suggestion of elfin cynicism, but he is direct, as a child is direct. He has written two dedicatory poems for books to be given to children; they are slight things, but they are a revelation of their author's power to do what only a very few poets can do, that is, to enter into the heart and mind of the child, following that advice which has its literary as well as moral significance, to "become as a little child."

And in many of Hilaire Belloc's poems by no means intended for childish audiences there is an appealing simplicity that is genuinely and beautifully childish, something quite different from the adult and highly artificial simplicity of Professor

THE POETRY OF HILAIRE BELLOC

A. E. Housman's *A Shropshire Lad.* Take that quatrain *The Early Morning.* It is as clear and cool as the time it celebrates; it is absolutely destitute of rhetorical indulgence, poetical inversions or "literary" phrasing. It is, in fact, conversation —inspired conversation, which is poetry. It might have been written by a Wordsworth not painfully self-conscious, or by a Blake whose brain was not as yet muddled with impressionistic metaphysics.

And his Christmas carols—they are fit to be sung by a chorus of children. Can any songs of the sort receive higher praise than that? Children, too, appreciate *The Birds* and *Our Lord and Our Lady.* Nor is that wonderful prayer rather flatly called *In a Boat* beyond the reach of their intelligence.

Naturally enough, Hilaire Belloc is strongly drawn to the almost violent simplicity of the ballad. Bishop Percy would not have enjoyed the theological and political atmosphere of *The Little Serving Maid,* but he would have acknowledged its irresistible charm. There is that wholly delightful poem *The Death and Last Confession of Wandering Peter*—a most Bellocian vagabond. "He wandered everywhere he would: and all that he approved was sung, and most of what he saw was good." Says Peter:

"If all that I have loved and seen
  Be with me on the Judgment Day,
I shall be saved the crowd between
  From Satan and his foul array."

Hilaire Belloc has seen much and loved much.
He has sung lustily the things he approved—with
what hearty hatred has he sung the things he dis-
approved!

V

Hilaire Belloc is not the man to spend much time
in analysing his own emotions; he is not, thank God,
a poetical psychologist. Love songs, drinking
songs, battle songs—it is with these primitive and
democratic things that he is chiefly concerned.

But there is something more democratic than
wine or love or war. That thing is Faith. And
Hilaire Belloc's part in increasing the sum of the
world's beauty would not be the considerable thing
that it is were it not for his Faith. It is not that
(like Dante Gabriel Rossetti) he is attracted by the
Church's pageantry and wealth of legend. To
Hilaire Belloc the pageantry is only incidental, the
essential thing is his Catholic Faith. He writes con-
vincingly about Our Lady and Saint Joseph and
the Child Jesus because he himself is convinced.

[76]

THE POETRY OF HILAIRE BELLOC

He does not delve into mediæval tradition in quest
of picturesque incidents, he merely writes what he
knows to be true. His Faith furnishes him with the
theme for those of his poems which are most likely
to endure; his Faith gives him the "rapture of an inspiration." His Faith enables him, as it has enabled
many another poet, to see "in the lamp that is
beauty, the light that is God."

And therein is Hilaire Belloc most thoroughly
and consistently a democrat. For in this twentieth
century it happens that there is on earth only one
genuine democratic institution. And that institution is the Catholic Church.

THE CATHOLIC POETS OF BELGIUM

A T A recent meeting of the English Poetry Society, Mlle. Coppin, a distinguished Belgian poetess, who now, like so many of her compatriots, is a refugee in London, said: "I believe we have been too prosperous, too fond of pleasure. We are being purged, and in our adversity we have found our nationality. If ever England, France, and Russia make a new Belgium, we shall be more simple and hard-working."

Those of us who believe that the character of a nation is, to a great extent, revealed in its literature cannot doubt that Mlle. Coppin's words are true. Surely the sick fancies of Maurice Maeterlinck (to mention the most conspicuous of Belgian men of letters) could come into being only in a land suffering from over-much civilisation, in a land whose citizens are too sophisticated for common and wholesome delights. Even more than the elaborate obscenities of Iwan Gilkin and Albert Giraud, Maeterlinck's morbid studies of mental, spiritual, and physical degradation belong to that sort of lit-

[78]

erature which is called "decadent." And decadent literature usually is produced for and by people who need to be, in Mlle. Coppin's words, "more simple and hard-working."

That the great tragedy which has overtaken Belgium will have a beneficial effect upon its literature is not to be doubted. Of course, the first result is an almost total cessation of creative activity; one cannot handle a rifle and a pen at the same time. But with the return of peace must come the development of a new Belgian literature, a literature which is not an echo of the salon-philosophies of Paris and Berlin, but a beautiful expression of the soul of a strong and brave race.

It is possible that when the poets of a re-created Belgium are singing their clear songs, the world, comparing them with Gilkin, Giraud, Maeterlinck, and the Verhaeren of *Les Débâcles* and *Les Flambeaux Noirs,* will say: "Now, for the first time, Belgian poetry deserves the attention of those who are interested in other than the pathological aspects of literature! Not until the land had been purified by blood and flame did the Spirit of Beauty come to dwell in Flanders!"

But this criticism will be unjust. Great literary movements do not spontaneously come into being;

they develop slowly and surely through the centuries. If all the poetry of Belgium were the work of charlatans and vicious men, then, not even this tremendous war could stimulate it into healthy life. The fame of Maeterlinck's dismal dramas, and of the least worthy poems of Emile Verhaeren, should not make us oblivious of the fact that Belgium has, and has always had, its small, but brilliant, company of sincere and gifted writers, men who have not debased their art, but have held in honour the sacred traditions of their high calling. He who, neglecting the productions of the symbolists, decadents, and similar phantasists, turns his attention to the authentic literature of the Belgian people, finds a strain of poetry white and beautiful, and as fervently Catholic as the immortal songs of Crashaw and Francis Thompson. It is not the disciples of Baudelaire and Mallarmé who have planted the seeds of poetry that soon shall burst into splendid bloom, but men like Thomas Braun and Georges Ramaekers, men who, serving faithfully their Muse, have never wavered in their allegiance to the Mistress of all the Arts, the Catholic Church.

It must not be thought that these poets write only religious poems. They have, indeed, produced such masterpieces of devotional verse as Braun's *Livre des Bénédictions* and Ramaekers' *Le Chant des Trois Regnes*. But when their poetry is not religious it is not, at any rate, irreligious; they "utter nothing base." And surely even the lightest of secular poems may do its author's Catholicism no discredit. As Francis Thompson said of poetry in the eloquent appeal to the "fathers of the Church, pastors of the Church, pious laics of the Church" with which his most famous essay begins, "Eye her not askance if she seldom sing directly of religion: the bird gives glory to God though it sings only of its own innocent loves. . . . Suffer her to wanton, suffer her to play, so she play round the foot of the Cross!"

Indeed, what is true of much modern English verse is true also of that of Belgium, there are Catholic poets who seldom in their work refer directly to their faith, and there are infidel poets who have laid impious hands on the Church's treasures and decorate their rhymes with rich ecclesiastical imagery and the fragrant names of the Saints. So we find, for example, Emile Verhaeren using the first chapters of Genesis as the theme of a poem that is anything but edifying, while that pious Catholic, Thomas Braun, writes a volume of verses about postage stamps.

ESSAYS

There are certain optimistic persons who believe that the general use in literature of sacred names and traditions augurs well for the spread of faith. A member of an Anglican religious order, who two years ago delivered a series of lectures in New York City, prophesied a mighty recrudescence of religion among the poets of England, and based his prophecy, apparently, on the fact that Mr. Lascelles Abercrombie and other brilliant young writers have made ballads out of some of the most picturesque of the legends about the Saints. He did not see that Mr. Abercrombie selected his themes solely because of their literary value. There are many poets who eagerly avail themselves of the stores which are the Church's heritage, who introduce the name of the Blessed Virgin into their verses exactly as they would introduce that of Diana, or Venus or any creature of fable. Personally, I have never been able to enjoy the recital, however skillful, of a sacred story by a poet who did not believe in it, and therefore I cannot grow enthusiastic over the knowledge that many Belgian poets, whose philosophies are hostile to the Church, like to write about monstrances and chalices and altars, and to tell ostentatiously "human" stories about sacred people in general and St. Mary Magdalen in particular. I find Thomas Braun's poems about postage stamps more edifying.

The modern Catholic poets of Belgium may be roughly divided into two groups, the mystics and the primitives. These terms are here used merely for the purposes of this classification, and cannot perhaps be justified by scientific criticism. Among the mystics I would include such writers as Georges Ramaekers, the brilliant editor of *Le Catholique,* and perhaps Max Elskamp, who use elaborate and complicated symbols, and, in general, may be said to do in verse what the late Joris Karl Huysmans, after his conversion to Catholicism, did in prose. Among the primitives I would place such poets as Victor Kinon and Thomas Braun, who look for their inspirations to the ancient religious life of Flanders, in all its picturesque simplicity, and are more concerned with celebrating the piety of simple Flemish peasants than with endeavouring to penetrate high mysteries.

It is to that valued friend of Belgian letters, Mr. Jethro Bithell, of Birbeck College, London, whose translation of Stefan Zweig's book on Verhaeren has recently earned him the gratitude of the English-speaking public, that we owe this excellent version of Thomas Braun's *The Benediction of the*

ESSAYS

Nuptial Ring, taken from this poet's *The Book of the Benedictions.* The directness and sincerity of this poem suggest the work of George Herbert.

THE BENEDICTION OF THE NUPTIAL RING

"That she who shall wear it, keep faith unchanged
with her husband and ever live in mutual love."
Almighty God, bless now the ring of gold
Which bride and bridegroom shall together hold!
They whom fresh water gave to You are now
United in You by the marriage vow.
The ring is of a heavy, beaten ore,
And yet it shall not make the finger sore,
But easefully be carried day and night,
Because its secret spirit makes it light.
Its perfect circle sings into the skin,
Nor hurts it, and the phalanx growing thin
Under its pressure molds itself ere long,
Yet keeps its agile grace and still is strong.
So love, which in this symbol lies, with no
Beginning more nor ending here below,
Shall, if You bless it, Lord, like gold resist,
And never show decay, nor flaw, nor twist,
And be so light, though solid, that the soul,
A composite yet indivisible whole,
Shall keep its tender impress to the last,
And never know the bonds that bind it fast.

In many of Thomas Braun's poems is to be found a quality suggestive of the folk song. Like the Verhaeren of *Les Flamandes,* Braun writes of those huge, boisterous farmers and merchants who live for us on the canvases of Brauwer and Jan Steen. But he writes of them, it need scarcely be said, in a very different spirit. Verhaeren saw only their gluttony, drunkenness, and coarseness; Braun sees their courage, industry, good-nature, piety. In fact, Verhaeren saw their bodies, Braun sees their souls.

In an essay on Verhaeren recently printed, I called attention to the fact that while Verhaeren wrote of the Flemings with enthusiasm, and with repulsively careful attention to detail, he did not write of them with sympathy. He does not join in the revels about which he writes; he is interested in his loud purple-faced peasants, but with his interest is mingled a certain scorn. Thomas Braun, on the other hand, is thoroughly in sympathy with the life of which he writes; the reader feels that such a poem as *The Benediction of Wine,* for example, was written by a man who is artist enough to share actually in the strong simple piety of the keeper of the vineyard. The quaintness of Thomas Braun's poems, which is emphasized by the woodcuts made to accompany them by his brother who is a Benedictine monk, is not an affectation, it is a quality proper to the work of a man who, like Wordsworth, sees beauty chiefly in simplicity. Like Coventry Patmore, he has "divine frivolity," he is acquainted with the mirth of the Saints. In his own beautiful words, he knows how to play in the straw with the Child of Bethlehem.

Georges Ramaekers is a poet whose verse is for the most part too obscure to lend itself readily to translation. He will write a poem, for example, on mushrooms, and the reader will think after several minutes that he is being told merely about the common fungi. Then it comes to him that it is the Tree of Life that these maleficent growths are attacking; then they cover the columns of the Church and actually reach the Host Itself. The poem is, it seems, a denunciation of certain heresies, or of sloth, indifference, and other spiritual evils, but its meaning cannot adequately be given in an English translation.

Here is a similar poem, which, in Mr. Bithell's translation, shows Georges Ramaeker's symbolic method at its best and clearest.

THE THISTLE

Rooted on herbless peaks, where its erect
And prickly leaves, austerely cold and dumb,
Hold the slow, scaly serpent in respect,
The Gothic thistle, while the insects' hum

Sounds far off, rears above the rock it scorns
Its rigid virtue for the Heavens to see.
The towering boulders guard it. And the bee
Makes honey from the blossoms on its thorns.

Victor Kinon, like that very different poet, Albert Giraud, the chief Belgian disciple of Baudelaire, is of Walloon descent. Mr. Bithell calls this poet a "fervent Roman Catholic," but the poems which he has selected for translation are entirely secular in theme and treatment. They show, however, that their author is free from the vices of extreme realism and hysteria, which afflict many of his contemporaries. Sometimes it is fair to judge a poet's whole attitude toward life from his love poems. When decadence and feverish eroticism are in fashion, it is refreshing to come upon a poet sane enough to write so honest and delicate a poem as this of Victor Kinon.

HIDING FROM THE WORLD

Shall not our love be like the violet, Sweet,
And open in the dewy, dustless air
Its dainty chalice with blue petals, where
The shade of bushes makes a shy retreat?
And we will frame our daily happiness
By joining hearts, lips, brows in rapt caress
Far from the world, its noises and conceit.

[87]

Shall we not hide our modest love between
Trees wafting cool on flowers and grasses green?

In Victor Kinon's poetry is shown a knowledge
of nature like that possessed by that American poet
whose death the world of letters has not ceased to
mourn, Madison Cawein. He sketches a landscape
in a few vigorous lines, and the picture is vivid and
true. This little poem might be a lyrical rendition
of a Monet painting.

THE SETTING SUN

The stainless snow and the blue,
   Lit by a pure gold star,
   Nearly meet, but a bar
Of fire separates the two.

A rime-frosted, black pinewood,
   Raising, as waves roll foam,
   Its lances toothed like a comb,
Dams the horizon's blood.

In a tomb of blue and white
   Nothing stirs save a crow,
   Unfolding solemnly now
Its silky wing black as night.

It is difficult to resist the temptation to read into
the Catholic fold many Belgian poets who do not,

perhaps, belong there. There is scarcely a man of
letters in Belgium who does not owe his introduction to literature to the Catholic Church. The
Catholic schools and universities of Belgium have
given a knowledge of art and poetry to many a poet
who now pays for the gift his little stanzas of abuse.
But some of them, and among them must be counted
Emile Verhaeren, seem to be thinking of their old
faith, now that the need of faith has become terribly
apparent to them. Verhaeren, especially, seems to
be about to stop in his weary flight from the Hound
of Heaven. For many years he was a writer of
poems that seemed to betray a mind absolutely dis-
eased. There were realistic studies of human vice
that seemed like pages of Zola done into verse, and
there were extraordinary attempts (of which Stefan
Zweig speaks approvingly) to "chisel a new face
of God." But since his retirement to his little cottage at Caillou-qui-Bique, he has written poems
that are for the most part exaltations of pure love,
as lofty in thought as they are finished in composition. Mr. Bithell's translation of this little song
of wedded love shows that Verhaeren has left far
behind him the grossness of *Les Flamandes* and the
morbidness of *Les Flambeaux Noirs.*

ESSAYS

This is the good hour when the lamp is lit.
  All is calm, and consoling, and dear,
And the silence is such that you could hear
  A feather falling in it.

This is the good hour when to my chair my love will
      flit
  As breezes blow,
  As smoke will rise,
  Gentle, slow,
She says nothing at first—and I am listening;
  I hear all her soul, I surprise
  Its gushing and glistening,
  And I kiss her eyes.

This is the good hour when the lamp is lit.
  When hearts will say
  How they have loved each other through the day.

And one says such simple things:
The fruit one from the garden brings;
  The flower that one has seen
  Opening in mosses green;

And the heart will of a sudden thrill and glow,
Remembering some faded word of love
  Found in a drawer beneath a cast-off glove
  In a letter of a year ago.

  But the poem which indicates most clearly the
[90]

tremendous change that his nation's tragedy has brought to Verhaeren, is that inspired by the demolition of the Cathedral of Rheims. A year ago, it may be, Verhaeren would have thought of this cathedral merely as a beautiful piece of architecture, as an ancient and lovely landmark. Now that it has suffered from the cannon of an invading army, he remembers suddenly the high use for which it was intended, the destruction of the sacred images and vessels reminds him, in spite of all his sophistry, that these things were not mere works of art. Once more, as in those far-away years when, with Georges Rodenbach, Charles Van Lerberghe, and Maurice Maeterlinck, he learned of literature and life at the Jesuit College of Sainte-Barbe, he is able to understand that most necessary of all acts, worship. The poem is so significant, so important to all who desire an insight into the psychology of Verhaeren and of literary Belgium, that I venture to quote here my own translation of it. It by no means does justice to the beauty of the original.

THE CATHEDRAL OF RHEIMS

He who walks through the meadows of Champagne
  At noon in Fall, when leaves like gold appear,
    Sees it draw near
Like some great mountain set upon the plain.

From radiant dawn until the close of day,
  Nearer it grows
  To him who goes
Across the country. When tall towers lay
  Their shadowy pall
  Upon his way,
  He enters, where
The solid stone is hollowed deep by all
Its centuries of beauty and of prayer.

Ancient French temple! thou whose hundred
    kings
Watch over thee, emblazoned on thy walls,
Tell me, within thy memory-hallowed halls
What chant of triumph or what war-song rings?
Thou hast known Clovis and his Frankish train,
Whose mighty hand Saint Remy's hand did
    keep,
And in thy spacious vault perhaps may sleep
An echo of the voice of Charlemagne.
For God thou hast known fear, when from His
    side
Men wandered, seeking alien shrines and new,
But still the sky was bountiful and blue
And thou wast crowned with France's love and
    pride.
Sacred thou art, from pinnacle to base;
And in thy panes of gold and scarlet glass
The setting sun sees thousandfold his face;
Sorrow and joy in stately silence pass

THE CATHOLIC POETS OF BELGIUM

Across thy walls, the shadow and the light;
Around thy lofty pillars, tapers white
Illuminate, with delicate sharp flames,
The brows of saints with venerable names,
And in the night erect a fiery wall.
A great but silent fervour burns in all
Those simple folk who kneel, pathetic, dumb,
And know that down below, beside the Rhine—
Cannon, horses, soldiers, flags in line—
With blare of trumpets, mighty armies come.
Suddenly, each knows fear;
Swift rumours pass, that every one must hear,
The hostile banners blaze against the sky
And by the embassies mobs rage and cry.
Now war has come and peace is at an end.
On Paris town the German troops descend.
They are turned back, and driven to Champagne.
And now as to so many weary men,
The glorious temple gives them welcome, when
It meets them at the bottom of the plain.

At once, they set their cannon in its way.
　　There is no gable now, nor wall
　　That does not suffer, night and day,
As shot and shell in crushing torrents fall.
The stricken tocsin quivers through the tower;
The triple nave, the apse, the lonely choir
　　Are circled, hour by hour,
　　With thundering bands of fire
And Death is scattered broadcast among men.

    And then
That which was splendid with baptismal grace;
The stately arches soaring into space,
The transepts, columns, windows gray and gold,
The organ, in whose tones the ocean rolled,
The crypts, of mighty shades the dwelling places,
The Virgin's gentle hands, the Saints' pure faces,
All, even the pardoning hands of Christ the Lord
Were struck and broken by the wanton sword
    Of sacrilegious lust.

O beauty slain, O glory in the dust!
Strong walls of faith, most basely overthrown!
The crawling flames, like adders glistening
Ate the white fabric of this lovely thing.
Now from its soul rose a piteous moan,
The soul that always loved the just and fair.
Granite and marble loud their woe confessed,
The silver monstrances that Popes had blessed,
The chalices and lamps and crosiers rare
Were seared and twisted by a flaming breath;
The horror everywhere did range and swell,
The guardian Saints into this furnace fell,
Their bitter tears and screams were stilled in
    death.

Around the flames armed hosts are skirmishing.
The burning sun reflects the lurid scene;
The German army, fighting for its life,
Rallies its torn and terrified left wing;

And, as they near this place,
The imperial eagles see
Before them in their flight,
Here, in the solemn night,
The old Cathedral to the years to be
Showing, with wounded arms, their own disgrace.

Of Verhaeren's school-fellows at Sainte-Barbe, one, Maurice Maeterlinck, is already enjoying a fame which exceeds his deserts and is not likely to endure. Georges Rodenbach, who died in 1898, wrote, like Verhaeren, of Flemish peasants, but he gave them a romantic glamour which has alienated critics who admire naturalistic poetry. Stefan Zweig has little use for him, and Jethro Bithell speaks of his "weary Alexandrines," and says that his reputation has waned considerably since his death. But Charles C. Clarke, of the Sheffield Scientific School, in the course of an illuminating article on Belgian literature, says that Rodenbach's poems have considerable vogue in France. From his discussion of Rodenbach I quote this felicitously phrased paragraph:

"Morbid and mystic like his prose, Rodenbach's poetry has a delicacy and a silvery tone that are inimitable. Out of almost nothing it weaves thoughts and calls up memories of wonderfully melancholy beauty. In it water is always stagnant, giving chill reflections of the sky through trees; lights are dim, footsteps noiseless; rooms are repositories of reminders of the past, where silence speaks to the heart through sad aspects. The extent to which Rodenbach uses such notes constitutes his originality. His skill in avoiding every common formula and his delicate choice of metaphors seem really inspiration. No one has imitated his poems of gray tints and muffled sounds, his mourning designs of dull filigree, without falling into monotony and trifling. It is not enough praise for a poet to say of him that he was unapproachable in picturing the accessories of melancholy; but Rodenbach deserves no more, unless it be our gratitude for preserving in literature something of ancient Flanders which battle and flame have destroyed beyond material restoration."

Another school-fellow of Verhaeren, Charles Van Lerberghe, can scarcely, I believe, be called a Catholic poet, although, like Dante Gabriel Rossetti, whose disciple he was, his verse is filled with Catholic symbolism. In a country like Belgium, in which nearly all the education is Catholic, and in which nearly every poet is, at any rate nominally, a Catholic, it is sometimes difficult to distinguish between writers who have a genuinely devotional spirit, and those who merely like to play with mysticism. There are, for example, the amazing poems of Max Elskamp. He writes simple and charming poems about the Blessed Virgin and the Christ Child, and seems, indeed, to have the hardy faith of his Flemish ancestors. But the simplicity of his poems is not always convincing; the reader remembers that the late William Sharpe wrote, as "Fiona MacLeod," poems that seemed to flame with all the piety of the Gael. And William Sharpe was, as he took care to let the world know, a "pagan." The feeling that Elskamp's interest in religion is chiefly literary is strengthened when we learn from Mr. Bithell that most of the sacred names in his poems have a symbolic meaning, that the Blessed Virgin means merely "the pure woman," and the Christ Child simply "the delicious infancy." Intellectual caprices like this seldom accompany genuine devotional feeling.

But at any rate there is nothing to disgust or pain the reader in Elskamp's verse; whether or not he believes in the sacred personages of whom he writes, he does not treat them irreverently. His Catholicism, however, is not so convincing as is that of Thomas Braun and Georges Ramaekers.

It is good to find that in Belgium, a country the literature of which must inevitably reflect from time to time the strange fashions of Germany and France, there has been preserved through the years the poetry of Catholic tradition. Belgian poetry must become more and more spiritual; the poets have seen and felt things mighty and terrible, and they can no longer concern themselves with erotic fancies and the nuances of their own emotions. In days to come, historians of literature will perhaps see that on the thought of Belgium as on the thought of all Europe, this war has had a clarifying and strengthening effect. Good still comes from evil, sweetness from force, and honeycomb out of the lion's carcass. Belgium may say, in the words of one of the truest poets of our time:

> Sweet Sorrow, play a grateful part,
> Break me the marble of my heart
> And of its fragments pave a street
> Where, to my bliss, myself may meet
> One hastening with piercèd feet.

LETTERS

To Charles Willis Thompson

THE NEW YORK TIMES.
November 1, 1914.

Dear Charlie—

Can you lend me $1.00? I wish to go to New Brunswick, N. J. Help me to gratify this strange whim!

J. KILMER.

To Shaemas O'Sheel

Mahwah, N. J.

My dear Shaemas—

Aline and I are heartily glad of the splendid fortune that has come to you and Blanche. I am sure you will enjoy Washington—it's a very lovely city as I remember it—I was there for two days at the age of four.

With love from Mayor Gaynor, Cale Young Rice, Alfred Noyes, Madison Cawein, B. Russell Hertz and Harriet Monroe,

I am,
Yours,

JOYCE.

[101]

LETTERS

The New York Times.
February 12, 1916.

Dear Shaemas:

I have been thinking a good deal about you for the last day or so, and might therefore have known that a message from you was on its way. The Minaret is a fine adventure, and God knows Washington needs adventures more than any other city in the United States. There is some beautiful writing and some brave and direct thinking in the copies you sent me, and of course I enclose my subscription for a year. I'd support any enterprise of yours, so long as it wasn't a scheme to make the Kaiser Mayor of Mahwah, New Jersey. I also enclose a poem, with my blessing.

But why do you let your young collaborator—I suppose he is responsible—be so damned vindictive! No poet has any right in the world to knock the work of another poet who is honest. Vachel Lindsey is, in my opinion, a sincere artist, whose work sometimes—as in "The Chinese Nightingale"—glows with genius. That is of course only my own opinion—but it is not merely a matter of opinion, but a matter of absolute fact, that he is an honest man, consistently serving his ideal, earnestly endeavouring to express the beauty that is in him.

[102]

And abuse is not what he should receive from his brother poet.

However, go ahead, and good luck to you. But lay off the hammer! Poets have enough to suffer without being castigated by other poets. Keep out of jail, and give my love to Blanche and Patrick Wilhelm.

> Yours as always,
> JOYCE KILMER.

To Louis Bevier, Jr.

> NEW YORK TIMES.
> November 28, 1916.

My dear Louis:

I am sending you by this mail a copy of my book "The Circus and Other Essays," which our friend Laurence has just published. I had intended to dedicate it to your father and yourself, but I suddenly discovered that I had never dedicated a book to my own father. So I have dedicated this one to him, and will dedicate to your father and yourself one of the two books coming out in the Spring— either the poems or the interviews.

At any time you wish, I will buy you a drink.

> Yours sincerely,
> JOYCE KILMER.

[103]

LETTERS

NEW YORK TIMES.

February, 1916.

Dear Sara:

I don't know that POETRY could use a Valentine poem, but if it could do so, it ought by all means to use it long after Valentine's day, for timeliness, the greatest curse of our much cursed magazines, is certainly not one of POETRY'S vices. And how do you like it? It's the first free verse I've written since free verse made a special label for itself—it's a highly artificial poem, and yet passionately sincere.

I've quit being a critic, thank God! I resigned from the *Bookman* and *Book News Monthly,* and I no longer review poetry for the *Times.* I still run the *Digest's* "Current Poetry" department, but that's not criticism, it's just an exhibition. I merely hold up for admiration the best poetry I can find, saying nothing about inferior stuff. And I can do that without losing my self-respect. But criticism of poetry is no task for an enthusiastic poet, however little he may deserve the title.

Aline is still in hospital, impatient for the new baby. She likes to receive letters.

YOURS, JOYCE.

LETTERS

To Katherine Brégy

THE NEW YORK TIMES,

Times Square.

November 6, 1914.

My dear Miss Brégy:

It is delightful to find on my desk this morning your letter telling me of the honour in store for me. Of course I am reading with enjoyment the "Opera" in *America;* how valuable a friend Catholic poetry, that is poetry, has in you!

A verse-maker, I suppose, is an unskillful critic of his own work. But in reply to your question, I will say that I am greatly pleased when people like "Trees," "Stars" and "Pennies," when they see that "Folly" is a religious poem, when they praise the stanza fourth from the end of "Delicatessen," and understand stanza three of section four of "The Fourth Shepherd."

Before what Miss Guiney calls my "great leap into Liberty" I published a book of verses called "Summer of Love"; but I do not think it would interest you; it is, for the most part, a celebration of common themes. If you have not a copy of "Trees and Other Poems" please tell me and I will send you one. I will send also "Summer of Love" if you wish it, for some of the poems in it, those inspired

[105]

by genuine love, are not things of which to be ashamed, and you, understanding, would not be offended by the others.

Your sincerely,
JOYCE KILMER.

May 18th, 1917.

Dear Katherine:

Naturally I'm expecting to go to the Wars, being of appropriate age and sex. I was going to Plattsburg to try for a commission, but for many reasons—one of them being that I didn't want to be an officer in charge of conscripts (the democratic bluff again! says Katherine)—I gave up the idea. So a month ago I enlisted as a private in the Seventh Regiment, National Guard, New York. We were reviewed by your friend Joffre—in 1824 we were reviewed by Lafayette. We go to training camp in a week or so—where I don't know—and then we are mustered into Federal service. We may be sent to France, we may be sent to Russia, or it may be Mexico or Cuba—nobody knows.

Please come to New York and let me take you to luncheon. And give Mrs. Coates my love.

JOYCE.

LETTERS

To Amelia Josephine Burr

Headquarters Company, 165th Infantry,

A. E. F., France.

My dear Josephine:

That is a magnificent piece of knitting—I am delighted to own it. Thanks ever so much! And I will thank you ever more for your book of poetry, which you promise to send me. I enjoyed your recent poems in the *Outlook*—you are one of the few American poets who should be allowed to write war songs. Your letter came up to the specifications of the order—it was highly entertaining and therefore genuinely appreciated. I sympathise with you in your trials in addressing camp audiences, though I don't know as you deserve any sympathy. I think you have a pretty good time. And I know the audiences do.

I wouldn't be surprised to hear of you coming over here as a nurse or something. Nice country, nice war. I wouldn't be back in the States having meatless, wheatless, boozeless, smokeless days for anything. I am a Sergeant now. I spend my time working at Regimental Headquarters while we are in reserve, and in training and when we are in action I am an Observer in the Regimental Intelligence Section—very amusing work. I had a fine time during the recent activities of our regiment, activities of which you probably read in the papers. In the dug-out I wrote a poem I think you'll like— "Rouge Bouquet" is its name. I expect to remain a Sergeant (unless I'm reduced), for to get a commission I'd have to leave the Regiment and go to a training school for several months and then I would be sent to some regiment other than this. And I'd rather be a sergeant in the 69th than a lieutenant in any other outfit.

Give my love to anybody you meet who would appreciate that commodity. And write often to
Yours,
JOYCE.

To Howard W. Cook

Headquarters Company, 165th Infantry,
A. E. F., France.
June 28, 1918.

Dear Mr. Cook:

Your letter of May 31 has just arrived. I am afraid that such information as I can send you will reach you too late to be of use, but anyway I'll do what I can.

You ask first for biographical details. All this
[108]

material you will find in Who's Who in America, except the information that I am the father of four children, named respectively Kenton Sinclair, Deborah Clanton, Michael Barry and Christopher.

Second, you ask for comments on myself and something about my earlier efforts in poetry. That's harder to answer. How can I make comments on myself? I'll pass up that part of the questionnaire, if I may, but I'm willing to write about my earlier efforts in poetry. They were utterly worthless, that is, all of them which preceded a poem called "Pennies" which you will find in my book "Trees and Other Poems." I want all my poems written before that to be forgotten—they were only the exercises of an amateur, imitations, useful only as technical training. If what I nowadays write is considered poetry, then I became a poet in November, 1913.

Now, as to your other questions. I'll take them in order. 1. What has contemporary poetry already accomplished? Answer—All that poetry can be expected to do is to give pleasure of a noble sort to its readers, leading them to the contemplation of that Beauty which neither words nor sculptures nor pigments can do more than faintly reflect, and to express the mental and spiritual tendencies of the people of the lands and times in which it is written. I have very little chance to read contemporary poetry out here, but I hope it is reflecting the virtues which are blossoming on the blood-soaked soil of this land—courage, and self-abnegation, and love, and faith—this last not faith in some abstract goodness, but faith in God and His Son and the Holy Ghost, and in the Church which God Himself founded and still rules. France has turned to her ancient Faith with more passionate devotion than she has shown for centuries. I believe that America is learning the same lesson from the war, and is cleansing herself of cynicism and pessimism and materialism and the lust for novelty which has hampered our national development. I hope that our poets already see this tendency and rejoice in it—if they do not they are unworthy of their craft.

2. What is American poetry's influence to-day? Answer—This question I am ill-prepared to answer, but I would venture to surmise that the extravagances and decadence of the so-called "renascence of poetry" during the last five years—a renascence distinguished by the celebration of the queer and the nasty instead of the beautiful—have made the poet seem as silly a figure to the contemporary American as he seemed to the English-

man of the eighteen-nineties, when the "æsthetic movement" was at its foolish height.

3. What of American poetry's future? Answer —To predict anything of American poetry's future requires a knowledge of America's future, and I am not a student of political economy. But this much I will tell you—when we soldiers get back to our homes and have the leisure to read poetry, we won't read the works of Amy Lowell and Edgar Lee Masters. We'll read poetry, if there is any for us to read, and I hope there will be. I believe there will.

Sincerely yours,

JOYCE KILMER.

To Thomas Walsh

Headquarters Co., 165th Infantry,
A. E. F., France.

April.

Dear Tom:

Where will you be, I wonder, when this letter reaches you? Perhaps in the Brooklyn sanctuary (this term is here used in a purely literary sense) reading reviews of your newest book of verse— pleasant reading indeed, judging by those I have

seen. Perhaps you will be in your Sabine farm at
Lake Hopatkong—if that is the way that strange
word is spelled. Perhaps the postman will give it to
you just as you parade away from your home, and
you will take it with you to the palatial new Columbia University Club, and glance at it over your
turtle soup and sherry and steak and mushrooms
and corn and sweet potatoes and chaveis—but I'm
breaking my heart describing this meal of yours.
Soon the mess call will sound and I'll take my aluminum meat dish and canteen cup, and wade
through the mud to the mess-line. And I'll get a
plate of stew and some milkless tea or coffee, and
I'll stand in the mud or sit down in the mud and
consume it.

Nevertheless, it's a nice war and I'm enjoying
most of it. Our time at the front—of which the
newspapers have by this time informed you—was
a wonderful experience. I had the privilege of
spending a week as observer in the Regimental
Intelligence Section—lively and interesting work.
I'd love to see you at an observation post, Tom,
you'd get as thin as I now am.

Send me your book, will you, Tom? I enjoy
poetry more now than ever before—I suppose it is
because I get it so seldom. When I'm writing verse

and reviewing verse and talking about verse and to verse-makers all the time, I have not the enthusiasm for it I have over here, where most of the poetry is unwritten and undiscussed.

Nevertheless, it's a nice country. I'd like to buy you a litre of red wine—for a franc and a half— with a dash of syrup in it. Also I could introduce you to the results of the labours of a few accomplished cooks, some of them soldiers, some of them French women.

Fr. O'Donnell quotes you to the effect that Louis is now in this land, or on his way hither. I hope to see him. He ought to be sent to an Officer's Training School soon—I think that will happen. He is the sort of fellow who ought to have a commission. I might possibly be allowed to go to an Officer's Training School, but I wouldn't do so, because if I did so I'd be sent—whether or not I got a commission—to some Regiment other than this. And I take no pleasure in the thought of soldiering in a regiment of strangers. I like the crowd in this outfit very much and would rather be a sergeant—as I am—here than be a lieutenant in any other Regiment.

If you are ever minded to send me papers, please let them be *Times* Book Reviews or other sheets of

a decidedly literary flavour. Occasional copies of
The Bookman would be welcome. I like a bit of
concentrated literature now and then.

Remember me, please, to your sisters and brothers and to any of my other friends whom you may
meet. And believe me

Always yours sincerely,

JOYCE.

To Robert Cortes Holliday

Headquarters Co., 165th Inf.,

A. E. F., France.

May 7, 1918.

Dear Bob:

I have not the time now to write you the letter
I'd like to write—chiefly about your characteristic
and delightful Tarkington book, which I greatly
enjoyed and expect to enjoy during many re-read-
ings. What I write now is merely a note in answer
to your letter of April 12. This you will please
communicate to Mr. Doran and regard as final.

The only way I can give you any material for a
book is as I am doing now—sending you every six
months or so some verses or an introspective essay
which you can syndicate and eventually turn into a

[114]

book. I sent you a prose sketch "Holy Ireland" (which represents the best prose writing I can do nowadays), another prose sketch, and (by way of Aline) a poem, "Rouge Bouquet," which you ought to be able to do a good deal with. It is probably the best verse I have written. I never planned doing war-correspondence work—if I had I'd have come over as a correspondent instead of as a soldier. Many circumstances, including the censorship, the rules governing a soldier's conduct and other things, prevent me from trying to make a consecutive narrative now, even if I so desired. I am a poet at present trying to be a soldier. The experience may naturally be expected to result in a book—of some kind, at some time. I am not going to try to "cover" the war or my Regiment's share in it. But the title "Here and There With the Fighting Sixty-ninth" may probably be taken as well as any other to cover what, if I survive, I shall probably, in the course of time, write. My days of hack writing are over, for a time at least.

To tell the truth, I am not at all interested in writing nowadays, except in so far as writing is the expression of something beautiful. And I see daily and nightly the expression of beauty in action instead of words, and I find it more satisfactory. I am a Sergeant in the Regimental Intelligence Section—the most fascinating work possible—more thrills in it than in any other branch except possibly aviation. And it's more varied than aviation. Wonderful life! But I don't know what I'll be able to do in civilian life—unless I become a fireman!

Please give my love to Stella and believe me always your affectionate and grateful friend

JOYCE.

To Reverend Edward F. Garesché, S.J.

Hq. Co., 165th Inf.,
A. E. F.
Jan. 29, 1918.

My dear Father:

I have to thank you for three letters, for two poems, for the proof sheets of your book and for your beautiful Christmas gift, which I treasure and have with me always. The poem "To Rose in Heaven" is so exquisite that I cannot write or speak all my deep appreciation of it. But I know that it is not my personal feeling alone that makes me consider it one of the noblest elegiac poems in our language. I wish that I were still in the book-reviewing game—I'd like to express my opinion of your new book. My column in the *Literary Digest* is now conducted by Mrs. Edwin Markham. However, I occasionally send in some clippings and comment, and I'll try to get some of your book quoted. I congratulate you on your book; it is an achievement for which you must be deeply grateful; of course none of us rhymers can really be proud if we're true to the traditions of our craft. You see, I'm not in "The Proud Poet" mood now. I'm neither proud nor a poet—I've written only one poem since I sailed, a little thing called "Militis Meditatio."

We all are well and happy—I do not think that any one of us can honestly say that he has not enjoyed this Winter. The trials and hardships of the life are so novel as to be interesting. But I imagine that one enjoys very little his tenth year of soldiering. It is especially pleasant to be in France and the part of France that we are in. I am surprised, I acknowledge, by the passionate Catholicity of the people. Even "Holy Ireland" can scarcely be more Catholic than rural France.

Tell my friends my address and urge them to write to me. Pray for me, and believe me always
Yours sincerely,
JOYCE KILMER.

LETTERS

Headquarters Company, 165th Infantry,
A. E. F., France.
May 6, 1918.

My dear Father:

It is very comfortable to dwell in so genuinely Catholic a land as this; to be reminded in every room of every house, and at every cross-road of the Faith. I do not know when you last visited France, and perhaps you are already familiar with conditions here, but I do not cease to be surprised and delighted to see the number of people receiving Holy Communion not only on Sunday, but every day. And you will find soldiers of this Regiment in church whenever and wherever there is a priest to say Mass. I think that most of us are better Catholics now than when we were at home—certainly we should be.

My own work is growing steadily more interesting. For a while I worked, as you know, in the Adjutant's Office, having special charge of recording and reporting statistics. But this I gave up recently to enter (as a Sergeant) the Regimental Intelligence Section. This is much better for me, since it is open-air work of an intensely interesting kind, and I think that I am now more useful to the Regiment. My newspaper training, you see, has

[118]

made me a competent observer, and that is what I am nowadays—an observer of the enemy's activities. I have already some strange stories to tell, but for telling them I must await a time when censorship rules are abrogated. I have written very little—two prose sketches and two poems since I left the States—but I have a rich store of memories. Not that what I write matters—I have discovered, since some unforgettable experiences, that writing is not the tremendously important thing I once considered it. You will find me less a bookman when you next see me, and more, I hope, a man.

Pray for me, my dear Father, that I may love God more and that I may be unceasingly conscious of Him—that is the greatest desire I have.

Your affectionate friend,
JOYCE KILMER.

To Reverend James J. Daly, S.J.

Cragmere, Mahwah, New Jersey.
Oct. 7, 1912.

My dear Father Daly:

I hope that I interpret your letter of September 20th correctly in thinking that it means that you will permit me to write to you occasionally, and that you will write me in return. Of course I know that your work occupies much of your time, and that you have pleasanter uses for your leisure than writing letters to some one you have not seen. So do not feel obliged by courtesy to answer me at length.

I am glad that you like some of my work. My present occupation is that of assistant editor of *The Churchman,* an Anglican weekly paper. It is a Church Newspaper, with some literary features. Did Grey tell you that I was not of your Communion? I hope that this knowledge will not shut me out of your regard.

Your remarks, in your letter, on the fact that many of our most famous writers to-day are anti-Christian, are certainly justified. Still, do you not think that a reaction is coming? Already we have Chesterton, and Belloc, and Bazin, and Miss Guiney, and Fr. Vincent McNabb, and a number of other brilliant writers who not as theologians but purely as literary artists express a fine and wholesome faith. People are beginning to tire of cheap eroticism and "realism" and similar absurdities.

Yours sincerely,
JOYCE KILMER.

JOYCE KILMER, AGE 5

FROM A PHOTOGRAPH
IN THE POSSESSION OF
MRS. KILBURN KILMER

New York,
Dec. 14, 1912.

My dear Father Daly:

The cards are rather laconic, but they are supposed to convey the information, as you thought, that my family is the larger by one. I have already a little boy, who will be four next March. His name is Kenton Sinclair. I married when I was twenty-one, immediately after my graduation from Columbia. Then—since you have twice asked for biographical information—I taught school in Morristown for a year, came to New York, went to work on the Standard Dictionary, and after three years took my present position on *The Churchman*.

Do you know the Rev. Michael Earls? I recently received a copy of his book of verse. He is a member of your Society—I think he is at Georgetown. The poems about children are very delicate and sympathetic—one called, I believe, "An Autumn Rose-bush" is admirable.

I see Grey frequently—I hope to take breakfast with him to-morrow. A number of us have the custom of breakfasting on Sunday mornings on the excellent Irish bacon to be procured at Healy's, on 91st St. When you return to New York, you must join us. Do you know Thomas Walsh? He is with us occasionally—you should know him, and his translations from the Spanish, and his verse. I hope you are coming East soon.

Yours sincerely,
JOYCE KILMER.

Cragmere, Mahwah, N. J.
July 24, 1913.

Dear Father Daly:

I do not like to burden my friends with my troubles, but you have certain opportunities that I lack, so I am asking you the greatest favour. Please pray for the healing of my little daughter Rose. She is dangerously ill with infantile paralysis. This is a disease that has appeared among mankind only recently, and physicians are uncertain how to treat it. She is staying in New York with her mother to be near the doctor and I am staying here nights to take care of my other child. Of course the maid is here during the day so the house is kept up. But Rose cannot move her legs or arms —She was so active and happy only last week— she cannot even cry—her voice is just a little

[122]

whimper—the danger is of its reaching her lungs and killing her. I cannot write any more. You know how I feel. Pray for her.

JOYCE KILMER.

Aug. 30, 1913.

Dear Father Daly:

There is not, it seems, any danger of the death of Rose now. And she has regained her strength. Her arms and legs have been left paralysed but her hands and feet move. It will take a year's time for us to know whether or not this paralysis is permanent.

I am deeply grateful to you for your compliance with my request. I know that your prayers were of value in keeping her alive. Apologies for the brusqueness of my letter asking your aid, are, I think, not necessary—you were the only man to whom I could appeal for the special help needed, and I was in bitter grief and anxiety.

My wife asks me to express her sincere gratitude to you.

Now that the crisis is past, we have a strange tranquillity.

And we have acquired a humility that is, I think,

[123]

good for us. Well, these are things not readily expressed—accept our heart-felt thanks.

Yours sincerely,

JOYCE KILMER.

New York.
Oct. 6, 1913.

Dear Father Daly:

This is to express our gratitude for your prayers. They have helped us in our trial—they are helping —and I know that in part to your efforts Rose owes her life and we our peace of mind. For fifteen or sixteen years she will, the doctors say, remain paralysed, unable to move her arms or legs. But her mind is active and we will keep her happy. I think that there are compensations, spiritual and mental, for the loss of physical power.

My wife and I are studying Catholic doctrine and we hope to be received this Autumn.

Yours sincerely,

JOYCE KILMER.

New York.
Dec. 5, 1913.

Dear Father Daly:

You may be amused by the circular which I en-

[124]

close. You know, we have been having a plague of
white-slave plays in New York this season—"The
Lure," "The Fight" and the rest; and now they
are giving white-slave moving pictures—"The
Traffic in Souls" they are called. I think that "The
Drama as a Factor in Sex Education" is ridiculous
—and I'm going to say so. Most of the other people who are to speak at the Academy of Medicine
are very serious-minded settlement workers, ready
to save the world by means of eugenics and inex-
pensive divorce. So I don't think I'll make myself very popular. But I hope to have a lot of fun.

My wife and I are very comfortable now that we
are Catholics. I think we rather disappointed
Father Cronyn (the Paulist who received us) by
not showing any emotion during the ceremony.
But our chief sensation is simply comfort—we feel
that we're where we belong, and it's a very pleasant
feeling.

I wonder if the enclosed verses will shock you. I
am very much bored by the praise of suicide so common in "æsthetic" circles. Many of my friends like
to think themselves "decadents" and they are most
enthusiastic over the work of such third-rate versi-
fiers as the late Richard Middleton, who killed himself at the age of thirty. It seems to me that suicide

is the most absurd of all sins. There is, undoubtedly, pleasure in many sorts of evil; many crimes
are reprehensible but not ridiculous. But suicide is
a stupid sort of sin—the criminal gets no fun at all
out of it. I have tried to put this idea into verse—
and you should have heard the criticisms when the
poem was read aloud at a meeting of the Poetry
Society!

Yours sincerely,
JOYCE KILMER.

New York, Dec. 22, 1913.

Dear Father Daly:

I am grateful to you for your sound criticism of
"To a Young Poet Who Killed Himself." It had
previously been criticised by "pagans" who thought
that suicide was romantic and charming. You gave
me just what I needed—an analysis of its "philosophy." Of course I'll leave it out of my new book
of verse, or else, as you suggest, make it the utterance of someone not myself.

You will be glad to hear of our Christmas present
from Soeur Therese. Rose can lift her left fore-
arm. I know that you have been getting her aid for

[126]

us. Please tell us how to show our gratitude to her and to you.

A picture of Rose and her mother is going to you for Christmas. I hope that it may be a mirthful feast for you. We can honestly say that we have never before been so happy.

Yours sincerely,
JOYCE KILMER.

Mahwah, N. J.
Jan. 9, 1914.

Dear Father Daly:

At last I have leisure to thank you for your Christmas gifts. I did not know that such beautiful cards were made. How is it that in Prairie du Chien—a place of which the name suggests Indians and tomahawks and Deadwood stage-coaches— you can procure better cards than I can get in New York? The medals are highly valued—the workmanship on them is admirable—they will be worn properly as soon as I can afford to buy some silver chains—and that will be next Tuesday.

Of course you understand my conversion. I am beginning to understand it. I believed in the Catholic position, the Catholic view of ethics and æsthetics, for a long time. But I wanted something not intellectual, some conviction not mental—in fact I wanted Faith.

Just off Broadway, on the way from the Hudson Tube Station to the Times Building, there is a Church, called the Church of the Holy Innocents. Since it is in the heart of the Tenderloin, this name is strangely appropriate—for there surely is need of youth and innocence. Well, every morning for months I stopped on my way to the office and prayed in this Church for faith. When faith did come, it came, I think, by way of my little paralysed daughter. Her lifeless hands led me; I think her tiny still feet know beautiful paths. You understand this and it gives me a selfish pleasure to write it down.

I was very glad of your criticism of "The Young Poet Who Killed Himself." I need some stricter discipline, I think, and it's hard to get it. I enjoy Father Cullem's direction very much, he is a fine old Irishman with no nonsense about him. But I need to be called a fool, I need to have some of the conceit and sophistication knocked out of me. I suppose you think this is "enthusiasm"—that much heralded danger of converts. Perhaps it is, but I don't think so. I know I'm glad I live two miles from the Church, because it's excellent for a lazy person like myself to be made to exert himself for religion. And I wish I had a stern mediæval confessor—the sort of person one reads about in anti-Catholic books—who would inflict real penances. The saying of Hail Marys and Our Fathers is no penance, it's a delight.

Forgive this egotistical letter! I am praying that the New Year may bring you much happiness.

Yours sincerely,

JOYCE KILMER.

Mahwah, N. J.
July 14, 1914.

Dear Father Daly:

If you read my "Some Mischief Still" I hope the strong language of my janitor didn't shock you. I've written to my long-suffering confessor to ask whether or not I can let characters in my plays and stories "cuss" when they feel so disposed. I fear that I introduced a new sin to him—vicarious profanity.

You asked me several questions recently. Let me see if I can answer them. In the first place, you asked me why I addressed the Holy Name Society of Suffern, New York. The answer to that is, why not? I go to Sacred Heart Church in Suffern. My parish church is in Ramsey, New Jersey, but we Mahwah Catholics (those of us who go to Church) are allowed to go to Suffern, which is much nearer. Ramsey has only a small Mission Church, to which comes the priest from Hohokus.

Furthermore, I tolerate no levity on the name *Suffern!* especially from a dweller in Prairie du Chien (named after a ridiculous vermin) who has been visiting a place called Pilsen (named after a beer) and conducting a retreat in a place called Peoria (obviously a corruption of Peruna, a patent medicine of ill repute).

You ask me if I know what a retreat is. I do, because long before I was a Catholic, before I was a wild-eyed Socialistic revolutionary, I was a ritualistic Anglican, and I went twice up to Holy Cross Monastery at West Park. This is an Anglican institution, which observes a modification of the Benedictine rule. And there I learned about imitation retreats, anyway. I must go to a regular retreat sometime.

I don't expect to take any vacation this Summer, but I'm going to spend several Saturdays fishing. I hope you do not scorn that wholesome and unliterary diversion. Most writers of my acquaintance consider it lamentably base.

I hope you were satisfied with your efforts at Peoria. I did what you asked. By the way, when you pray for the Kilmers, please include a new Kilmer, who is coming, we hope, in October. He— or she—will have Barry among his or her names, after the family from whom my wife is descended.

Yours affectionately,

JOYCE KILMER.

Mahwah, New Jersey.
Nov., 1914.

Dear Father Daly:

We are now back in Mahwah, thank God! It's the chief thing I thank Him for, of all the splendid things He's given me—this home of mine. My children are all well, and my wife. Prayer has given Rose the almost normal use of one arm and the power to sit up. And prayer will do more.

Yours affectionately,

JOYCE.

This is a postscript, to say that the smug young person portrayed in the *Citizen* resembles me only "as the dew resembles the rain." I am fat and gross,

[131]

and I have "elastic and rebellious hair," like M.
Baudelaire's cat. Someday I'll have a decent picture and courageously send it to you. In my young
youth, I was slightly decorative. But now I drink
beer instead of writing about absinthe. And therefore —

June 15, 1915.

Dear Father James:

Your suggestion as to a lecture tour is character-
istically kind. I am already on the books of a lecture manager named Feakins, who manages Chesterton, Barry Pain and other people. I'll probably
lecture before Catholic organizations as well as secular ones, because I need the money, but I don't
want to for reasons you will, I know, understand.
In the first place, I don't want in any way to make
money out of my religion, to seem to be a "professional Catholic." In the second place, I have delight chiefly in talking veiled Catholicism to non-
Catholics, in humbly endeavouring to be an Apostle
to Bohemia. I have no real message to Catholics,
I have Catholicism's message to modern pagans.
So I want to lecture chiefly to Pagans.

The Prairie du Chien correspondent of the Police
Gazette has cabled that you are to read a paper at

the St. Paul Educational Conference.   Congratulations!   And I'll try to help you to the extent of my power—but you don't need help as I do.

Yours affectionately,

JOYCE.

Good Samaritan Hospital,
Suffern, N. Y.
August 2, 1916.

Dear Father James:

I am sorry that you received exaggerated reports of my accident.   All that happened to me was the fracture of a couple of ribs, and I have been very comfortable in a delightful hospital.   My secretary comes out several times a week, so I am keeping up with my work.

Remember me, if you please, to Mother Mercedes and Father O'Reilly.

Yours affectionately,

JOYCE.

Mahwah, N. J.
Aug. 10, 1916.

Dear Father James:

This is to say that I am rapidly recovering my health, and hope to be in my office in a week.   I

[133]

had a fine time in the hospital, a comfortable place run by particularly amiable Sisters of Charity. It may interest you to know that I had received the Blessed Sacrament half an hour before the train struck me, and that to this fact I attribute my escape from death—since at the place where I was struck several men have been killed, being thrown forward and under the wheels, instead of, (as I was), to one side.

Affectionately,

JOYCE.

(Aug 8, 1917).
Monday.

Dear Father James:

Your letter was opened and read by one Private Kilmer, a hardened military cuss, unused to literary activities. This is the first literary labor he has essayed for a month, aside from studying Moss's Manual of Military Training and the art of shooting craps.

We're still in New York—at the Armory from 9 A. M. to 4.30 P. M., but we usually get home at night. Young Louis is in the same company as myself. We probably will go to Spartansberg, North Carolina, about Aug. 17, but we may be here till

[134]

October, or we may go to France to-morrow. Nobody knows. I find that there are many Catholics in the Seventh. It's amusing that our training camp is in North Carolina—nothing to drink and no Jesuits! Bishop is a Benedictine mitred abbott—it's in Belmont Abbey.

Before mobilisation I finished editing "Dreams and Images," an anthology of Catholic verse written since (but including) Patmore. Terrible rush job, but pretty good book. Do you mind having it dedicated to you? Wanted to include some of your stuff, but didn't have time to get any. Have dedicated it to you, but can change it, if you wish. Don't hesitate to say so! Can't hurt my feelings! Hard military character, seriously considering acquisition of habit of chewing tobacco.

This is an absurd note, but I find myself very stupid at writing. Perhaps after drill becomes easier, I'll have more of a mind left at night. Fr. Dwight honoured me by asking me for a sonnet on St. Ignatius for *America,* but I fell down on the assignment. I could not write even a limerick on St. Ignatius in my present mental state! But it's a comfortable life physically—mentally too, I guess, and as for spiritually, why, pray for yours affectionately, JOYCE.

[135]

LETTERS

(Sept., 1917).
Thursday.

Dear Fr. James:

I never expected to write to you on lined paper or Y. M. C. A. paper—uses of adversity! The Y. M. C. A. gives us poor "dough boys" the only place we have to sit down and read and write—so far the Knights of Columbus have not been in evidence in this highly papistical camp. I am, as you know, a member of the 165th Infantry, U. S., formerly the 69th New York. I have recently been transferred from Co. H. to Headquarters Co., and exchanged my 8 hours a day of violent physical exercise (most deadening to the brain, a useful anodyne for me, coming as it did after my grief) for exacting but interesting statistical work. I am called Senior Regimental Statistician, but in spite of all these syllables still rank as a private. My work is under the direction of the Regimental Chaplain, Fr. Francis Patrick Duffy. The people I like best here are the wild Irish—boys of 18 or 20, who left Ireland a few years ago, some of them to escape threatened conscription, and travelled about the country in gangs, generally working on the railroads. They have delightful songs that have never been written down, but sung in vagabonds' camps

[136]

and country jails. I have got some of the songs down and hope to get more—"The Boston Burglar"—"Sitting in My Cell All Alone"—they are fine, a veritable Irish-American folk-lore. Before I was transferred to Headquarters Co., I slept in a tent with a number of these entertaining youths, and enjoyed it tremendously. We sang every night from 9 to 9.30. Now I am in more sophisticated but less amusing company—ambitious youths, young office men, less simple and genial than my other friends.

I get to New York for part of Saturday and Sunday. Aline is staying with her mother in New York. It is good that I am not with the 7th Regiment in Spartanburg—as it is I can telephone to Aline every night. I will send you a picture of Rose soon. Her death was a piercing blow, but beautiful. It happened at the best time. Aline was there and I and our parish priest. Rose was happy but did not want to get well. "I'll drink it in another house," she said, when the nurse coaxed her to take some broth. Perhaps she meant the new house in Larchmont which we move to in October. And perhaps not. There was a Mission in our parish-church, just a couple of blocks from the house, and while Rose died the voices of the Sisters singing "O Salutaris Hostia" could be heard in the room. I thank you for your letter, beautifully inter-pretative. Certainly Rose makes Heaven dearer to us.

Yours affectionately,

JOYCE.

Headquarters Company, 165th U. S. Infantry,
Camp Albert E. Mills, New York.
October 28, 1917.

Dear Father James:

I hope you don't mind being typewritten to by an unskillful typist. I have learned all I know of this art since I became a soldier. It is ridiculous for a newspaperman to learn typewriting in the army, but I never had the time to learn it before—I found it better to have an expert typist for a secretary and dictate my stuff to him. I used to turn out four or five thousand words an hour when Watts was work-ing for me. I haven't much speed as yet but I ought to be pretty good at it when I get back. There are two things I always wanted to learn—how to typewrite and how to serve Mass. I'm learning the one and I'm going to get Fr. Duffy to let me pinch-hit for his orderly at Mass some mornings. So I'll be an accomplished cuss when I

[138]

come back from the Wars—I'll know how to typewrite and to serve Mass and to sing the Boston
Burglar.

Numerous philanthropic citizens are sending
cigarettes to soldiers, and pipe-tobacco (in which
last bounty I often share). But some enlightened
person should start a nation-wide campaign for
sending cigars to Senior Regimental Statistical
Representatives. I am Senior Statistical Representative of the 165th U. S. Infantry, I am!

Yours affectionately,

JOYCE.

Headquarters Company,
165th Infantry,
A. E. F., France.
April 5, 1918.

Dear Father James:

When I next visit Campion, I will teach you (in
addition to "The Boston Burglar") an admirable
song called "Down in the Heart of the Gas-House
District." I sing it beautifully. Its climax is,
"If you would meet good fellows face to face, Just
hang around Jimmy Cunningham's place, For it's
down in the heart of the Gas-house district, In Old
New York."

LETTERS

I received two most welcome letters from you recently. One had to do with the case of ———. It contains excellent advice, and I am carrying it in my pocket, intending to clip your name and the name of the college from it and to give it to him. I am deeply grateful, my dear Father, for your great and characteristic kindness in this matter. I think we'll yet see him practicing and teaching philosophy. You see, in his veins is a dangerous mixture of bloods—like my own—German and Irish, perhaps that accounts for his troubles. Gaelic impetuosity and Teutonic romanticism—no, sentimentality—no, self-pity—no, what is it that makes Germans German? I mean Sturm und Drang, Sorrows of Werther and that sort of thing. Well, it doesn't matter what it's called. But all people with any German blood have a bit of it. And highly diluted it's rather nice. Which reminds me that Father Duffy says I'm half German and half human.

I wrote a poem called "Rouge Bouquet." I'll ask Aline to send you a copy—it's long—and you remind her. It will tell you of an incident which will indicate to you that handling statistics in Regimental Headquarters isn't the dry task you imagine it. The statistics aren't dry—they're wet—

and red. Also, I'm attached to the Regimental Intelligence Section, which is exciting. I had a very
thrilling week not long ago—I'm not allowed to
write about it yet. I'll tell you about it some day.
By the way, it was at that time—Feb. 26, that you
wrote to me. I wasn't in the office then, I was out
working as an observer—finest job in the army!
By the way, I'm a Sergeant now. I'll never be anything higher. To get a commission I'd have to go
away for three months to a school, and then—
whether or not I was made an officer—I'd be sent
to some outfit other than this. And I don't want to
leave this crowd. I'd rather be a Sergeant in the
69th than a Lieutenant in any other regiment in the
world. Get Aline to send you a copy of "Holy Ireland"—it will explain, somewhat.

Please give my love to anybody who will accept
it. Remember me with special fervour to Sister
Eugene and Sister Stanislaus. I enjoy reading the
Campion, and am glad to see the newspaper has become a reality.

You speak of French anti-clericals in your letter.
They all must be in Paris. I haven't found any in
my rather extensive wanderings around France.
As a common soldier, I have the privilege of intimacy with the French peasants—and I find them

edifyingly good Catholics. Pray for me, dear
Father James.

Affectionately,

JOYCE.

April 8, 1918.

My dear Father James:

I am sending you with this letter some verses that
will, I think, interest you. They are my first attempt at versification in a dug-out—a dug-out not
far from the event of which the verses tell. I have
sent a copy to Aline, but since the trans-Atlantic
mails are so uncertain, will you be so kind as to
write to her asking if she has received it?

Somewhere within a radius of five miles from
where I write now slumbers (for it's long after bed-
time for soldiers who keep regular hours) one
Drury Sheehan. Every day he meets someone from
my outfit and asks after me and says he's coming to
see me. And some days ago I—riding on a truck
—passed and was passed several times by his outfit. And I paged him, so to speak, unavailingly.
Also numerous letters from the States tell me that
young Father Charles O'Donnell is somewhere
near. We'll have a great reunion one of these days.
I wish you'd be in it! But one of these nights I'll

[142]

jump off a freight at Prairie du Chien, break a pane of glass in a basement window and go to sleep in the Bishop's room. The Brother will be aghast next morning at discovering a ragged mustachioed shaven headed soldier in such a place—I'll try to explain to him that I'm an adopted alumnus of Campion—I'll probably use French in my excitement—and he will promptly shoot me. Then I'll spend two months in the Campion Infirmary, which is, I am told, a very nice place.

I am having a delightful time, but it won't break my heart for the war to end. I feel much comforted and strengthened by many prayers—those of my wife and little children, those of many dear friends, mostly priests and Sisters. I value highly my share in your Masses. Always pray hard, my dear Father, for

Your affectionate friend, Joyce.

May 15, 1918.

Dear Father James:

I thought you'd like to see how I looked after six months of soldiering. I'm having a lot of fun (I'm a Sergeant in the Regimental Intelligence Section now, you remember) but I haven't been to Mass

for *three weeks!* It so happened that I was away
from churches (except the ruins thereof) and from
Fr. Duffy. So you'll have to be praying doubly
hard for your affectionate friend,

JOYCE.

To Mrs. Kilburn Kilmer

To My Mother, on Her Birthday, 1914, With a Book of Poems

Gentlest of critics, does your memory hold
  (I know it does) a record of the days
    When I, a schoolboy, earned your generous
      praise
For halting verse and stories crudely told!
Over those boyish scrawls the years have rolled,
  They might not bear the world's unfriendly gaze,
  But still your smile shines down familiar ways,
Touches my words and turns their dross to gold.

Dearer to-day than in that happy time
  Comes your high praise to make me proud and
    strong.
In my poor notes you hear Love's splendid chime
  So unto you does this, my work, belong.
Take, then, this little book of fragile rhyme;
  Your heart will change it to authentic song.

LETTERS

To A. K. K.

AUGUST THE FOURTH
NINETEEN HUNDRED AND ELEVEN

Now the English larks are singing,
And the English meadows flinging
Scarlet flags of blazing poppies to the fragrant
　　summer air,
And from every tower and steeple
All the wondering English people
Hear a chime of fairy music, though no bell-ringers
　　are there.

What has caused this jubilation?
Days ago the coronation
Went with jewelled pomp and splendour to the
　　country of the past.
Is the land some Saint's Day hailing?
Or has some tall ship gone sailing
Through the hostile fleet to triumph, with the Union
　　at her mast?

Nay, it is no warlike glory,
Nor pale saint, of ancient story,
That has made the island blossom into beauty rare
　　and new.

[145]

We in this sea-severed nation,
Share with England our elation,
As we keep this feast, your birthday, and are glad
    with love for you!

"White Horse" of Kilburn

To A. K. K. on Her Birthday, 1912

Last night the beat of hoofs was heard upon the
    shaded street,
    It broke the silent brooding of the peaceful coun-
      tryside;
I looked and saw a horse that stamped its terrible
    white feet,
    A giant horse, as white as flame, long maned and
      starry-eyed.

"Who is this monstrous visitant?" said I, "Buce-
    phalus?
    Or Rosinante, looking for another crazy Knight?
Or (not to be conceited) may it not be Pegasus?
    This mighty horse, this glowing horse, so beau-
      tiful and white."

[146]

He proudly tossed his noble head, and neighed,
    "Across the foam
  My stable lies, with clouds for roof, and moun-
    tainous green walls;
I come to take your message unto Her, who near
    my home
  Will hold her Birthday feast before another eve-
    ning falls."

"Go back, O Horse," I said, "and seek your pleas·
    ant dwelling-place,
  And here's a gift for you to take, I trust it to
    your care;
Support this heavy load of love until you see her
    face,
  Then humbly kneel before her feet and lay my
    homage there."

Having English blood in her veins, Mrs. Kilburn Kilmer con-
siders herself something of a Yorkshire woman. The famous
White Horse she has climbed many times.

LETTERS

Valentine Written for My Mother, 1913

I will send my heart to England, and will make it
     learn to act
     Like a vacant minded vicar, or a curate full of
          tea;
I will make my heart talk Cambridgese, or York-
     shirish, in fact;
     I will make it be as British as a human heart can
          be;
I will dress my heart in roses, roses red and ever
     gay;
     I will steep my heart in scarletest of wine;
I will teach my heart to bow, and smile, and sing,
     and dance, and play—
     Just to make you take it for a Valentine.

Birthday Poem—1913

England! England! put your veil of mist away,
     Dress in green, with poppies in your hair.
England! England! let your birds sing "Holiday,"
     Let your lanes be jubilant and fair.
She is made of singing, therefore hail her with a
     song;
     Strew her path with loveliness, and crown her
          with delight.

[148]

Golden hours of joy and beauty should to her be-
  long.
  Everything that lives to-day must own her gentle
    might.
England! England! now the jocund feast is here.
  Now is time for frolicking and mirth.
England! England! now another turning year,
  Brings the day that celebrates her birth.

VALENTINE TO MY MOTHER, 1914

The English meadows call her, and the streets of
    London Town,
  And the pleasant little villages under the York
    shire Hills.
She can see the roads, like ribbons white, that stretch
    across the down,
  And the great slow turning sails of sleepy mills.
She longs for stately mansions, in whose eaves the
    pigeons coo,
  And she longs for yellow corn fields, where the
    scarlet poppies shine,
She loves the folk of England, and, of course, they
    love her too,
  But she lingers in America to be my Valentine.

Set to music by Mrs. Kilburn Kilmer and published in London
in the Spring of 1914.

LETTERS

"England," she said, "is surely England yet;
  Therefore it is the place where I should be.
  In spite of war, I know that tea is tea,
A cigarette is still a cigarette.

"Why should I worry over Wilhelm's threat?"
  And thereupon she said goodbye to me,
  And gaily sailed across the dangerous sea,
To where, among the Zeppelins, tea was set.

What if the sea foam mountainously high
  With waves that had in Hell their fiery birth?
What if black peril hover in the sky,
  And bursting shell wound deep the trembling
        earth?
All evil things must harmlessly pass by
  Her who doth bear the Talisman of Mirth.

Birthday Poem, 1915

To My Mother Singing

Out of the golden valleys of old years,
  You have recalled so many a lovely thing.

[150]

LETTERS

Forgotten splendours glimmer when you sing,
With their long vanished light of mirth and tears.
Gay lovers flout their love's delicious fears.
    The proud swords clash for Charles, the rightful
        King,
    A woman weeps, and turns her "Silver Ring."
The "Men of Harlech" charge with level spears.
Yet, I crowned with my crown of vanity,
    Have been more happy when you sang and
        played
The songs wherein your art had succoured me.
    As starry note on starry note was laid,
Then my chained rhymes, by your designs set free,
    Flew Heavenward on the radiant wings you
        made.

To My Mother, October, 1915

There fell a flood of devastating flame
    On half the world, and all its joy was dead.
    The sky was black, the troubled sea was red,
And from all mouths a lamentation came.
But you, in calm and hurricane the same,
    Went with gay lips, brave heart and unbowed
        head.

LETTERS

What was the charm, from which all danger fled?
What did you say, what cabalistic name?

It was my love that sent its quickening breath
    On all the waves that bore your ship along.
My love held out, against the flying death,
    That clove the sea, a shield than steel more strong,
Bringing you back, where no war harrieth,
    Stars in your eyes, and in your heart a song.

August Fourth, Nineteen Sixteen

The Berkshire Hills are gay
With a gladder tint to-day,
    And Mount Graylock rears his mighty head in
        pride.
For the lady that they knew
Long ago, to them is true,
    And has come within their shadow to reside.

And across the troubled sea,
Yorkshire hill and Cambridge lea,
    Send their love to you by every wind that blows.
And a greater love than these
Hurries Northward on the breeze
    From the little hills they call the Ramapos.

[152]

LETTERS

If some day, as you idly turn the pages,
   Whereon my verses are,
You find a flower where angry winter rages,
   On the black earth a star;
If in dead words you come on something living,
   Some fair and vibrant line—
It is the message that my heart is giving,
   It is your Valentine.

March, 1918.

Dear Mother:

The sweater arrived, and it certainly is a magnificent specimen of knitting, and the wristlets are wonderfully purled—whatever purling may be. Probably I shall need both sweater and wristlets for many weeks, for although it is Spring now, it often is cold.

Under separate cover I am sending you my warrant as Sergeant. I thought you might like to have it framed to hang in the Old-Fashioned Room. The "drafted" in the corner means that the regiment was drafted into Federal Service; that is, made a part of the United States Army instead of a part of the New York State National Guard.

[153]

LETTERS

I suppose that you have read in the newspapers of the Regiment's recent activities. Now we are taking it easy in a very pleasant little town. I hope we may stay here at least a month, as it is hard to work when the Regiment is moving about the country. I had a week's respite from office work some time ago and spent it doing what is called "observation" work for the Regimental Intelligence Section. It was most interesting.

Did Aline tell you of Kenton's success in school? It seems that he won a gold medal for being the best pupil in the school. I was delighted to learn it. So nearly as I can remember, I was not an especially keen student when I was his age, although I became one later.

There is practically no chance of my rising any higher in the Regiment than Sergeant, and I am perfectly content. To become an officer I would have to go to school away from the Regiment for several months, then if I failed to pass my examinations and win a commission, I would be sent to some other Regiment than this, and if I succeeded I would be sent as an officer, not back to the 69th, but to some other outfit, and I want very much to stay with the Regiment. I have many good friends here, and I would feel lost in any other military organization.

[154]

I am looking forward to receiving the photographs you have had taken. By this time you must have received the one I sent you. I hope you like it.

Your letters are very gratefully received, and I am looking forward specially to receiving the cake and the candy you sent me. Everything else you have written of in your letters has arrived in good condition, and a day or two ago I got five big jars of excellent tobacco from the Dickens Fellowship . . . a most intelligent gift.

Affectionately yours,

JOYCE.

May 15th, 1918.

Dear Mother:

As to your "War Mother" poem, I hesitate to tell you how much I like it, because I am afraid you may think I am trying to flatter you. It certainly is the best poem you ever wrote—beautiful, original and well sustained. I have seen no recent war verse I like so well. There is no question but what you will sell it to some good magazine. I certainly congratulate you, and congratulate the magazine fortunate enough to print your poem.

I am very glad to hear of the deserved success

your songs made at Lakewood, and in general of your triumphs at the Dickens Fellowship, and elsewhere. I wish I could have witnessed them, but I will be seeing more of the same sort next winter. That is what we like to hear about over here—triumphs and celebrations, and in general the pleasant and prosperous course of civilian life.

Of course we soldiers are undergoing hardships and privations—we expect to, but we don't spend our time advertising them. But in the States when you find they must do without quite as much wheat, or meat, or something of the sort, instead of just going without and keeping their mouths shut, they advertise their remarkable abstention by having "wheatless days" and "meatless days," and all that sort of hysterical rubbish, and fill the papers with the news, thereby disgusting us soldiers and undoubtedly comforting the enemy. I think I will start a "strawberryless, ice creamless, sodaless day" for the army. It would be as sensible as what the people at home have been doing. If you (I don't mean you personally, of course) have to eat hardtack instead of butter-raised biscuits, why eat the hardtack and shut up about it, but don't be such an ass as to have a "butter-raised biscuitless Monday," and don't shut down on theatres and amusements;

[156]

and don't deprive people of their honest drink. Merely making stay-at-homes dismal does not help the soldiers a bit. England's early "Business as Usual" scheme was more practicable, and this is something of a concession for me to make. There is quite a sermon on economics for you! Kindly read it to my father, whom it will edify and instruct. A recent letter from him shows that he utterly misunderstands my point of view on this subject, the result of lamentably careless reading by him of one of my letters in which I contrasted the gaiety and common-sense of the French, through years of starvation and ruin, with the wail which a little self-denial brought from the States.

Send your picture soon.

Affectionately yours,

JOYCE.

May 27th, 1918.

Dear Mother,

I presume by this time you have received the humorous photographs of myself I sent you.

I am delighted to know of the Kilburn Hall project. By all means buy the Hall; it will be an excellent investment. Property is now very cheap in

[157]

England, and prices will rise as soon as the war is over. I hope to be able to spend my summers in France after the war, and I have the place in mind —only about a day's run from London. I am absolutely in love with France, its people, its villages, its mountains, everything about it. America would do well to copy its attitude in the war. It has suffered tremendous hardships with dignity and humour, and kept its sanity and faith. America, to judge by the papers, grows hysterical over a little self-denial; can't do without an extra lump of sugar in its tea without a band and speeches and "sugarless" Sundays. It is funny and rather pathetic to us soldiers. But I honestly think, although it may seem conceited to say so, that when we soldiers get back from the war we will do the spiritual and intellectual life of the States a lot of good. France has taught us lessons of infinite value.

I am having an absolutely Heavenly time since I joined the Intelligence Section. I wouldn't change places with any soldier of any rank in any outfit. This suits me better than any job I ever had in civil life.

The cake is not yet here. I will soak it in wine all right, don't worry about that. Speaking of wine, enclosed find some flowers given me by a very nice wine-shop girl in a city near here. "Madelon" is a perfectly respectable song, but "Madelon" is not a gun or anything else of the sort; it is the name of the girl who serves wine to the soldiers, as the song clearly states.

Yours affectionately,

JOYCE.

June 14th, 1918.

Dear Mother:

There is a chance that I will be able to get to England on a seven days' leave in a few weeks. In that case I shall probably spend most of my time in London, with a possible visit to Oxfordshire, where my friend Mrs. Denis Eden lives. I wish there was something I could do for you to expedite the purchase of Kilburn Hall, but since the Archbishop of Yorkshire is in the States you should, yourself, be able to make a deal with him. English real estate is a wise investment these days; it will go up fifty per cent in a year's time. I wish I could afford to buy some property in this country. I certainly would like to live here. If the States go "dry" I honestly think I will move my family over here. I can write for American papers without living in

America. Then if you move to Kilburn Hall I will be only a day's trip away from you, and you will love rural France almost as much as you love rural England.

Learn to sing "Madelon."

Affectionately yours,

JOYCE.

June 28, 1918.

Dear Mother:

I received three letters from you yesterday and to-day, the first I have had from you in a long time. Your letters always come in bunches like that. And this morning I received two admirable boxes of Mirror Candy, in perfect condition. I certainly was delighted to get it, as it is a long time since I have had any candy. My gratitude is so great that I even will refer to it as "Sweets."

I was also glad to get your picture, taken on shipboard. You must send to Larchmont another copy of the picture of yourself looking at my photograph, which you sent me some weeks ago, as I had to remove it from its mount and cut it down to make it fit into my wallet. All the rest of the fellows in the Intelligence Section (there are nine of us, nearly all

[160]

college graduates, and men of some standing—editors, brokers, etc.), have pictures of their mothers, but none of them so good looking as mine.

You would be amused at some of the scenes when your picture is exhibited. Tired from a long hike from a stay in the trenches, I am having an omelet, and some fried potatoes, and some vin rouge, beau coup, le vin rouge in some French peasant's little kitchen. It is a cottage such as you and I often visited in Derbyshire and Cambridgeshire; a low grey stone building with rose trees against the wall, a tiny garden, and a geometrically neat path. The kitchen floor is of stone, the table without a cloth, but shining from much polishing. The only thing to distinguish it from the typical English rural cottage is the crucifix on the wall, and the wooden shoes at the door. (People wear sabots out of doors, cloth slippers in the house, leather shoes on Sunday). Well, after such a repast as I have described, I take out my wallet to pay my bill, and the sharp eyes of little Marie, or little Pierre, intently watching this strange soldat Americaine espy the picture. At once an inquisitive, but delighted, infant is on my knee demanding a closer inspection of the picture; the Maman must see it, and Grandpere, and Veuve Vatre from across the street (the man of the house can't see it; he is away from home on the errand that brought me across the sea). Well, they all say "Elle est jolie, ma foi, et jeune aussi." These comments have been made on your picture many times in many towns, which I will one day show you on a map of France.

I have not much anxiety for my father, for I look on his condition as a state of rest really necessary to a mind so constantly busy. But I am glad that from you I have inherited the power of readily escaping from worry and work; of entering with enthusiasm into whatever mirth I find around me; in finding good and true and merry friends everywhere. I think that some of this quality would have helped my father very much, and increased his bodily and mental health. I worried grievously about you for a while, and wished I could have been with you when my father was taken ill, but I don't worry now—you are too spirited and courageous for anybody to worry about. I certainly admire you more than ever, and look forward eagerly to regular banquets at Henri's and Rector's with you.

I want you to meet all the Regimental Intelligence Section—a fine bunch of brave men, and good comrades. We have taken big chances together,

[162]

and it has made us the best of friends. You will like them all and they will like you.

Affectionately yours,

JOYCE.

To Kenton Kilmer

Heaquarters Co.,
165th Infantry,
A. E. F.
Nov. 28, 1917.

My dear Kenton:

I hope that by this time you have entirely recovered from your illness. I remember that I had whooping-cough when I was about your age. If you are back in school, send me some of your monthly reports. The address you must put on letters to me is just what you see at the top of this sheet, except that you must put before it "Private Joyce Kilmer."

There is a school in the building where I work, much like the school you attend, except that there are no nuns here for teachers. When the weather is wet, the children wear wooden shoes instead of rubbers. They go to school at eight in the morning and don't leave until five. You wouldn't like that, would you?

LETTERS

This letter ought to reach you about Christmas time. I am not sending you anything at once, but I will later. And I know that your mother and all your grandparents will give you things, and so will Saint Nicholas.

Be a good boy, and pray to St. Francis and Our Lady to help you. You ought to go to Mass every morning, since you live so near the church. Take care of Deborah and Christopher and Michael, and do all you can to make things easy for your Mother.

From Your affectionate Dad.

To Kenton Kilmer

January 10, 1918.

My dear Kenton:

Your plan for ending the war is very good. I showed your letter to Sergeant Russell, who fought in the Spanish-American war, long before you were born, and he said that your plan was the one that the American Army would adopt.

I am glad to see that you can write and typewrite so well. I hope that you will get Fr. Morris to teach you how to serve Mass, we live so near the church that you can easily serve his Mass and get your breakfast and get to school on time, and if you are

[164]

a priest when you grow up you will be glad you had such practice when you were young.

Take care of Deborah and Michael and Christopher and your mother and don't forget to pray for
Your affectionate Dad.

To Deborah Kilmer

Headquarters Co.,
165th Inf.,
A. E. F., France.
May 27th, 1918.

My dear Deborah:

About a month ago, I sent you a rubber doll. If you didn't get it, let me know and I'll send you another one.

Yesterday morning about six o'clock I climbed down the mountain to go to Mass. And just outside the village where the church is, I met a young lady and walking beside her was a pleasant young pig with a pink nose.

"Bonjour, M'sieur!" said the young lady.

"Bonjour, Mam'selle!" I replied.

"Bonjour, M'sieur!" said the pig.

"Bonjour, M'sieur!" I replied.

And the young lady and the pig threw back their

heads and laughed heartily and went on to breakfast. And I went on to Mass.

Remember me to young Michael and young Christopher, and believe me

Your respectful Dad.

To Mrs. Joyce Kilmer

Nov. 11, 1917.

This is what is technically known as a hurried scrawl. It is to the effect that I have arrived, in excellent health and spirits. I have recently read the Censorship Regulations, and am in doubt about what I can say—God help the people who have to interpret them! I mailed a postcard two weeks ago, which you should now receive. Also I'll try to cable you soon, if it is allowed. I have not yet consulted the adjutant on the subject, but so far as I have been able to find from a diligent study of the censorship regulations, I am allowed to say that I love you. Accordingly, I state it, with considerable enthusiasm. Also, I have a certain regard for Kenton, Deborah, Michael and even Christopher. I hope to write you again very soon. You know my address—same as before, only American Expeditionary Forces. I enclose some verses which may

[166]

entertain you. The brief one is a memory of the days when I used to drill. I don't feel that way about a typewriter—which instrument I now use with accuracy and speed. Send me some magazines now and then, and *Times* REVIEW OF BOOKS. And love me exceedingly.

Headquarters Co.,
165th Infantry,
A. E. F.
Nov. 24, 1917.

I am having a delightful time out here—absolutely beautiful country and very nice people. I am short of money, but I believe we'll be paid soon and I've borrowed 80 francs from Fr. Duffy. That isn't as much as it sounds—you get 5 francs and 70 centimes for a dollar at the Y. M. C. A. I enclose a bill I received for two enormous boxes of cakes I hired an old lady to make for me. I furnished the sugar—you know there was a bag of it in the box of groceries my mother sent me just before I left. I meant the cakes for dessert for Thanksgiving dinner, but with the help of my friends I've already eaten most of it. There is a rumour to the effect that we are to have duck for dinner to-morrow, and the Regiment is much more excited about it than about the good news of the War in yesterday's paper. We get the Paris editions of the London *Daily Mail*, New York *Herald* and Chicago *Tribune*, and before long I suppose we'll see the magazines when the Y. M. C. A. opens up its local tent. I never thought I'd regard the Y. M. C. A. with such esteem—I wish the Knights of Columbus had a chance to do as much work for us.

I haven't written anything in prose or verse since I got here—except statistics—but I've stored up a lot of memories to turn into copy when I get a chance. The Colonel occasionally speaks of my historical work, but I doubt if it will be feasible to publish any part of it except some very general stuff until the war is over. I asked Thomas Hughes Kelley to send me a history of the 69th published some years ago, and another copy to you, to make sure. I think it will be useful in preparing the introductory chapters.

I love you very much indeed and see you clearly always and have a conviction that I will be with you soon—sooner than you expect.

LETTERS

I was delighted to receive the other day (December 7th, the day after my birthday) a batch of letters, including two from you. I am glad Kenton is getting along well; I was worried about his illness. It is fortunate you were able to get a good nurse.

You ought to be receiving some money from the government soon. I made over half my pay to you, and the government is supposed to add to it so much for you and so much for each youngster. The whole thing will come to about $57 a month, I believe! I personally am not in need of money—I am getting a book of traveller's cheques from my father and before I heard he was sending it I wrote to John Timpson Co., and asked them to open an account for me in some Paris bank. Also we are paid in francs, which makes us feel wealthy, as there are 5.70 of them in a dollar. And I could live comfortably without any spending money—all there is to buy is candy and canned stuff and wine and an occasional meal when the business of my department takes me to a nearby town.

Fr. Garesché's poem certainly is beautiful; by far the best thing he has done. I am enclosing a letter from Sister ——— which I think you will enjoy. Delightful old person, nearly blind, but tremendously energetic. Harriet Monroe was one of her pupils. Probably you remember her book on Fr. Tabb.

Your Christmas presents probably will reach you in time for Easter. I hope to get a pair of wooden shoes for Deborah.

I am having a fine time. My statistical work occupies me in the evening as well as all day, but it's interesting, and will be increasingly important, since the Statistical Department really is the only link between the soldier and his family.

I hope as soon as we get settled I'll be able to do some writing, I've been too busy so far. I love you very much, and always think of you.

In your letters you spoke of sending me some stuff. Send anything you think of as soon as you think of it—don't wait to find out if I want it, because the mails take too long. Just now I want snap-shots of you and the children, especially Deborah, and tobacco. I love you.

December 17.

I hope you are getting the letters I send you from time to time. I got one admirable batch of letters from you by way of birthday present—they came on the day after my birthday. Perhaps I'll get another batch for Christmas—it's December 17th now, and we should receive another mail soon. I hope to send you a photograph soon. I believe personal pictures may be sent through the mail. It will be a beautiful sight. I got a Sing Sing haircut recently and am growing a corsair moustache. This is the pleasantest war I ever attended—nothing to do but fall in, fall out, pound a typewriter 13 hours a day and occasionally hike across France and back carrying a piano. However, I do really enjoy it, and the work is different in kind from newspaper work, and so a rest from it. By the way, I sent you some time ago a poem called *"Militis Meditatio."* Please send a copy of it to a magazine and tell them to send the check for it to you. I hope to be able to do some writing as soon as we get settled and I get some of my statistical work out of the way. You ought to get your allotment this month, with additions from the Government (I hope you and the children are not yet in the poorhouse, or at any rate that you have struck a comfortable poorhouse). Send me pictures of yourself and the children, especially Deborah. I have made a nuisance of myself telling my bored friends about her intelligence in naming her doll "Hugh and Mrs. Leamy." Also send me some tobacco, enough to fill a bedsack (also love me

[171]

as intensely as possible; I love you more than ever
before and think of you all the while). ....

Christmas Eve.
The enclosed clippings may amuse you—after
you read them you'd better send them to Bob Holliday. They came with a raft of letters a couple of
days ago. It's very nice the way feasts seem to be
marked—I last heard from you just before my
birthday, and I got three letters from you by way
of Christmas present. There must be a lot of par-
cels awaiting me, judging from information in your
letters and those of my father and mother. We
may get the packages to-night, in which case I'll
have some hours hard work, for all the Adjutant's
office helps in assorting mail. But I don't think the
packages will come until after Christmas. I suppose that you and the children are in New Brunswick now, and will go to Midnight Mass at St.
Peter's and pray for a vagrant verse-maker who is
trying to be a soldier. We may have a Midnight
Mass in the church here to-night. Fr. Duffy has
had a choir practising for it, and we possess a tenor
soloist. He is an Italian, a barber when not singing
or soldiering.

[172]

LETTERS

I have allotted half my pay to you, and the Government's addition to that will bring it, I believe, up to about $60—enough to pay the rent. But don't worry if there is delay in receiving it. It takes a long time, usually, to set things like that in motion. I recently read that a veteran of the Civil War had just received a check for $12 from Washington, representing his pay for his last month of service.

I am glad you are sending me some tobacco—I suppose it's in the five truck loads of Christmas packages said to be awaiting us at a town some miles away. I have been able to get American tobacco, I am glad to say, but not my favourite brand. Also I'll be glad to get the cigars my father has sent me —I have smoked all of Fr. Duffy's. But be sure that tobacco or anything else you send me, such as Michael and Deborah, is very securely wrapped and tied, as the journey is hard on packages and many of them go to pieces.

I am hoping to get more letters from you soon— write as often as you can. I'd rather get a letter from you than anything else now possible. (I love you more than ever before).

Jan. 18, 1918.

Virginia is an excellent State. One evening last week I met by chance a Sergeant Interpreter named Nicholson Barney Adams. And he didn't know my name and I didn't know his—he is not connected with the 69th. And he said, "I see by the *Times* that Joyce Kilmer has enlisted." And furthermore, thereafter, he put me up in his place—he and two other fellows have a room together—and I had admirable things to eat and drink, and slept in a bed, for the first time in over three months. And he came from Lynchburg, Virginia.

You will find with this letter $50 in American Express checks. Put the place and date in the upper right-hand corner when you cash them. You see, I had written to John Timpson for some money before I got a book of checks from my father, so I find myself having more money than I need.

I wrote this letter—the first part of it—this afternoon. Now it is evening, and five ambulance-loads of mail have arrived and I have helped distribute it. I got a November *Harpers* from my father and a copy of Frances Huard's "My Home In the Field of Mercy" from Doran. To-morrow we get 14 more ambulance loads, they say—I hope I get some packages, but I especially desire letters from you.

[174]

LETTERS

My last letter from you—dated Dec. 12—contained a very noble poem by you—"High Heart." I was delighted to get it, I felt admitted to a realer intimacy than I had known since I crossed the ocean. Please send me all your poems, sad or spirited. I cannot write verse, but enjoy reading it more than ever before. And you happen to be my favourite poet.

I bought a copy of Conan Doyle's new "Sherlock Holmes" book in a nearby town recently, in the Conrad edition. A French publisher named Conrad has taken over the Tauchnitz business—you remember the Tauchnitz books, don't you? Also I've been reading Harry Leon Wilson's, "The Spenders"— an entertaining imitation of Mr. Howells, and re-reading "The Cardinal's Snuff Box"—most delightful.

I love you very much, and I am very sorry for you—you aren't having the amusing adventures I am having—but you're able to write nice things, and that's a consolation. I hope to see you and your admirable babies soon.

JOYCE KILMER.

LETTERS

Jan. 21, 1918.

Two or three days ago I received from you an admirable letter, dated December 12, and yesterday arrived our long errant Christmas mail—many trucks of it—and in it several letters from you dated about Thanksgiving. It is strange that my letters take so long to reach you, but you must have some of them by now. I certainly was glad to get ten cans of tobacco from you, I have wanted a pipe full of that excellent tobacco for months. I got a thousand stogies from Fr. Daly, a box of cigars from my father, another from John B. Kennedy and another from one Romaine Pierson, one of my father's friends, who sent me also a large can of tobacco. Also I got a lot of jelly and candy from my mother and a little book of "Maxims of Fr. Faber" from Eleanor Rogers Cox, and enough scapulars to sink a ship.

It certainly gives me the keenest delight to read your poetry. The poem about the Christmas Tree has —— backed off the map. Also "High Heart" is very noble poetry. I envy you your power of writing poetry—I haven't been able to write a thing since I left the ship. Also I envy you your power of being high hearted and, wholly legitimately, aware of your own high heartedness. Not that I

[176]

am low spirited—I am merely busy and well-fed and contented. I am interested but not excited, and excitement is supposed to be one of war's few charms. The contentedness is not absolute, of course, for I have, when away from you, always a consciousness of incompleteness. But I have not had the painful and dangerous times I expected to find as soon as we reached this country.

I am keenly interested in the novel you and Margaret are writing. But don't plunge too deep into occult studies in getting dope for it. Don't attend any seance of any kind or use Planchette or try automatic writing or make any experiments of a supernatural kind. If you do, I swear that if I do get shot I won't haunt you—and I'm conceited enough to think I can't make a worse threat.

By the way, Kenton's suggestion that you send me a checkerboard is excellent. I'd like it very much.

I love you.

Feb 5, 1918.

I am enclosing a letter from Helen Parry Eden which should be put in the autograph-letter file. A good way to keep author's letters is to paste special envelopes for them on the inside of the covers of author's books. Do not use the original envelopes for this purpose. But probably this plan is unsafe in a library frequented by wild babies. But at any rate try to get the stuff stowed away safely and neatly. Bob Holliday could advise you intelligently as to the proper preservation of autographed letters.

It is about a week now since I heard from you, and I am eagerly awaiting to-day's arrival of mail. I work in the place to which the mail is brought for assortment, so I get my letters without much delay —that is, delay after they reach the Regiment. The first delayed batches of mail are still arriving—I get a November letter one day, a January letter the next, a December the next.

Send me by all means all the verse you write—I find I enjoy poetry more these days than I did when I made my living largely by making it and writing and talking about it. But I wish I could make it as I used to—I have not been able to write any verse at all except *"Militis Meditatio"* which I sent you. I wrote a brief prose sketch which is still in process of censuring—the censorship regulations may or may not be so interpreted as to exclude it. I think I'll be allowed to print it, however, as it is really not a writing on military subjects, but an introspective essay written by a sort of soldier. If it gets by, it will go immediately to George H. Doran to be censored.

The second package of tobacco has arrived. The package containing it was broken, but in the bottom of the mail bag I found all ten cans of tobacco. I certainly am glad to get it—after ten years this kind still seems to me to be the best tobacco in the world.

I am not especially delighted with the circumstances of my work just at present. I am perfectly comfortable, have good meals and quarters and my work is not at all hard. But I want to get into more interesting and important work—perhaps it will be all fixed up by the time I write to you again. I love you.

JOYCE KILMER.

February 22d, 1918.

My dear Aline:

It is a long time since I have heard from you— about three weeks. But I suppose that I will receive a number of letters at once. I do not yet know whether or not you have received the two batches of American Express Company checks, amounting in all to $100.00, which I sent you some time ago. But I am not worrying about it, if the checks are lost it still is possible to recover the money. I sent you two lots of prose and verse recently, and in the envelope containing this letter is a quaint supplement to one of my little sketches—that called "Breakfasts." It is a letter to Kenton from the little girl who lives in the house by the Fountain, where Farrell and Driscoll and I used to eat every morning in our last station. I showed Solange (an excellent, demure and pious infant) Kenton's photograph, and told her that he studied French in school. He is supposed to answer in French, tell him—of course his French teacher must help him. I saved the censor trouble by clipping from Solange's letter the name of the town honoured by her presence, but I guarantee (with St. Anthony's aid) the safe delivery to her of any epistle he may entrust to me.

The town we are in now has no Solange—or has revealed none to me as yet—but in a certain Cafe which I much frequent is Antoine, aged two, who can salute in the French manner, *comme ca* (illustrated) or in the American manner, *comme ca,* (illustrated). No, not with the left hand! good Heavens, child! *Sacre bleu! nom d'un nom!*

[180]

Quelle dommage! Well, if you are going to cry about it, you needn't salute at all. Here, shut up and drink the dregs of my *vin rouge et sirop. Fini, bebe!*

Also there is an admirable child named Jean who has six months. He wears a lavender cloak with a hood attached. His home is a barber shop, the most beautiful and extraordinary barber shop in the world. His father the barber has gone to the Wars —remain madame, grandpere, and M. Biebe. It is a very modern barber shop, with mirror-walls, and powdered soap in silver salt cellars. Grandpere sits by the stove all day long and says that there are many American soldiers in the town. Madame exhibits le petit Jean and asks if it is ever as cold as this in America. I shave with six razors if I desire, and wash in *beaucoup de l'eau chaud.* And Madame deftly swinging le petit Jean over her left shoulder opens a secret drawer under a mirror and proffers me a tiny tube of *fixative* for my moustache.

I have a delightful delusion now and then—I see you walk into the Adjutant's office, past the Sergeant Major's desk, and to me. The building in which we work was once a palace—but its inlaid floor never supported a duchess (gold powdered though her hair were, and light her laughter as champagne bubbles) so precious as this fleeting vision of you.

JOYCE KILMER.

Note.—Three small, spirited pen drawings are incorporated into this letter at the points indicated in the printed text.

A. E. F.

Dear Aline:

Sorry to use this absurd paper—but none other is accessible. I'm in a hospital at present—been here for three days with a strained muscle. It has been delightful to sleep between sheets again—I have rested up beautifully, I go back to the regiment to-morrow.

I sent you two batches of copy recently—or three, rather. Hope you get them—but if you don't, I'll write some more—like Caterina, you know when she was defending her husband's castle against the enemy. The enemy took her six children as hostages. "Surrender the castle, or I'll kill the children!" said he. "Go ahead, kill 'em!" said Caterina. "I can make more!"

As to your plan of renting a house at Shirley—wherever that is—for the Summer, go ahead, if you

[182]

must—I don't think there is any chance of my getting home this Summer. If I do come home, I'll cable you in time for you to get back to Larchmont before my arrival. Larchmont is just about far enough from New York. Not for many a year will I consent to spend a day in any place more rural. I have had enough of wildness and rawness and primitiveness—the rest of my life, I hope, will be spent in the effetest civilization. I don't want to be more than an hour's distance from the Biltmore grill and the Knickerbocker bar. And God preserve me from farms!

I love you.

JOYCE.

March 12, 1918.

Dear Aline:

I receive your letters frequently and regularly, and they are delightful, stimulating, typical. Today I returned from a week's sojourn in a charming hospital (a strained muscle, now healed, sent me there) and I found two letters from you awaiting me, the latest dated February 12. Let me congratulate you on your aviation poem—most beautiful

[183]

and true, the most intellectual poem you have made. By all means put it in your book.

I received Francis Carlin's wholly heavenly book just before I went to the hospital, and have read it many times with delight. When you see him, give him my homage. He should be walking goldener floors than those of a mortal shop—he should rather be over here with us, whatever his convictions may be. For it is wrong for a poet—especially a Gael —to be listening to elevated trains when there are screaming shells to hear, and to be sleeping soft in a bed when there's a cot in a dug-out awaiting him, and the bright face of danger to dream about, and see.

I treasure your picture, and Christopher's shadowy profile—send me more photographs. Love me constantly, never let a day pass without going to church for me.

JOYCE.

March 14, 1918.

Dear Aline:

I enclose some verses that you may like very much. That is, I think I enclose them—I have yet to consult with our Regimental censor as to whether

or not I may send them. If the place name is cut
out, put in its stead any French proper name that
rhymes and do with the poem as you will. Perhaps
the best thing to do with it will be to hand it to Bob
for publishing.

As to my book—why don't worry about it—we
all will live just as long and just as happily and
probably be just as wealthy—or poor—if it is never
written. I am cheerfully neglecting it, for many
reasons. One is, of course, the censorship, which
prevents the sending out of articles sufficiently topical and specific to be interesting. Another is a
military regulation which forbids an officer or enlisted man from acting as a correspondent or writing for publication on a military subject. This will
not, I suppose, prevent the publication of such of
my verses and essays as are inspired by my experiences. But it will prevent my making for serial
publication any consecutive record of events. What
I will do will be to assemble, after the war is over,
or after I have returned from it, such random essays
or rhymes as I have made and bind them together
with a thread of reminiscence—partly introspective, partly—what is the word? extraspective? ex-
ternal, at any rate. I shall write nothing that has
any news value. I believe in my vanity that it will

be a most charming book, not without its high lights
of something more than charm. It really is the sort
of book I'd like greatly to read, and I think that it
will reach a public tired of the many war-narratives.
And don't think people won't read it after the war
is over! They will! The only sort of book I care to
write about the war is the sort people will read after
the war is over—a century after it is over! And
that is the sort of book I am going to make. A
journal intime, but as close to literature, as carefully thought and wrought as I can do. It will be
episodic—chaotic, perhaps—no glib tale, no newspaper man's work—but with God's help, a work of
art. So clamour not for copy! My enclosures of
some weeks ago may have pleased you, but you'll
like this better.

Which for no reason brings me to the subject of
growing middle-aged, an experience which you are
enjoying, I trust; I know I enjoy it. What an ad-
vantage we have over our children! While they, to
their embarrassment, grow up—voices changing,
legs and arms becoming too obvious, self-consciousness and shallow romanticism seizing them—we
gracefully, comfortably, grow down. Perhaps it is
as a protective measure that I, a private soldier,
grow vain—as snails develop shells—but I confess

[186]

it is with consummate pleasure that I contemplate my senility and, may I say, mediævality. I picture myself at forty, rotund but eminently presentable, moustache and hair delicately grayed, tailored admirably, with the leisurely power no young man may have. I picture myself at sixty, with a long white moustache, a pale gray tweed suit, a very large Panama hat. I can see my gnarled but beautifully groomed hands as they tremblingly pour out the glass of dry sherry which belongs to every old man's breakfast. I cannot think of myself at seventy or eighty—I grow hysterical with applause—I am lost in a delirium of massive ebony canes, golden snuff-boxes, and daily silk hats.

And as for you! My God! what a vision! That dear autumnal hair silvering—the mouth of my delight exquisitely etched with honourable lines—each one the record of a year's love—those eyes richer in their mystery—but I cannot write of this—for the thought might give me power to sweep away the years and make me find you, when I come back from the Wars, becapped and tremulous and leaning on two sticks! NO! I don't want you to be old now— I want you to be the innocent sophisticated young woman you are in the little picture I carry (traditionally!) over my heart. But I want to watch you grow old—if I can watch you and at the same time hold you in my arms.

JOYCE.

April 1, 1918.

Dear Aline:

This letter is written to you from a real town—written, in fact, above ground. You may be surprised to know that recent letters to you were not written in these conditions. They were written in a dug-out, but I was not permitted to tell you so at the time. In a dug-out, also, were written the verses I sent you some two weeks ago—you may remember their damp-clayey flavour. I slept and worked (the latter sometimes for twenty hours at a time) in this dug-out for a month, except for one week when I was out on special work with the Regimental Intelligence Section. You don't begrudge me that week, do you? I cannot now describe it, but it was a week of wonder—of sights and sounds essential, I think, to my experience. For there are obligations of experience—or experiences of obligation—to be distinguished from what I might call experiences of supererogation or experiences of perfection—but what rubbish this is! Let us rather con-

[188]

sider my present great luxury, and the marvels of
which it is composed. In the first place, one room
(not a cot in a crowded barrack, not a coffin-like
berth in a subterranean chamber) but a real room,
with windows and a large bed and a table and chairs
and a practical wash stand. The bed I share with
one L—— D——, an amiable gamin, about to be
made a Corporal. I am a Sergeant—with stripes
some five days old. (It is the height of my ambition, for to be commissioned I'd be sent to school for
three months and then, whether or not I succeeded,
be assigned to another Regiment. And I'd rather
be a Sergeant in the 69th than lieutenant in any
other outfit.)

To continue—I also eat from a table excellent
meals, with a napkin on my knees. I have soldiered
pretty hard for some months now, taking everything as it came, and I think I've honestly earned
my stripes. Now I'm going to have an easier life
—not working less hard, but not seeking hardships.
So I am paying seven francs a day for meals, and
six francs a week for my share in a bed-room. And
it's delightfully refreshing. Also, I yesterday had a
hot shower-bath—very much a novelty!

This morning I received two letters from you, to
my great joy. The pictures of the children are ex-

[189]

cellent. I am glad to see Deborah's hair so long and lovely. Do, by all means, send me pictures of yourself and Deborah in a leather case, as you promise. I can imagine no possible gift I'd rather receive. Mail is coming here every day now, so I look forward to frequent messages from you.

What a cheerless place the States must be these days! Don't send me American papers (except the *Times Book Review*) for they depress me, showing me what a dismal land you live in. This meatless, wheatless day business is very wearying. It can do no earthly good—it is merely giving comfort to the enemy, who undoubtedly know all about it. I wish—aside from the obvious greatest reasons— that you were here in France—you'd like everything, but especially the gentle, kind, jovial, deeply pious people. Time enough—to resume—for wheatless days when the enemy takes your wheat. Until then, carpe diem!—that is, eat buckwheat cakes with plenty of syrup.

I am disgusted with all I read in the American Magazines about the Americans in France. It is all so hysterical and all so untrue. It isn't jealousy that makes me say this—I have no desire to compete with newspaper-correspondents—but it annoys me to see the army to which I belong and the country on and for whose soil we are fighting so stupidly misrepresented.

I hope you received "Rouge Bouquet"—if you did receive it I know you liked it. General ——— (I forgot, I mustn't name generals lower in rank than Major-Generals) had twelve copies of it made. I sent it to you two weeks ago—you should be receiving it now. The newspapers by now have rerevealed its meaning to you, if any explanation was needed. It was read at an evening entertainment at one of our camps at the front. Father Duffy read it, and taps was played on the cornet before and after. I couldn't get down to hear it—I was further front, at work in the dug-out that night.

I think most of my war book will be in verse. I prefer to write verse, and I can say in verse things not permitted to me in prose. You remember— no, probably you don't—Coventry Patmore and his confessor. The confessor objected to the passionate explicitness of some of Coventry's devotional poems—they dealt with things esoteric, he said, and should be set forth in Latin, not in the profane tongue. And Coventry replied that for most people poetry was an incomprehensible language, more hidden than Latin—or more hiding.

And speaking of Coventry Patmore, the best

way to fry potatoes is to have deep oil or butter violently boiling in a great pot, to slip the slices of
potatoes into it and stir them persistently, never
letting them touch the pot's bottom, to lift them out
(when they are golden brown) by means of a small
sieve, and to place them on paper so that the grease
may be absorbed.

The best news I've had since I reached France is
about Kenton's medal. I'm going to write to-day
and tell him so.

I love you,

JOYCE.

April 19, 1918.

Dear Aline:

My chief occupation at the present time is awaiting a letter from you.

It is several hours since I wrote the first paragraph of this letter. I have been to supper (I am
hitting the mess-line these days, for my money gave
out and I didn't want to borrow any more) and
ridden in a motor-cycle-side car all over the countryside—through a dozen little villages, every one
full of French and American soldiers, with a sprinkling of coolie labourers, in quest of a certain village

[192]

which holds two companies of a certain outfit with which I had to have a conference. The village was hard to find (their names all sound alike, and old French ladies, when interrogated as to direction, always point in a direction in which there is no road and say something that sounds like "Honk! honk! Ba! ba!") and also the night was cold. I have enjoyed many rides more. Returning to the office (I sleep in the same building) half frozen and weary, I found that not two truck-loads, but two sacks of letters had been delivered, and that I had received three letters. I leaped at the letters—one was an invitation to a Ladies' Day at the Columbia University Club, another was from my mother, another from Fr. Garesché. None from You! You accused me in one of your letters of writing to you when I was depressed—well, I'm depressed now, all right! I'll wait until to-morrow morning to finish this letter, I guess, or else I'll give you real cause for complaint. Not that I blame you, or think you haven't written often—it's the mail system's fault. Good night!

I hope Kenton has learned to serve Mass by this time. I wrote to him a long time ago and told him to see Fr. Morris about it, but I fear that he would be too shy to do this unless some pressure were

brought to bear. If you would ask Fr. Morris to
teach him how to serve Mass, and persuade him to
ask Kenton to come to see him about it, so that the
initiative would seem to come from Fr. Morris, I
think things would work out well. I pray for Kenton to have the grace of a vocation to the priesthood
—I hope he may have a Jesuit vocation—and I
think it is good to do all we can toward the fulfill-
ment of this desire—this is, I think, a supplementary way to "sway the designs of God." I think of
the children often and can visualise them well in
spite of my long absence from them, that is, all except young Christopher. I am aware of Kenton's
gravity and of his thoughtful and radiant smile, of
Deborah's vivacity and exquisite colouring (she is
like one of her mother's gay thoughts), of Michael's
magnetic rotundity, of his blue eyes, of his charming habit of toppling over like a toy tumbler of lead
and celluloid. And of Rose I am nearly always
conscious, delightfully, when I am awake and often
when I am asleep, and especially when I am in the
church—which is twice every day, to receive Holy
Communion immediately after Reveille and to pray
for a few minutes in the evening. We have a
magnificent old church in this town, as near to
where I am now as the church is to our house in

[194]

Larchmont. And right by the tower-door is a big statue of St. Nicholas of Bari, in his episcopal robes, and hopping around his feet are two little bits of babies he saved and brought back to life after they'd been cut up and pickled. Very nice! You'd like it! Pray to St. Nicholas for me, and to St. Stephen, St. Brigid, St. Michael, St. Christopher, St. Joseph, St. Anthony of Padua, St. Teresa, and all our other good friends in Heaven, and love me.

JOYCE.

April 21, 1918.

Dear Aline:

I am glad of the auspicious beginning of Eleanor's romance. I would so regard it, for I cannot understand the interpretation which makes marriage the termination instead of the beginning of a splendid adventure. If there should ever be the perfect novel of love, it would begin rather than end "And they were married." Would the phrase continue: "And lived happily ever after"? I doubt it—but that depends upon the definition of happiness. I know that you dislike the symbolism which is the basis of Coventry Patmore's greatest poems, but I think you will admit that there is this truth in his idea—the relationship of man and wife is like that of God and the soul in that it must be purified and strengthened by suffering. Also—to put it on a lower plane—Eleanor is enough of a poet to take some enjoyment out of being the wife of a soldier gone to the wars—or Irish enough, which is the same thing.

As to the matter of my own blood (you mentioned this in a previous letter) I did indeed tell a good friend of mine who edits the book-review page of a Chicago paper that I was "half Irish." But I have never been a mathematician. The point I wished to make was that a large percentage—which I have a perfect right to call half—of my ancestry was Irish. For proof of this, you have only to refer to the volumes containing the histories of my mother's and my father's families. Of course I am American, but one cannot be pure American in blood unless one is an Indian. And I have the good fortune to be able to claim, largely because of the wise matrimonial selections of my progenitors on both sides, Irish blood. And don't let anyone publish a statement contradictory to this.

Speaking of publishers, please be very careful that there is nothing in the book you and Margaret wrote to offend, in the slightest degree. I would go so far as to say that if the spirit of the book is not obviously and definitely Catholic—readily so recognised by Catholic readers—it would grieve me to see it published with your name attached—grieve me deeply. I don't want anyone to say of you, "There is nothing about that novel to show she is a Catholic." I don't think Catholic writers should spend their time writing tracts and Sunday-school books, but I think that the Faith should illuminate everything they write, grave or gay. The Faith is radiantly apparent in your last poems. It is in Tom Daly's clowning as it is in his loftier moods. Of course anyone would rather write like Francis Thompson than like Swinburne. But I can honestly say that I'd rather write like John Ayscough than like William Makepiece Thackeray—infinitely greater artist though Thackeray be. You see, the Catholic Faith is such a thing that I'd rather write moderately well about it than magnificently well about anything else. It is more important, more beautiful, more necessary than anything else in life. You and I have seen miracles—let us never cease to celebrate them. You know that this is not the first fever of a convert's enthusiasm—it is the permanent conviction of a man who prayed daily for months for the Faith before that grace was given

[197]

him. The Faith has done wonderful things for you, but I think since I have been in France it has done more for me. It has carried me through experiences I could not otherwise have endured. I do not mean that it has kept me from fear—for I have no fear of death or wounding whatever. I mean that it has helped me to endure great and continued hardships. These hardships are now past—they belong to last December—but I cannot forget what made me live through them and bear myself like a man. Therefore—for this and a multitude of other reasons, among which let me put that it is my most earnest request—be zealous in using your exquisite talent in His service of Whom, I am glad to have said, Apollo was a shadow. If what you write does not clearly praise the Lord and his Saints and Angels, let it praise such types of Heaven as we know in our life—God knows they are numerous enough.

Does this sound like the writing of the least desirable of your aunts? Forgive me if it does, and heed my request even if it seem unreasonable—the request, I mean, not to sign your name to the book if it is not Catholic in spirit. I can honestly offer "Trees" and "Main Street" to Our Lady, and ask her to present them, as the faithful work of her poor unskilled craftsman, to her Son. I hope to be able to do it with everything I write hereafter— and to be able to do this is to be a good poet.

Speaking of Poetry, I have read with exquisite relish, several times, the copy of the Bulletin you sent me. And always I stop reading—prevented from continuing by irresistible mirth. God help us! Let all the world, especially all of it that deals in thought, beat its breast and repeat after me "God help us." Here are young men battling in a strange land to win back for the people of that land their decent homes. Here are French peasants (old men, children and women) kneeling at mass in a church with a yawning shell hole through the tower. Among them are American soldiers. And other American soldiers (God rest their brave young souls) rest in new graves by a fair road I know. We hear the crash of shells, the tattoo of machine guns, we see unearthly lights staining the black sky. And—Oh, God help us! Send me more bulletins! I want to read more about Mr. —— whose "mystic" (of course!) poems, seem to . . . "to challenge comparison with the works of Tagore." I want to read more about . . . chaunting to crowds of old ladies who stink of perfume and cold cream and gasoline, while a young female shakes her shanks

and "gives a visual embodiment of the poet's idea."
I want to read about A . . . "What a privilege
to be at once a poet and a fairy godmother! " And
I want to read about W . . . going West and
—just being himself! God forgive me for being a
Pharisee, and keep me from judging others! But
I do love to read about these things and then go
across the street and drink a large drink with Joe
Brady, meanwhile singing a coarse ballad entitled
"The Old Gray Mare."

We're going to be paid to-morrow, I'm glad to
say, so I'll be able to have a few meals indoors.
This roadside picnic stuff is all right in fair weather,
but French weather is not always what it should be.
I hope your allotment is arriving, but I doubt it. I
think we'll collect it in our old age. I read recently
that a Civil War Veteran had just succeeded in
collecting some pay due him in 1862—perhaps we'll
be as lucky. We'll buy a carton of cigarettes for
Christopher's youngest son with the first payment.

Your poem "Experience" has lodgment in my
brain and heart and soul. "She walks the way
primroses go." Simple—isn't it? that line—to
make it nothing much was required—genius merely.
Thank God there's you in a world of ——s and
——s. Do you mind being considered the "one just

man"? Figuratively I kiss your hand—it was absurd of me to preach to you who are my mistress in the art of devotion as in the art of poetry.

JOYCE.

April 27th, 1918.

Dear Aline:

Some mail came to-day and in it was a package containing ten boxes of tobacco, Merci bien! (when I get back I'll talk just like —— or ——.) I received a box of admirable cigars yesterday (they were originally awarded to Father Daly in payment for a contribution to *America,* and he kindly directed that they be sent to me).

We are in a new town now (new to us, that is) a little bit of a place. We have been recently in a rather large town, where I lived very comfortably. I am comfortable here (especially since yesterday afternoon, when I had a hot shower bath and had my clothes sterilized) but not luxurious. But I'm looking forward to a much easier and vastly more interesting time for the rest of my stay in France. I have asked to be relieved from my office job, and my request has been granted. I hope on Monday (this is Saturday night) to become a member of the Regi-

[201]

mental Intelligence Section, and the Adjutant tells me I am to be transferred as a Sergeant, although I was willing to give up my stripes for the sake of getting into this work. So henceforth I'll be peering at the Germans through field glasses from some observatory instead of toiling in a dugout or crowded office. You wouldn't want me to come back round-shouldered and near-sighted, would you? Well, that would be the result of keeping on this statistical job much longer. The intelligence work is absolutely fascinating—you'll be glad I took it up.

You would have liked the gutter-babies in our last town. About a dozen of them used to come out at meal times and besiege our mess-line. They brought their dad's canteens to be filled with coffee, and they accepted, politely, bread and karo. They were very nice, and fat, as all French babies are. I don't know whether the French are so devoted to my dear patron St. Nicholas of Bari, because they love children, as he does, or are devoted to children because they love him. Anyway they have the nicest children there are outside of Larchmont Manor and Heaven (these words mean nearly the same thing) and they treat them most enthusiastically. Large crowds of men and women stand for half an hour in a busy city street watching a young baby learn to walk, the baby being decorated, for the occasion, with his big sister's broad-brimmed hat. And also nearly every church has a statue or window representation of St. Nicholas of Bari with the three babies he restored to life. It helps me to feel at home. I hope you and Kenton pray to him often, he is a very generous saint and has treated me beautifully.

I had a quaint experience to-night. There is no priest now in this town, but there is a fine old church, with God in it. Since there is no priest, I can't get my daily communion, but I go in occasionally to say my prayers. Well, to-night there was a very old lady in the church. She was so crippled with age and rheumatism that she could not kneel, so she was huddled up on a bench near the rail. And she had a white cap on, and she carried a tall staff with a crutch top such as witches use. She was very pious, and prayed audibly, making pious ejaculations, like an old Irish lady. For some time she didn't know anyone else was in the church. But when she found I was there, she waited until I had said my beads and then she came over to me (rising with great difficulty and putting on the heavy wooden shoes that lay beside her). Then she ex-

[203]

tended to me her beads. The link between two of them was undone, and she asked me to mend it. I tried to do so, but my clumsy fingers had little success. So I gave her my rosary in exchange for hers —which I can easily mend with a pair of pincers— and she was very grateful. But I feel that I got the best of the bargain, for there may be a special sort of a blessing attached to beads worn by the gnarled fingers of one so near God. I could make a rhyme out of this experience, but it would seem a profanation. You see some of the possible interpretations of it, don't you?

The news about D—— is interesting—well, he is trying to serve his conscience, and I am trying to serve mine, and that's all a gentleman can do. And since we're both suffering, I believe we've both followed the right course. There are many ways to Heaven, but only one Lamp—as I once said in some verses.

But as to suffering—don't be pitying me! It's you that are doing the suffering, you with no exhilaration of star-shells and tattoo of machine-guns, you without the adventure. I feel very selfish, often.

I love you and you are never away from me.

JOYCE.

LETTERS

April 29, 1918.

Dear Aline:

For Heaven's sake, don't tell me about how bad tea rooms are! I admit that I used to scorn them. Now I could live in one, enthusiastically. I wouldn't mind at all the closeness, the bad service, the soiled table linen. Why, Max's Busy Bee sounds better to me now than Sherry's used to sound.

"She walks the way Primroses go" reechoes in my soul. What a delightful poet you are! Send me some more poems, at once, please.

It's time I heard from you again. Some mail came to-day, but I got nothing from you. You should write me long letters often. *By all means* take up Fr. Hayes' lecture offer. You can make your lectures chiefly readings. Get Dr. Pallen to help you make a circular, and put on it testimonials from whomever he suggests. Get Bob Holliday's advice as to form of circular. You will find valuable suggestions as to engagements in my correspondence files, wherever they are.

(Here I paused to eat ten cakes purchased at the Y. M. C. A. for a franc.)

Young —— is in a nearby town—an amiable child indeed he is. I saw him twice, and he presented me with a bag of cakes and a box of cigars.

[205]

He reminds me very much of Kenton, but is in many respects his inferior. I'd like to see Kenton and Fr. Daly and Deborah and Michael and Christopher and Sister Emerentia and some Bass' Ale and some dry sherry and a roast of lamb with mint sauce and Blackwood's Magazine and the bar in the Auditorium Hotel in Chicago and a straw hat and the circus. And I really wouldn't mind seeing you.

JOYCE.

May 15, 1918.

Dear Aline:

Your friends are a bit impertinent, I think. I don't claim to be a learned French scholar (although I have talked French every day for six months). But I do claim to know the name of the place where I lived in constant danger of death for six weeks, where many of my friends gave their lives for their country. It is Rouge Bouquet, not Rouge Bosquet. I'll be deeply grieved if it appears in print incorrectly. Also, I wish the grace in "Holy Ireland" to stand as I wrote it. It is just as Frank Driscoll said it on that unforgettable night—it is the grace used in Jesuit houses. Please

[206]

see to this, and don't let all the world revise my mss.
I rather expected you'd like the poem better, but
perhaps the reason the fellows in the Regiment
liked it so much is because we all felt keenly the
event it memorizes.

I'll write to you more to-morrow. I love you.

JOYCE.

The above is rather stern and brusque, is'nt it?
Well I wrote it in rather stirring times—now only
memories. I am resting now, in a beautiful place—
on a high hilltop covered with pine and fir trees. I
never saw any mountain-place in America I thought
better to look at or from. I sleep on a couch made
soft with deftly laid young spruce boughs and eat
at a table set under good, kind trees. A great improvement on living in a dug-out and even (to my
mind) an improvement on a room with a bed in a
village. I am not on a furlough, I am working, but
my work is of a light and interesting kind and fills
only six out of twenty-four hours. So I have plenty
of time for writing, and have started a prose-
sketch (based on an exciting and colourful experience of the last month) which I will send you soon.

[207]

Everything I write, I think, in prose or verse, should be submitted to Doran first.

I wish I could tell you more about my work, but at present I cannot. But there are advertised in the American magazines many books about the Intelligence Service—get one of them and you'll find why I like my job. The work Douglas is doing is not allied to mine. Only I suppose he'll have a commission. I won't work for one, because I don't want to leave this outfit. I love you more than ever, and long for the pictures you promise me. You will be amused by the postcards I enclose.

JOYCE.

Say, the stuff about your not appreciating "Rouge Bouquet" was written before I got your delightful letter of April 13, admirable critic!

Dear Aline:

I have just received your letters of April 1st and April 5th. "Moonlight" is noble, like its author. As to being worried about you because it expresses pain, why, I'd be worried only if you did not sometimes feel and express pain. Spiritual pain (sometimes physical pain) is beautiful and wholesome and in our soul we love it, whatever our lips say. Do you not, in turn, worry because of my foolish letter to you from the hospital. At that time I was just an office hack—now I am a soldier, in the most fascinating branch of the service there is—you'd love it! It is sheer romance, night and day—especially night! And I am now therefore saner than when I wrote to you from the hospital. I've had only a week of this work—but I'm already a much nicer person.

> "For Sergeant Joyce is three, and Oh,
> He knows so much he did not know!"

As to the picture I sent you, why, surely I have a moustache, and not a "morning pout." *Mechante.* A long moustache I have (illustration of moustache) *comme ca.* Also, I have thick hair which stands up (illustration) *comme ci.* I had my head shaved last November, you know, and it had a good effect. My letter is thrilling, isn't it, with all these martial details? A veritable cross-section of battle, a flower from No Man's Land. Well, I am sending some battling picture-postcards soon which you will find amusing, I think—portraits, in two striking histrionic poses, of myself. You know now, from my previous letters, that I am no longer (I thank God!) doing statistics, so gently, but widely

[209]

and most firmly, correct the statement that I have a bullet-proof job. I had one, but succeeded, after two months' intriguing, in getting rid of it. It wasn't a shell-proof job—nothing in a real regiment is. (Such jobs are in the Ordnance or Supply Departments, back of the lines.) It wasn't shell-proof, I say, and if I should be squashed by a shell, wouldn't you hate to have it said that I was nobly holding my post in the office, or bravely manning my typewriter? Now, I'm doing work I love—and work you may be proud of. None of the drudgery of soldiering, but a double share of glory and thrills. But it is not so glorious and thrilling as you.

JOYCE.

May 24, 1918.

Dear Aline:

I don't know just what kind of a mental picture you have of my present life—to be accurate it would need to be rather kaleidoscopic, for my activities and the spheres of them vary frequently and greatly. But this afternoon you (or perhaps not you, but readers of Empey and Private Peat and the rest of that mob of war writers—thank God, let me Pharisaicly say, that I am not one of them—

would do so) would have been amazed at the martial picture before you, had you seen me. Just outside the edge of the forest of firs and spruce in which we fourteen men live is a lovely meadow. There, among the knee-high buttercups, lay in the May sunshine all afternoon three warriors—myself being one. Whiles we smoked and gazed at the lovely valley miles below us—whiles we took turns in reading aloud from—what do you suppose? The Oxford Book of English Verse! We read Gray's Elegy, the first chorus from Atalanta in Calydon, "They told me, Heraclitus," that witch poem of William Bell Scott, "Love in the Valley," "Lake Isle of Innisfree," "Keith of Ravelston," and half a dozen other poems, all of which brought you most poignantly and beautifully before me. No, they didn't bring you before me—you are always before me and with me and in my heart and brain—but it's dangerous to write this—it draws so tight the cords that bind me to you that they cut painfully into my flesh. Well, we are to be together sometime, inevitably, and soon in terms of eternity. For we are absolutely one, incomplete apart, and in Heaven is completeness. How unhappy must lovers be who have not the gracious gift of faith!

There is to be an Homeric banquet at our house

one day—the day when I exhibit to my comrades the glory of my life—yourself. You will like them all—Watson (a gifted artist from Richmond, who is now at work on a fine drawing which must accompany Rouge Bouquet in *Scribner's*), Bob Lee, Titterton (my especial friend), Beck, Mott, Kerrigan, Levinson—say a prayer for them all, they're brave men and good, and splendid company. They are all men of education, and breeding, and humour, and we have fine times. Dangers shared together and hardships mutually borne develops in us a sort of friendship I never knew in civilian life, a friendship clean of jealousy and gossip and envy and suspicion—a fine hearty roaring mirthful sort of thing, like an open fire of whole pine-trees in a giant's castle, or a truly timed bombardment with eight-inch guns. I don't know that this last figure will strike you as being particularly happy, but it would if you'd had the delight of going to war.

Right here I had to pause to discuss theology with Watson, Titterton, Levinson and Jongberg. Jongberg is up here for a brief spell; he is a Swedish-Irishman, and now he is posing for St. Michael for Watson, using a bayonet for a sword. Levinson (in full uniform, including belt and helmet) is being model for the soldiers leaving Rouge Bouquet

[212]

for Heaven. He is a quaint little French-Jewish-American, with whom we have a lot of fun. They all trooped into the room where Titterton and I sit writing to our respective sweethearts, to ask about the style of St. Michael's sword and that of his halo. These questions settled, Watson became enamoured of the idea of angels saluting, and devised a whole manual of arms for angels—as "Angels, attention! Wings raised, by the numbers. 1 up! 2 down! Wings flap! Hey you down there! what's the matter with you? Don't you know enough to keep your hands down when you flap your wings? Awkward squad for you to-morrow!" Then they went back to their work.

Well, I don't know how long the Intelligence Section is to stay in this lovely summer resort of a place, but it's certainly fine while it lasts. And I am very fortunate to have such a crowd as this to work with. I never was with so congenial a company in civilian life. Fr. O'Donnell came up to see us yesterday—he is stationed not far away. Fr. Duffy has an assistant—Fr. Kennedy—a Jesuit, thank God! I have not met him yet. He is a brother of the publishers of Barclay Street. I have a new stripe—an inverted chevron of bright gold on the left cuff for six months service. Let you be proud of that too, please, and let my children be proud of it. That is all the news except that I love you.

JOYCE.

Dear Aline:

To-day I was made very happy by receiving two nice little ridiculous letters from you—one of which considered itself to be long. As to Sr. Mary Leo— if you happen to be writing to her (you will be, for I told her to ask you for "Rouge Bouquet") ask her by all means to tell you how her grandmother taught her geography. It's an absolutely delightful story, and she's a delightful old saint.

You say Tad will go "in a few months." I'm glad I'm not Tad. There are many reasons for this, of course, but I mean I am especially glad I'm not to go in a few months. I'm glad I'm a Sergeant in the 69th, a volunteer regiment, the bravest and best regiment in the army. I'm glad I have a golden service chevron on my left arm—that means six months service in France, and is better than two bars on my shoulder, which would mean only three months stay at Plattsburg. If I get an honorable wound that will unfit me for soldiering but not for civilian work, that civilian work will not be hack-

[214]

writing. It may be straight reporting, or editing, or writing (*Evening World* at $80 a week, for instance) a weekly essay-column, or dramatic criticism (this last appeals to me strongly). Also I'll do less lecturing and more oratory—bombastic, thundering, literary, Henry Woodfin Grady oratory! It is exciting, and lecturing isn't, especially.

Meanwhile I find myself approving your plan of getting literary work, although doing it makes me feel like a coloured man approving his wife's plan of taking in washing. You relieve my mind greatly by your willingness to keep your name off the book. I thought I would acknowledge to you the pleasure I got from "A Wind Rose in the Night." It is a holy and dear poem.

Please see that Kenton learns to serve Mass, won't you? Sorry to keep teasing you about this, but you never write anything about it.

Your poem "To a Sick Child" is beautiful, and "cookies" is the making of it. I love you.

JOYCE.

May 18, 1918.

Dear Aline:

I didn't get your letter expressing enthusiastic approval of "Rouge Bouquet" until I had received

[215]

two others just mentioning it. I certainly am glad the poem "got" you, as it got me. The Regiment —and soldiers outside the Regiment as high as a Brigadier General—are wonderfully enthusiastic. The Brigadier General had twenty-four copies made to send his friends. Of course we are especially moved by it because the event is so close to us. But to appreciate it you should have heard taps played and at a soldier's funeral. P. C. ought to know the distinction between peacemakers and pacifists. I wonder he didn't include St Michael in his catalogue of pacifists. We are peace-makers, we soldiers of the 69th, we are risking our lives to bring back peace to the simple, generous, gay, pious people of France, whom anyone (knowing them as I have come to know them in the last six months) must pity and admire and love. They are an invaded people—and invaded people *always are right.* The careful study of certain ghostly villages (I cannot forget them) has taught me where I would have stood in the 60's and that is on the side of the invaded Southern States. God keep me from ever being ordered to take part in an invasion of a peaceful land! So long as I am helping drive out the invader, I know I'm right—and all questions of international politics are of no importance whatever.

[216]

LETTERS

Here are nice old ladies, fat babies, jovial humorous men, and little girls just after making their First Communions. They've been driven out of their pretty sleepy little villages. They want to get back and mend the shell holes in the roof and go to school and take their place drinking red wine of an evening according to their tastes and ages. Well, we men of the 69th are helping to give these people back their homes—and perhaps to prevent our homes from one day being taken from us by the same Power—of whom nothing at all worse need be said than that it is an invader. And St. Patrick and St. Bridgid and St. Columkill and all the other Saints are with us—they are no more pacifists than they are Roycrofters! And God keep us from Washington Square! No Man's Land is a damn sight healthier place—I have tried both, and I know what I'm talking about.

And as for you, you young flippertigibbet, you won't be middle-aged, you say? Well, we'll see about that! I'll probably come back with one eye, one arm, one leg and a horrible temper, and turn your hair white in a day. Stop calling any child of ours "Billy." When you referred to "Billy" in previous letters I thought you meant some rather unfortunately named dog or cat. Now I am annoyed to find out you meant Michael. The habit of so designating him probably started humorously— please stop it at once.

I have not read "The Tree of Heaven," to which you refer in a recent letter. But I have read Carnival—and if when I get back to the States I find that you really think such books are "fine," as you say in your letter, I'll grab a baby (probably young Michael) and start for whatever South American Republic or other bellicose land has need of the services of a ranting, roaring, slashing, dashing young Sergeant, fresh from the ranks of the quarrelsome Irish, veteran of the Great War.

JOYCE.

May 27, 1918.

Dear Aline:

I enclose three bits of verse by various hands. "A Nun's Prayer for a Soldier" is by dear old Sister Mary Leo. The flattering sonnet was sent to me by Sr. Mary Emerentia, having been copied from a paper published by the girls of St. Mary's College, Notre Dame, Indiana. I destroyed Sr. Emerentia's letter before I copied down the author's name, so I couldn't write to thank her, un-

[218]

fortunately. "The Green Estaminet" I want carefully preserved, for it must go in every anthology made by you or me or anybody we know. I like it better than any war poem I've read since I became a soldier, and I deeply regret that I didn't write it. Many and many a jovial evening I have spent in just such bistrals as the poet describes. Dear old Madame—she always has that "strange disease," and she finds that white bread is good for it—and in exchange for that white bread (from army kitchens) she gives the delicious soft-crumbed brittle-crusted war-bread, better than any bread in the States. "The great round songs begin"—they do, indeed! "Bing Bang Bingen on the Rhine!" "Down in the Heart of the Gas House District," "Sidewalks of New York," and always "Madelon," in which the French soldiers in the corner enthusiastically join. Cecil Chesterton told me he always judged a country by its drinking-places. Well, here are the merriest, bravest drinking places in the world. If the States go dry, I'm going to bundle all you young critters over here to live—a comfortable, humorous, Catholic country. Honestly, the only drawback to living in this country is the absence of you and your gang. I'd like a house on the very mountain top I now inhabit, and I know you'd enjoy it tremendously. I'm perfectly serious about this, and look forward to bringing you here.

Write oftener, and longer! I love you.

JOYCE.

June 1, 1918.

Dear Aline:

A terrible thing, this war, what with a pine forest to live in, all the latest novels to read, and bridge every evening. And now I am preparing for a short week-end in a certain nice small city, an hour's walk through the forest and across the mountains. It is a lovely forest in which to wander of a June day—so deliberately European—a forest whose tall evergreen trees and smooth brown floor suggest all the folk tales I ever heard your dear voice beautify for our children's delight. Reaching this certain town, I have interesting things to do—to collect my pay for one thing. To get mail—I hope from you. To go to confession to Fr. Duffy or Fr. Kennedy, S.J., our new assistant chaplain, or to some curé with thin hands and long white hair. To drink a bottle of beer at the Sergeants' Club—among my brother noncoms, French, Italian and American, in horizon blue, green and olive drab respectively. To

[220]

mail to you this letter and a splendid drawing for "Rouge Bouquet," by Emmett Watson, of ours. To dine sumptuously on steak and fried potatoes and Pinard at a merry bistral on a side-street, where Madame la patronne will present me with a sprig of lilies of the valley, which I (imagine a boutonierre with an American uniform!) will present to the baby of the tailor's daughter. To attend the movies —two sous! To sleep between clean sheets in a hotel-bedroom—half a franc! And to-morrow to be (gold service stripe flashing in the sunlight, trench-stick jauntily swinging) a part of the many-coloured Sunday afternoon procession along a certain broad avenue. Then back to my forest-lodge for supper.

I have written a long topical poem about a hike which I'll send you soon.

I love you.

JOYCE.

A. E. F., France.

Dear Aline:

So far, I have told about six people about your rejoicing in the fact that the possession of a kitten justifies you in purchasing a bird-cage. An absolutely delightful character-revelation—that is, the revelation of a delightful character. And the most genuine sample of you I have had since last November.

I am writing this letter in the end of one of our barracks, which its partition cuts to make an airy office for the Supply Sergeant of Headquarters Company. You'd like him very much—a very beautiful person of about my age, a playwright by profession, educated in Paris. At the other end of the long table sits a bridge party, of which the members are the Supply Sergeant (Lemist Esler is his name), Howard Young (who was a Marine before he became a fighting Irisher), Sergeant Kenneth Russell (a wealthy and charming business man of very literary taste, who knows most of the living poets we know and revels in the Oxford Book of English Verse), and Tom O'Kelly, who has the most beautiful tenor voice you ever heard. He is a professional singer from Dublin, with very tightly curled close-cropped hair, a reddish brown face, and the build of a prize-fighter. In the lulls of the game he sings snatches of "Digging for Gould" and other nice ballads. Admirable person.

I am with the Regiment now—the Intelligence Section is back from its Post, the beautiful place

"HE LIES BURIED ON THE RIGHT,
BESIDE LIEUTENANT OLIVER AMES,
AT THE EDGE OF A LITTLE COPSE
KNOWN AS THE WOOD OF THE
BURNED BRIDGE, CLOSE TO THE
PURLING OURCQ"

from which I wrote you many letters. Now we are in very flat country, the flattest I ever saw. Very violent flowers, chiefly scarlet poppies and small blue things, cornflowers, I believe. Gloriously hot, with good swimming nearby, and the best sort of shower-bath, obtainable by merely sitting under the spout of a pump while an obliging friend turns the handle.

Your letter of May twenty-sixth came after I had received a June letter. I am delighted to hear of Kenton's confirmation and of his choice of a name —St. Stephen is a gallant gentleman and a true friend and does wonderful things for me.

I'm not very enthusiastic about that group picture of office-workers in which I appear—I like myself better as I am now, a soldier instead of a clerk, visiting the office only occasionally—to work on my history. And I'm ever so much happier now than when the picture was taken.

Is Kenton serving Mass yet? *Please* have him do so. And please send me my Anthology—I believe restrictions no longer keep packages from soldiers. I love you.

JOYCE.

MISCELLANEOUS PIECES

A BALLAD OF NEW SINS

PRELUDE

I am sick of the riotous roses of rapture,
Of sibilant serpentine lips,
Of the wine cup
And murder
And all that mid-Victorian stuff.
I will sin large purple sins
American
And new.

THE SIN OF SOUTH BEND

Clandestinely, by night,
I will board a train
And be borne, palpitant and eager, over the shud-
    dering rails,
Until
In the chaste stillness of Sunday morning
I am hurled into the blushing station of South
    Bend, Indiana.
Thence I will speed to the Hotel Mortimer
And, leering with hot lips,

[227]

Rubbing with tremulous hand my rough jaws
(For this is the shameful signal,
Immemorial, inevitable),
I will ask the way to the barber shop.
The liveried menials will blench,
But one of them, hardened in crime,
Will feverishly seize my proffered gold,
And lead me, on tiptoe,
To the barber-shop's secret door.
There, in a dim back room,
Screened, impenetrable,
A barber (artfully disguised in a black coat and no
    chewing gum)
Will (now and then peering nervously out beyond
    the screen, fearful of spies and policemen)
Give to me, for twenty-five cents,
The forbidden delight
Of a Sunday morning shave.

II

THE WICKEDNESS OF WASHINGTON

What wickedness is more witchingly wonderful
Than the wickedness of Washington,
Where it is heinous to hock
And perilous to pawn?

A BALLAD OF NEW SINS

I will go to Washington
And offer my watch to an usurer.
"Wait here," he will whisper,
"And give me ten cents!"
Then will a messenger, winged like a swallow,
Carry my watch over meadow and hill
Over the riotous River Potomac
To the Virginian Shore;
He will return with a lavender ticket;
He will return with a five-dollar bill;
He will return (Oh, the logic of law!)
He will return with the watch
And the pawnbroker will lock it away.

III

THE IMMORALITY OF INDIANAPOLIS

I will go to Indianapolis,
And there sin strangely
By crossing the street catty-cornered
Instead of at the crossings,
And I shall be hanged.

MISCELLANEOUS PIECES

WAR SONGS

I—WATER-COLOUR

Pushing my way through the chattering throng of my brown-clad mates to the rail of the troop-ship, I look at still water, greasy and opaque. A touch of sunlight makes it splendid with rainbows, a great prismatic expanse, beautiful, more beautiful than clear water could be. Broken oars shatter the rainbow, bringing a black, clumsy rowboat close to our ship's side. Around the black boat the rainbow settles. The rower rests his oars and lifts graceful en‧treating arms. He wears pale blue overalls. In the stern of his boat is a little girl in a cardinal cloak. On her head is one of the caps that make the French sailors look so gay and gentle, a flat, round, blue thing with a red pompom. She claps her hands when cooks lean through the portholes and throw loaves of bread to her father.

II—BREAKFAST

I may breakfast in either of two ways. I may, as I pass a steaming field-kitchen, hold out by its long handle a shining aluminum basin. John Wilkert

[230]

will put into it a big ladleful of rice, and Leo Maher will pour golden syrup over it. Also, before I leave the line I shall have three long strips of broiled bacon and two thick slices of white bread, and a canteen cup full of hot, sweet coffee. The breakfast room is a meadow or the roadside across from the barracks. There is good company, hungry and mirthful. And over our heads noisy battalions of crows maneuver, advancing, retreating, hoarsely shouting down to us news of what awaits us beyond the frozen hills.

Or I may go to the House by the Fountain. Pierre's "permission" is over, so he will not come in from the stable to smoke my tobacco and tell me of life and death in the trenches. *Grandpere* sits by the fire, now and then blowing it to flame by forcing his scant old breath upon it through a long hollow tube, and toasting for me a thick slice of warbread. Madame superintends the heating of the big iron pot of this morning's milk and the three-legged pot of coffee. Now my bowl—a little precious sugar in the bottom—is filled with hot milk. Madame deftly pours black coffee into it, and it becomes richly brown. I break my toast into it and eat eagerly—more eagerly than does demure little Francine, who sits opposite me, her school books beside her on the bench. She has large innocent brown eyes like her father's. Her hands are so tiny that I am surprised at her dexterity with the large pewter spoon. I am afraid that if I stare at her I shall embarrass her and make her spill *cafe au lait* on her immaculate pinafore. On the great stone mantel over the fire are a spent seventy-five milli-metre shell curiously engraved with wreaths of roses, a pink china pig and a brass crucifix. A bugle sounds by the barracks. I give Madame her half-franc. I take my belt and rifle. "Bon jour, Monsieur," says Madame, "A demain!" Some day instead of "a demain" they will say "au revoir."

"TRY A TIN TO-DAY"

"AND NOW," said John Potts, whirling around on the piano-stool and throwing his lank forelock back with a jerk of his head, "we will interpret Grace Mallon's soul!"

"Oh, wait till she comes, John!" boomed the Rev. Morris Gildell. "She was at the Karl Marx Forum in our parish-house last night, and she said positively she'd be down here this afternoon."

"Yes, do wait!" said Mrs. Anna Watkins Wilbur, placing her fat hands, covered with rings set with semiprecious stones, over those of the pianist. "Do wait! It will be wonderful for her to hear it!"

The host of the occasion was Edwin Marmaduke, painter. He was at present engaged in spooning Arabian incense out of a cocoa-tin and putting it into a large bronze thurible, which hung before a plaster replica of Rodin's "Le Baiser." The incense caught fire, and dense clouds of fragrant smoke filled the little studio. Then Marmaduke turned his pale but agreeable face to his guests.

"No, do it now!" he commanded. "Perhaps you and Arthura will bring her with it."

So John Potts struck a few minor chords, and Arthura Lewis lifted her pale-green mantle in both thin arms, smiled at the low ceiling, closed her eyes, and danced. She did not really dance. She merely bent and kicked and gestured, approximately in rhythm with the music.

She was not really Miss Arthura Lewis, either. Her first name, which she had discarded as too usual, was Alice and her last name was Potts, for she was the pianist's wife. They were known to live together in the little apartment across Patchin Place from Marmaduke's studio, but the fact of their marriage was scrupulously kept a secret from the other members of their emancipated circle. No liaison was ever hidden from the world more zealously than was the regularity and mid-Victorian respectability of this seeming "free comradeship."

So John Potts played and Arthura danced, and the theme they were interpreting was Grace Mallon's soul. Edwin Marmaduke's eyes were turned toward Arthura, but he did not see her. Nor did he see Grace's soul. He saw her eyes—very gray and lovely—and her hair, which was golden-brown and had an indefinable air of mirth about it.

Marmaduke loved Grace better than cigarettes, or incense, or art; better even than the school of

[234]

painting of which he was the acknowledged master, the school which proudly accepted a name first derisively given it—the Incomprehensiblists. So, while Arthura twisted and turned and John Potts hammered out discords, he thought of Grace's beauty and charm.

To do him justice, he did not think of her great wealth. In fact, he did not like to think of her wealth, for that wealth came from her father's success in a most unesthetic business. Grace was the daughter of "Try a Tin To-day" Mallon, who was known in the world of canned goods as the Salmon King.

There was no vulgar hand-clapping after the artists had finished their interpretation of Grace's soul; but the Rev. Morris Gildell rattled his spoon against the sides of his teacup, while Mrs. Anna Watkins Wilbur sighed ecstatically and clanked her chain of heavy amber beads. Even in the act of lighting a cigarette, John Potts started dramatically and pointed toward the open window.

"La voilà!" he exclaimed. "We have summoned her! I hear the rumble of her chariot-wheels."

There did indeed come from the cobbles of Patchin Place the whir and snort of an automobile. Soon the great gong on the wall clanged viciously, causing Arthura Lewis to shudder and clasp her long, white hands to her eyes. Edwin Marmaduke sped down the four flights of stairs that intervened between his studio and the street door.

His deserted guests looked at one another expectantly.

"Dear Grace!" said Mrs. Anna Watkins Wilbur. "I hope she came alone. I can't stand that friend of hers—what is his name?—that Watson person."

"He is a terrible bromid," said Arthura Lewis, lighting a cigarette. "He's so very—so very, shall I say, salmony!"

This was said with humorous intent and received with kindly laughter.

"But what has Mr. Watson to do with salmon, anyway?" asked John Potts. "Does he catch them, or what is it?"

"Nothing so exciting as that," said the Rev. Morris Gildell, with a great chuckle. "He merely celebrates them. He is the advertising manager of the Mallon Salmon Company, and his chief claim to immortality is that he invented the 'Try a Tin Today' slogan. You know those great pink pictures of ridiculous-looking fish that we see in public vehicles and on the highways and byways, each one holding out a can bearing the legend, 'Try a Tin

To-day'? Watson is responsible for those mutila‐
tions of the landscape."

"Does Watson paint them himself?" asked Mrs.
Anna Watkins Wilbur. "He looks capable of it."

The Rev. Morris Gildell issued another of those
shouts of laughter which made the women's clubs
believe him masculine and hearty.

"Excellent!" he cried, putting an approving hand
on Mrs. Anna Watkins Wilbur's fat, bare shoulder.
"Oh, excellent! No, Watson doesn't paint them,
but he does worse—he inspires them. He persuades
some poor devil of an artist to make these hideous
caricatures of the truth. He is the Mæcenas of the
'Try a Tin To-day' school of painting."

After waiting for the murmur of amusement to
die down, the Rev. Morris Gildell continued:

"Grace brought Watson to the Feminist Confer‐
ence at our church last week, and several people
asked me what a rare, free spirit like her could see in
such a clod. I suppose she feels that she must go
around with him occasionally because he is so useful
to her father. But I hope she doesn't think of
marrying him!"

"Marrying him!" exclaimed Mrs. Anna Watkins
Wilbur, Arthura Lewis, and John Potts in unison.
"I hope not!"

"Why," said Arthura Lewis, "it would be a tragedy for an emancipated woman like Grace to marry at all! Not to speak of marrying such a soulless, brainless animal as that David Watson! I'd as soon see her—"

But the conversation was interrupted by the opening of the studio door and the entrance of Grace and their young host.

Edwin Marmaduke seemed somehow to look younger than before. He had lost a little of his expression of languor and disdain; and Grace was the very personification of radiant girlhood. In spite of her knowledge of her own good looks and good clothes, she was charmingly deferential to these people, whom she considered intellectuals. Her naively respectful greeting to the Rev. Morris Gildell seemed for the moment to restore to that drawing-room revolutionist some strange lost dignity.

Men and women alike greeted the young girl with genuine friendliness. When her gray motor-cloak had been hung over the corner of an easel, and she had been seated on one of the few real chairs the studio boasted, and served with sweet biscuits, a cup of tea, and a cigarette, then the great event of the afternoon occurred—the unveiling of Marmaduke's portrait of her.

[238]

"TRY A TIN TO-DAY"

The blinds were drawn—for the Incomprehensiblist painting is best appreciated in semidarkness. The incense-pot received some new fuel; John Potts played something "very golden" on the piano; and Edwin Marmaduke reverently drew back the gay Indian scarf that covered his masterpiece.

II

For a detailed description of Edwin Marmaduke's "Soul Study in B-Minor—for G. M.," the reader is referred to the introduction to the catalogue of the "Seven Rebels" exhibition at the Stein Galleries, or to the admirable essay "Incomprehensiblism—a Step Forward," which appeared in that sprightly but short-lived weekly review, the *Ultimate Democracy*. This at least was obvious—that the portrait was large and mauve; this at least was generally agreed upon—that it was wonderful.

The Rev. Morris Gildell defiantly, Mrs. Anna Watkins Wilbur cooingly, Arthura Lewis prayerfully, Grace Mallon respectfully, Edwin Marmaduke himself modestly—all said it was wonderful. And after Mrs. Anna Watkins Wilbur had embraced the young painter, and his other guests had clasped his hand, and they had all said "Wonderful!" many, many times, they clattered down the uncarpeted stairs to the street.

All, that is, but one—Grace Mallon. She still remained in the old Italian chair, holding an empty cup and an unlighted cigarette. She looked out of the window into dusty Patchin Place, and one slender, unjeweled hand lay on the sill. It was an attractive hand although the sun had turned it a shade darker than that of Edwin Marmaduke. It seemed firm and soft at the same time.

Edwin was, after all, human, and therefore he seized it; but Grace withdrew it from his grasp—not very abruptly, however.

"Now, Edwin," she said, "you must be very proper and mid-Victorian and all that sort of thing, since I'm being a reckless, forward young woman and staying here in your studio all alone with you. Now sit down there like a good boy and listen to me. Heavens! I wonder what David *would* say if he knew I was doing this!"

"Why do you care what David Watson would say?" asked Edwin, gently swinging the thurible to and fro before his goddess. "He's busy with his 'Try a Tin To-day' pictures. He isn't thinking about you or anything else that is beautiful."

"Stop swinging that incense thing around. You

make me nervous!" Grace replied irrelevantly. "I hate that stuff; it makes me think about when I had whooping-cough. Of course I don't care about what David thinks, silly! Last night he came up to the house, and he said something that hurt me very much."

She paused interrogatively. Edwin put the extinguished thurible on a teakwood stand, dusted his fingers on a yellow silk handkerchief, and sat down on a cushion at Grace's feet.

"Well, what did he say?" he asked.

Grace's colour had risen, making her more adorable than ever.

"Really, Edwin," she said, "I sometimes think that you are almost too skilful in repressing your emotions. I said he hurt me very much."

Edwin threw his cigarette into the coal-scuttle with a despairing gesture.

"My dear Grace," he said, "what would you have me do? Challenge him to a duel? Of course I'm tremendously sorry; but why do you talk to such an animal as Watson?"

Grace looked at him with a rather cynical smile.

"You men are pretty much alike, after all," she said. "What David said that hurt me was just like what you are saying about him. He made fun of

[241]

you and your painting—of course, that hurt me terribly—and then he actually had the nerve—the impudence to *forbid* me to come to your studio! Think of it! David Watson, whose only idea of art is a stupid fish holding a tin of dad's salmon and saying 'Try a Tin To-day'—that man to tell me what to do and what not to do! I'll tell you what I did. I forbade him ever to come to my home or to speak to me again! When I came down here this afternoon, I stopped at dad's office purposely. I know David was watching me when I left, and I said to Leon, 'Take me to Mr. Marmaduke's studio in Patchin Place'—loud, so he'd hear me!"

Edwin looked almost handsome as he smiled up at her from his cushion.

"That's my brave little comrade!" he said. "And soon we shall be married, sha'n't we? Remember, you'll keep your maiden name, and you won't promise to honour or obey me, or any of that cruel rubbish. Gildell will use that lovely, 'Polyrhythmic Ritual for a Free Mating,' and there'll be just the people we love best present. Arthura will dance, and it will all be wonderful!"

Grace gripped the arms of her chair and moistened her lips nervously.

"Edwin," she said, "I haven't told you yet why

I stayed here to-day. I told dad to come here at
six o'clock."

"Mr. Mallon coming here at six o'clock!" said
Edwin, rising to his feet. "Why, it's five minutes
to six now!"

"Yes, he's coming here right away. And, Edwin
—he knows," said Grace.

"You told him?" asked Edwin in unconcealed
amazement.

"Yes, I told him, idiot!" said Grace, springing up
from her chair. "How else do you suppose he
knows? Do you think he read my burning passion
written on my brow? Have some sense! Did you
never hear of a girl telling her own father that she
was engaged?"

"Of course!" said Edwin. "Of course! I understand. But what did he say, why is he coming here?"

"That's just it," said Grace, drawing on a white
glove hurriedly and splitting it in the process. "I
told him last night, right after David went away;
and he said he didn't like artists and didn't like you
—don't be angry, Edwin, he's only seen you three
times. I told him you were really a great painter,
and he said that he wanted me to be happy, and
that he'd have a talk with you and see what you were
made of."

"See what I am made of!" said Edwin with a sneer. "Why, does he think—"

"Now, Edwin, please, please, *please*, don't say anything bright!" said Grace. "You know dad has had only me to talk to since mother died, and he isn't used to bright people. He doesn't like them. Now be sensible, and—here he comes now!"

They had not heard the great motor-car swing around the corner of Jefferson Market and come to a stop at the entrance to Patchin Place; but they heard the clang of the gong on the studio wall, and together they went to the street-door and brought the Salmon King up the rickety stairs to the studio.

III

James Mallon was what is called a captain of industry. That is, he was one of those men who are always shown by the realistic cartoonists to be grossly fat, with very small heads, tremendous cigars, and suits of clothes covered with a chaste pattern of dollar-marks.

He no more looked the part, however, than you look the part of the *Common People*. He was slender, graceful, and modestly dressed; he had a neat, white mustache, thin gray hair, and a mildly

[244]

humorous expression. He loved his motherless daughter, his business, golf, pinocle, Smithfield ham, buckwheat cakes and maple-sirup, dry Sauterne, and detective-stories. He did not wear spats.

Mr. Mallon sat in the Italian chair, and after a brief survey of the room, turned to his postulant son-in-law a puzzled but amiable face.

"Mr. Marmaduke," he said, "don't you think that you and I could talk a little more comfortably if I sent this youngster of mine home? Run away, Grace, and have Leon take you straight to the house. I'll be back in time for dinner."

Grace gave her father that birdlike peck which is the traditional filial kiss, and ran down-stairs in accordance with his directions. She went to her car, and called Leon from his conversation with her father's chauffeur. There arose a rumble and a rasping roar, and her car sped over the cobblestones to the corner and up Sixth Avenue.

Oh, woman, in our hours of ease, what a double-faced hussy you are, anyway! Grace's car went away—presumably home—but Grace stayed behind. She had left the street-door of the house ajar. She tiptoed up the stairs to the top floor, where her father and her lover were engaged in important private discourse.

She came to a halt about three steps from the top, and perched in the dust with her golden-brown head on a level with the broad streak of light which marked the bottom of the studio door. A shameless eavesdropper, she listened greedily.

First she heard her father's voice:

"I have heard your paintings praised highly by critics whose opinions I respect," it said. "The fact that I myself fail to appreciate their merit is by no means to your discredit. I am not a connoisseur, and I am very old-fashioned in all my tastes. But I must say frankly that your success as a painter of ultramodern pictures scarcely seems to me to qualify you to marry my daughter."

She half hoped, half feared, that Edwin would say:

"I love your daughter and she loves me. That makes our union necessary and right."

But instead he said, in a low, tense voice which she had never heard him use before:

"But I may say without boasting that my art is not a failure, even financially. I have sold six paintings since last May, and the smallest check I received was for one hundred and twenty-five dollars."

"Indeed?" her father replied courteously. "I am

glad to hear it, Mr. Marmaduke—very glad to hear it. I did not know that the public was sufficiently fond of these new and unusual forms of art to invest money in them. I see that I was wrong. But you must forgive me, Mr. Marmaduke, if I say that in my opinion the demand for—what is it you call them? I am getting old, and my memory is not what it was—ah, yes, thank you—the demand for Incomprehensiblist paintings is not likely to be of great duration. The public is fickle, sir; it has no use for last year's novelties. Can you expect to invent new methods of painting yearly for its pleasure? You would have found it more profitable, in the long run, to paint in the traditional manner."

Edwin did not speak for several seconds. Then he said, with an air of deliberation:

"No, Mr. Mallon. I think you are wrong. I tried painting in the traditional manner, and I made much less money than I am making now. Except for commercial work, the only sort of painting that pays to-day is—well, what you would call freak painting."

"Ah!" Grace heard her father say. "Exactly— except for commercial work! There is a field for a young man! I cannot blame you for being an idealist; but you wish to marry my daughter, and I confess that I should prefer to see her married to a successful commercial draftsman—say, an artist connected with some sound advertising agency—than to—well, to an Incomprehensiblist."

The listening girl smiled at her father's words. Edwin Marmaduke and advertisements! It was an amusingly fantastic combination.

She heard Edwin cross the room and open a door. Then he seemed to be taking something from a closet. There was clattering and grating, as if canvases were being moved about.

"Before I show you these," he said, "I must ask you to promise to treat this matter as strictly confidential."

"Of course I promise, Mr. Marmaduke," said her father. "But really I am not competent to judge your work—"

Edwin made no oral answer. From the sounds that came to her Grace conjectured that he was lifting and placing one of his paintings on an easel. She wondered which one it was—certainly it could not be her portrait!

"Good Lord!" she heard her father say. "Good Lord!"

Then came silence.

IV

Frantic with curiosity, Grace rose from the step and tried to look into the room through the keyhole. The presence of a key made her effort unavailing. She heard the rustle of pictures hastily turned, and her father's iteration of "Good Lord!"

Then Edwin spoke.

"Now," he said, "you see that my work has some practical value, don't you? You recognise these drawings, don't you?"

"Recognise them!" said Mr. Mallon. "I should say I did. Do you mean to tell me—"

"Yes," said Edwin. "They're my work, all of them. Watson let the Parker Company handle their campaign, and I've done all their high-class work for the past three years."

The Parker Company! Grace dimly remembered hearing that name. Yes, David Watson had said something about the Parker Company.

"I don't sign any of this stuff," said Edwin, "but it's all mine. I originated that idea of the fish holding a can in his fin. I make all the 'Try a Tin To-day' pictures."

She was at first too stunned to move. Vaguely she heard her father's laugh, vaguely she heard him congratulating Edwin and inviting him to the house. Then, with a sense of walking in her sleep, she found herself at the foot of the stairs, fumbling at the catch of the street-door. She walked all the way home.

But it was a composed and apparently happy young woman who entered the Mallon house an hour later. Her father had already returned, and not even the fact that dinner had been delayed by her tardiness could account for his air of excitement.

"Grace," he said, "I was pleasantly surprised by that young man, that Edwin Marmaduke. He is no mere freak painter—he is a first-class commercial artist. He doesn't want it known, but—I should never have guessed it, it is a tremendous joke on me —he is the man who originated our 'Try a Tin To-day' posters! Did you know that?"

"Impossible!" said Grace. "Is dinner ready?"

"It's a fact," said her father. "He showed me the drawings. Of course, that changes things. I told him to call this evening—how does that strike you?"

Grace seemed passionately interested in her grapefruit. She looked steadily at it as she answered.

"Well," she said, "I'm afraid I won't be in this evening. You see, I met David Watson on the way home to-day, and he asked me to go to see 'The Boomerang' with him to-night, and I said I'd go."

"Oh!" said her father. "Then I'd better telephone Marmaduke to come to-morrow evening instead—or will you?"

"No," said Grace serenely. "To-morrow night won't do, either. David is coming to call."

Her father looked at her over his glasses. Then he took them off, polished them with a small piece of chamois, replaced them, and looked at her again.

"Oh!" he said.

SOME MISCHIEF STILL

CHARACTERS

MAXWELL JOHNSON
MRS. MAXWELL JOHNSON (*née* HELEN WHITE)
LIONEL MORRIS
JOHN RYAN
A POLICEMAN
PLACE: *New York; the upper West Side.*
TIME: *The present.*

SCENE—*The living room of a six-room apartment. On one side is a mahogany pianola; at the back is a doorway with a heavy portière, drawn aside to show a portion of the hall with a wall telephone. At the right of the doorway is a life size statue of a nude woman, the distance from her feet to her waist being four times that from her waist to her head, which is very small and has no features except a prominent nose. Her arms are stretched out at right angles to her body, and she has been painted a vivid purple.*

It is evening; the electric lamp is lit and there is a faint light in the hall.

[252]

SOME MISCHIEF STILL

MAXWELL JOHNSON, *a man of about thirty, is lying in slippered ease on a chaise-longue, smoking a cigar. MRS. JOHNSON is seated facing him on the bench by the pianola. She is a very pretty young woman, rather too highly coloured, wearing an extremely décolleté gown of pale green charmeuse, a long string of large jade beads and a broad silver bracelet. She has a profusion of bright yellow hair. One knee is crossed over the other, revealing green silk stockings and silver slippers.*

MAXWELL

But Anarchists don't ride in automobiles, do they, Nellie?

HELEN

Max, I do wish you wouldn't tease me about things that are sacred. If you don't want to get an automobile, just say so, but don't try to make fun of things you can't possibly understand!

MAXWELL

But, Nellie—

HELEN

It's hard enough for me to put up with your staying home and lying around and reading the paper while I go out night after night without you, and

[253]

wear myself out at the Settlement and the Ferrer School and making speeches and addresses and everything in the subway and back in it, and losing all the elation and social consciousness and everything, without having Anarchism and beauty and truth and everything that really means anything to anybody who tries really to think just made a joke of!

MAXWELL

Good heavens, Nellie, I'm perfectly willing to buy the automobile; and I'm not criticising any of your hobbies! I—

HELEN

Hobbies! Does one wear one's self out for a hobby? Does one die for a hobby? Is the vote a hobby? Is the Woman's Movement a hobby? Is Futurism a hobby? Is the Church of the Social Revolution a hobby? Is preaching the great truths of sex to one's unborn children a hobby? Is—

MAXWELL

All right, all right; let me slip in a word, won't you? I'm not knocking any of your—devotions. I'll get the automobile if you want it. I simply want you to make up your mind whether you want me to get it, or to use the two thousand for a bungalow at Amaranth, or wherever that crazy summer colony is.

HELEN

It would be lovely to have our own place at Amaranth—though I suppose you'd only come out for weekends—you know it's the most wonderful place, with the most wonderful scenery, and only really interesting people are allowed there, poets and sculptors and people who really do things; and there's to be a pageant this summer and Lionel Morris says he wants me to do my barefoot dance; but I do wish we had a car—it would be wonderful just to get into one's own car all the time and go anywhere, and I could take parties of interesting people out on tours to Ellis Island and the Night Court—

MAXWELL

The Night Court! Yes, I think if you run the car you will go on a tour to the Night Court pretty soon, and you'll have a special cop to take care of you, too. But you decide to-night whether you want the car or the bungalow, see? I'm game to spend two thousand dollars on one or the other, but you've got to decide. (*From the dining room comes the loud clink of the steam radiator.*) There's that

[255]

radiator again! (*The telephone bell rings.*) And there's the 'phone! (*He goes into the dining room and is heard muttering and pounding at the radiator, which continues to clink.* HELEN *goes to the telephone.*)

HELEN

Hello! . . . Yes; what is it? . . . Yes, I am Miss White. (*She turns and looks nervously toward the dining room.*) Yes, this is Mrs. Johnson, Sam. It's all right; I know what he wants. Tell Mr. Morris to come right up. (HELEN and MAXWELL *reënter the living room at the same time. The radiator still clinks, but less loudly, with longer intervals of silence.*)

HELEN

Max, Mr. Morris is coming up to take me to the Mortons' studio warming.

MAXWELL

Studio warming, hey? Well, I'm going down to get Ryan to come up and arrange a dining room warming. It's no use telephoning to him; he'll just promise to fix the radiator and then go back to his chair and fall asleep. I'll go down and drag him up by the throat. (*He goes out through the hall door, and is heard to open the outer door and speak to someone.*)   How are you, Mr. Morris?   Walk right in!   The madam's waiting for you.

LIONEL (*off stage*)

Ah, thank you, Mr. Johnson, thank you.

(*Enter* LIONEL. *He is a handsome, slender young man, very pale, with brown hair brushed straight back.*)

LIONEL (*lifting both of* MRS. JOHNSON's *hands to his lips*)

Ah, Miss White!   Dear Comrade White!

(*This hand-kissing and dearing business leads the audience to think that* MR. LIONEL MORRIS *is the villain of the play, a destroyer of homes, a desperate character. As a matter of fact, he is nothing of the sort. He is quite harmless, being a sociable young man of limited education who likes to take part in those radical movements which attract women. He writes obscene poetry and paints pictures and makes sculptures that would be disgusting if they were not so funny. He is a rather interesting hybrid, being part donkey and part tame cat.*)

HELEN

Dear Comrade Lionel!   See where I put your "Emancipation of Woman."

(*She leads him to the purple statue.*)

LIONEL

Ah! I never can interest myself in any of my work that is more than a day old. A poem or a picture that I have made bores me when the first flush of creation has passed. I feel toward it as I suppose a father felt toward his children, in those mediæval days when one had children. (*He touches the outstretched hand of the statue.*) But, dear Comrade White! Why do you make my "Emancipation of Woman" live with a Hiroshige colour print? A Toyokune I can endure, but a Hiroshige absolutely spoils the melody of her composition. Better the soft lyrical wall for a background, or perhaps a simple hanging of passionate black satin. Do you mind if I take this abomination down?

HELEN

Surely, surely; you are always so right about everything! Do change anything and everything that will make it more comfortable for your wonderful statue. She has meant so much to me since she came. . . .

LIONEL

I know, dear comrade.

(*He has moved the pianola bench to the wall and is standing on it taking down the Japanese print*

[258]

when MAXWELL *and* JOHN RYAN *come in.* RYAN *is a janitor, and looks like a janitor. He is in his shirt sleeves and wears a battered black derby. He is smoking—no, not a short clay pipe!—a cigarette. He takes off his hat when he sees* MRS. JOHNSON, *but instantly replaces it.*)

MAXWELL (*as he leads* RYAN *to the dining room*)
Come in here, Ryan. Did you bring your monkey wrench with you?

(RYAN *mutters something unintelligible. They go out into the dining room, from which come occasional murmurs of conversation and sounds of hammering.*)

LIONEL (*from the pianola bench*)
Do you know, I am not at all glad to see that man.

HELEN
Who? Max?

LIONEL
No, indeed! That dreadful janitor! Do you know, Miss White—that janitor—

HELEN
Don't talk so loud! Max doesn't like me to be called "Miss White." You know he's funny and

old-fashioned, and though he's willing for me to be a Feminist and to give money to the cause and everything, it makes him positively rage to hear me called "Miss White." I tell him that a woman doesn't give up her soul and her name and everything like a chattel mortgage just because she's married, but he says that I've got to be called "Mrs. Johnson" because I'm no more Miss White than he is.

LIONEL (*getting down from the bench and putting the colour print on the pianola*)

Ah, well, he'll wake up one of these days and learn what Feminism really is. Even the business men must wake up some time. There was a broker that marched beside me in the suffrage parade this year—a broker or a pawnbroker, I never know which is which.

HELEN

But what about Ryan? Why don't you like him?

LIONEL

That janitor! Do you know, he is simply a degenerate!

HELEN

A degenerate? Like Lombroso?

[260]

SOME MISCHIEF STILL

LIONEL

No. Worse than that. He actually has nine
children! Last week when I went around with
Comrade May Robinson Dannenberg and Comrade
Rebecca Idleheimer selling "Plain Facts about a
Great Evil" and working up enthusiasm for the suffrage rally at the Church of the Social Revolution,
I made a special effort to interest the janitors and
their wives. We went into every basement from
here to 125th Street, and we saw some things that
made my heart bleed. And in the basement of this
very house I saw this man Ryan rocking a cradle
and drinking beer out of a tin pail. His wife was
cooking something disgusting on the gas stove and
nursing a baby with her left hand. Comrade May
Robinson Dannenberg was treated with absolute
discourtesy by them; in fact, the woman told her to
"go to hell"!

HELEN

But then, those people, you know, they never do
anything or read anything or anything. They are
just like animals.

LIONEL

Yes, but you and I have got to keep them from
being animals! That's what Social Consciousness

means. I won't say duty—I hate the word—but it's your right to change the lives of those people and you absolutely must exercise that right, just as you absolutely must vote. There is that woman— a woman, the creature of all our dreaming—(*He points to the statue.*)—who might be out among the fields and the trees and the brooks and the birds and all the great and beautiful things of life, a sentient, social being; and what is she? What do we find her doing? Having a baby in a coalhole!

HELEN

I see what you mean. That dreadful janitor! I know; I tried to get her to come to my class in the Ferrer School, and she said she had too much work to do.

LIONEL

Exactly! Too much work to do! The thing that has crushed the souls and spirits and hearts of women throughout the generations! But we must stop all this. You must stop it. You must speak to the man—to Ryan—

HELEN

I speak to Ryan? What shall I say to him? He won't come to the Ferrer School.

SOME MISCHIEF STILL

LIONEL

The Ferrer School must come to him! You must go to him and say: "Ryan, woman is no longer your bond slave! You must have no more babies. You are killing your wife with soul-deadening drudgery. No janitor should have children; no janitor should have a wife. You must put Mrs. Ryan in a model tenement somewhere, and let her lead a normal, intellectual life. Society will care for the children. There are plenty of places where they can go and be studied by scientists and develop, perhaps, into useful members of the community. You will do your work as before, but you must keep Mrs. Ryan away from this drudgery somewhere where she can really live her life." Will you do this?

HELEN

Why, yes, I suppose I ought to . . . (*She picks up her cloak which has been lying on a chair and puts it on, with* LIONEL's *assistance.*) It's time we started, isn't it? But wait a minute! Max!

MAXWELL (*coming in from the dining room*)
Going? I hope you have a good time.

HELEN

Yes, we're going, but, Max, I want you to do

something for me. You know Ryan better than I do and you can talk to him. Mr. Morris says that he's been abusing his wife, and he thinks we ought to get him to put her into a model tenement where she can develop her soul. He's been overworking her and all that sort of thing, so you talk to him about it, will you? Mr. Morris knows a place where she can go, and we can put the children somewhere, and he can go on with his work, and it will be better for everybody. So you talk to him about it, will you?

MAXWELL

Ryan? Abusing Mrs. Ryan? Good heavens, I had no idea of this. Of course I'll talk to him about it. I'll put a stop to that, Nellie. Good-bye. Enjoy yourself. And you talk over that plan of ours with Mr. Morris and decide whether you want a bungalow or an automobile.

HELEN *and* MAXWELL

Good-bye.

(*They go out.* RYAN *comes in from the dining room.*)

RYAN

I guess that radiator'll be all right now, Mr. Johnson. There was a lot of air in the pipe and the valve was rusted tight, so I had a little trouble loosening it up.

(*He starts out.*)

MAXWELL (*frowning and looking at the floor*)

Wait a minute, Ryan. I want to talk to you about something. (RYAN *comes toward him and stands waiting.*) Ryan, I hear—don't you think— er—will you have a cigar?

RYAN

Why, yes, thanks.

(MAXWELL *goes into the dining room and brings out a humidor. He places it by the lamp on the table and opens it. Both men take cigars and light them.*)

MAXWELL

Ryan, what I want to talk to you about is the way in which you—it's about what I hear about the way you—Sit down, sit down!

(*He sits on the chaise-longue and* RYAN, *looking somewhat puzzled, sits on a chair on the other side of the table.*)

RYAN

What was it you want to see me about, Mr. Johnson? Any complaint?

Maxwell

Oh, no, not at all! Or, rather, yes, I have a complaint. It's rather a hard thing. I must say I'm surprised to hear about the way you treat your wife.

Ryan (*rising from his chair*)

What are you trying to give me? You mind—

Maxwell

Now, that's all right, Ryan; I'm not trying to start anything. I've lived in this apartment for five years and you know me. But they've been telling me that you don't treat your wife right, and I thought I'd tell you about it.

Ryan

Anybody that told you that, Mr. Johnson, is a liar, I don't care if it's man, woman or child.

Maxwell

Now, Ryan, will you just listen to me for a minute? This thing was sort of put up to me, and I've got to do it. Probably these people are all wrong. Just sit down and talk to me a minute. Have a drink?

Ryan (*sulkily, sitting down again*)

Yes, thanks. (Maxwell *brings in from the din-*

ing room a bottle, a siphon and two glasses.) Ain't you got any ice?

MAXWELL

Oh, yes, that's right.

(*He goes into the dining room again and comes back with a plate of cracked ice. Meanwhile* RYAN *pockets several cigars and pours a generous portion of whiskey into the glasses.* MAXWELL *sits down again, and as the men talk they drink, refilling their glasses from time to time.*)

RYAN

Now just what did these fresh guys say about me, Mr. Johnson? You know there's such a thing as a libel law in these here United States.

MAXWELL

Well, I'll tell you, Ryan. I don't know whether there's anything in it or not, and these people may have it all wrong, but they said that you were treating Mrs. Ryan very badly.

RYAN

I beat her up, I suppose?

MAXWELL

No, they didn't say anything like that. It's this

[267]

way, Ryan: These people are making a sort of special study of people that work hard for a living, and they say—I don't know whether they're right or not —that you're not treating Mrs. Ryan right to make her work so hard and have so many children and all that sort of thing.

RYAN

Mr. Johnson, if any man but you was talking to me like that, I'd knock his block off, the big boob! Why, whose business is it how many children I have? What do they expect she's going to do? Lie on a couch an' have me bring her ice cream all day long? I been married thirteen years next month, an' if anybody wants to know how I treat my wife I refer them to her, I do.

MAXWELL

Well, Ryan, as I said, I'm inclined to think that these people that were talking to me were a bit hasty. But see here; listen to me a minute. These people want to do you a good turn. You'll admit, I suppose, that it isn't the finest life in the world for Mrs. Ryan to be staying down there in the basement all day and all night washing clothes and cooking meals and tending to the children. She's sick every now and then, isn't she?

[268]

RYAN

Now and then.

MAXWELL

Well, the idea is this: These people are what they call philanthropists—that is, they're trying to make the world better, to make people happier. Now, they've built a very nice tenement house; it's called a model tenement; it's almost as good an apartment house to live in as this one. What they say is, that you can put Mrs. Ryan there, in a nice suite of rooms, with hot and cold water and a bathroom and electric light and everything for very little money— say five dollars a week. You can come there to sleep nights and you can get your breakfast and supper there with her in what they call the community dining room. You see, they do all the cooking for you and charge you just what the food costs for the meals. Your wife won't have any more cooking to do, and they'll give you better meals in that dining room than you've ever had before, believe me.

RYAN

I see. What about the washing?

MAXWELL

Well, they have a big laundry in the place and do

all your washing for you for about half what a regular laundry would cost you. That sounds like a
pretty good thing, doesn't it?

RYAN

A pretty good thing, and I suppose there's nurse-
maids and governesses for all the children, too, hey?

MAXWELL

Why, as a matter of fact there are—but not exactly in the way you mean. You see, they run a sort
of a boarding school, too, the people that run this
model tenement do, and they take care of all the
children there—keep 'em night and day, feed 'em
and dress 'em and teach 'em trades and all that sort
of thing. They let them come to see you on Sunday, but you're relieved of all responsibility and
your wife of all the trouble.

RYAN

I see. But what's to become of my job when
I'm going off to this here model tenement to sleep
nights? Don't you know that a janitor has to sleep
in the building he's taking care of?

MAXWELL

Well, you're not in love with your job, are you?
You'd be willing to do some other work where there

MAXWELL

No, I don't think he is.

RYAN

He came into my place the other day selling some sort of a little doctor book.

MAXWELL

I know; he does that because he's a philanthropist.

RYAN

Do people make a living by being philanthropists?

MAXWELL

No—well, as a matter of fact, many people do make a pretty fat living out of it, but Mr. Morris doesn't. He's a sculptor—a man that makes statues, you know.

RYAN

Oh, I know what a sculptor is, all right. What statues did Mr. Morris make?

MAXWELL

Why, he made that statue over in the corner, for one thing.

(RYAN *goes over and examines the purple statue.*)

RYAN

Do you like this statue, Mr. Johnson?

MAXWELL (*laughing*)

I'm not a judge of such things, Ryan. But people who know about art say that it's very good indeed.

RYAN

Is it a good likeness?

MAXWELL

It's not supposed to be a portrait; it's a sort of a fancy statue. It represents the "Emancipation of Woman"—woman freed, you know.

RYAN

Freed from what?

MAXWELL

Why, from overwork, and excessive child-bearing and all that sort of thing, you know.

RYAN

Well, that lady's freed from child-bearing, all right. She's perfectly safe on that score. (*He goes back to his chair and pours out another drink.*) But now let's get back to your friends' proposition.

[274]

I'm to get a day job and come home nights—is that right?

MAXWELL

That's right.

RYAN

The children are taken off my wife's hands, and she doesn't have to do any more cooking or washing or anything, hey?

MAXWELL

That's it, Ryan.

RYAN

And the place we'd live would be pretty much like this apartment, would it?

MAXWELL

Just as comfortable, at any rate.

RYAN

My wife would have no work to do; I'd work in the daytime and come home nights—there'd be no kids to take care of—it would be pretty much like the life that you and your wife have, wouldn't it, Mr. Johnson?

MAXWELL

Ah—why, yes, Ryan, pretty much the same. What do you think of the proposition?

[275]

MISCELLANEOUS PIECES

RYAN

Well, I'll tell you. Of course I wouldn't like to have the children go away—though they are a lot of trouble—but I suppose they'd be better taken care of than we could do, so, if that was all there was to it, I'd say go ahead. And it'd be all right for me, too, if I was a bachelor. But it's on account of my wife that I feel I've got to say, "Excuse me!"

MAXWELL

Why, you don't begrudge your wife a little rest, do you, Ryan?

RYAN

Would I begrudge the old woman a little rest? Yes, by God, I would, if a little rest meant having nothing to do all day except sit around and talk to her friends and run around town. It's just on that account that I say nix to your whole proposition. Now you think I'm a slave driver, I suppose. Well, I ain't, Mr. Johnson, but I've lived with a woman thirteen years, and what I'm telling you I didn't get out of no books—it's facts!

Listen, Mr. Johnson. What you want us to do is to live just the sort of life that you and your wife live—no children to take care of, no washing nor cooking nor nothing. Well, what I say is, excuse

me! That may be all right for you and your wife
—she don't need no housework nor children nor
nothing to keep her busy. Her time is full of all
sorts of useful things—I know that. (MAXWELL
stirs uneasily and looks at the floor.) But with
Annie, my wife, it's a different proposition altogether. She's one of them women—and there's a
lot more of them than you think—that can't stand
living in a nice regular apartment with nothing to
do. I know because we tried it when we was first
married. It's like what the old fellow said: "Satan
finds some mischief still for idle hands to do"!

MAXWELL

True enough! And—

RYAN

Listen, Mr. Johnson. When we was first married, Annie was one of these here idle hands they
tell of. She was an idle hand for three years, and
Satan, as the old fellow said, certainly found some
mischief for her to do. Not anything real bad—
there's no real harm in Annie—but it was mischief
all right. For the first three years we was living in
a nice apartment in Brooklyn. I wasn't a janitor,
then; I was driving a truck. I was out all day and

[277]

I got home every night at six or seven o'clock. All
Annie has to do is to get my breakfast and supper
and keep the place clean. Does she do it? Sure she
does, for the first four or five weeks! Then she gets
to making friends with other women in the building
and going out to matinees and vaudeville and all
that sort of thing. That's all right—I can afford
it—I don't care if she has a good time; but then
what does she do? I give her two dollars in the
morning to go out and buy a good supper for me
when I come home. I come home and she ain't in
yet, and the lady in the next flat gives me the
groceries that she's sent home. And what is they?
A little chipped beef and a box of Saratoga chips
and some baker's bread. About fifty-cent's worth.
When she gets home I ask her where she's been.
Why, Mrs. Eindorfer has took her to a spiritualist
meeting, and she's spent the rest of that money to
look into a glass ball or have her fortune told or
some such foolishness.

Now this goes on for nearly three years. It ain't
all spiritualists' meetings; it's all sorts of things.
She makes all sorts of friends, women and men, too;
I had to beat a couple of 'em up. The flat wasn't
kept up; I run into debt; my meals wasn't cooked
right or on time, and Annie was half sick all the

[278]

time just from running around entertaining herself. I ain't blaming her. She wasn't to blame. And what was to blame? The apartment house was to blame. When Peter was born, after we'd been married three years, and I gave up trucking and moved out of that apartment house and got a job as janitor, everything was all right. And everything's been all right ever since.

MAXWELL (*thoughtfully*)

And the apartment house was to blame?

RYAN

Believe me, Mr. Johnson, the only part of an apartment house to live in is the basement, where you can have a regular home. I been a janitor for ten years, and I seen these apartment houses do queer things to families. They don't seem to have no children when they live in apartment houses, that's one thing. And there ain't no coal to bring up and the washing goes out, and there ain't nothing for them to do but just make fools of themselves. And sometimes there's a good many divorces been caused by these here apartment houses. And there'd be a good many more divorces if a lot of husbands knew what went on when they was downtown at business.

Understand me, Mr. Johnson. I don't mean you and your wife at all. You ain't that sort of people, but what I do say is for my wife, and for a lot of women with more education and more money than she's got, the only sort of life is doing housework and taking care of children all day long. So Annie and me will stay down in the basement, much obliged to you, unless we go out of New York to live in a little house in the country sometime. And Annie'll have just as much work to do there. She's one of them women that wasn't meant to be idle. And now I guess I'll go downstairs.

(*He rises and goes toward the door.* MAXWELL *sits silent for a moment and then rises a little unsteadily. He holds out his hand to* RYAN *for a second and then drops it and starts.*)

MAXWELL

Ryan, I—er—why, I guess you're right, after all. I'll tell my friends what you said.

RYAN

All right. No hard feelings, I hope.

MAXWELL

Not at all; that's all right. Good night, Ryan.

[280]

SOME MISCHIEF STILL

RYAN

Good night, Mr. Johnson.
(*He goes out.*)

MAXWELL

There's a man that's master in his own home, at
any rate. (*He lights a cigar and walks around the
room with his hands in his trousers pockets, coming
to a halt in front of the purple statue. He looks at
it reflectively.*) Satan finds some mischief still—
(*A pause*)—for idle hands to do. For idle hands
to do. For idle hands to do. For idle hands—

(*The doorbell is rung violently. MAXWELL
starts and runs out into the hall. He returns with
HELEN, who is very much out of breath. As she
runs into the room the combs drop from her hair,
which falls over her face and shoulders. She throws
herself on the chaise-longue. MAXWELL sits beside
her and tries to push her hair back from her face.*)

Nellie! What's the matter?

(*HELEN sobs without answering.*)

HELEN

It's those nasty Martins and that nasty policeman and that nasty Lionel Morris.

(*The bell rings again. MAXWELL goes to the
door and admits LIONEL.*)

MISCELLANEOUS PIECES

LIONEL

Oh, I'm awfully glad you got back all right, Miss White. I jumped into a taxi as soon as that brute of a policeman came, and then I met all the rest of the crowd at the studio and everybody said, "Where's Miss White?" So I came right up here to find out if you'd got home.

MAXWELL

For God's sake, will somebody tell me what's happened?

LIONEL (*sitting on the pianola bench*)

Why, you see—

HELEN

Be still. You see, Max, we were all at the Mortons' studio, and Adrian Wolfe made a speech about those nasty striking miners in California or wherever it is that everybody is wearing mourning for and parading and all that and this—and Mr. Morris said: "Let's walk up to Union Square and hold an open air meeting to protest." So we went up there and I made a speech and there was a crowd and I saw a policeman there, but I thought it would be all right, and then Mr. Morris made a speech and he said something about trampling on a blood-stained flag, and the policeman told him to stop, and

[282]

he called the policeman a myrmidon, and some more
policemen came and broke up the meeting, and he
ran away and wouldn't help me; and I ran down
into the subway, and I don't see how he dares show
his face in here!

MAXWELL

I'll talk to him presently, but quiet down a little.
You'd better go in your room and fix up your hair.

(HELEN *rises to go out. She stops in the doorway and turns to* MAXWELL.)

HELEN

I won't go to that nasty Amaranth this summer,
Maxwell.

MAXWELL

No, you won't go to Amaranth.

HELEN

Then will you get an automobile?

MAXWELL

No, I won't get an automobile.

HELEN

Then what—

MAXWELL

I am going to take that two thousand dollars and
buy, with the assistance of the building and loan

association, a small house in a city called Joplin, in the State of Missouri. It will not be a large house, but I think that you will not find the time hanging heavy on your hands. My brother has a wholesale grocery there, and I dare say he will take me into the business, especially as I have a little money to invest. And I'll come home to luncheon every day. Missouri is a fertile State. My brother has six children.

LIONEL

But, Miss White—Mr. Johnson!

(HELEN *goes down the hall to her room.* MAXWELL *walks up to* LIONEL.)

MAXWELL

My wife's name is not Miss White but Mrs. Johnson—Mrs. Maxwell Johnson, of Joplin, Missouri. Get that? Do you know what keeps me from dropping you down the elevator shaft?

LIONEL

What—what do you mean?

MAXWELL

It's the janitor. Yes, Ryan, the fellow down in the basement with nine children that you and Mrs. What's-her-name wanted to segregate. He told me

[284]

all about you to-night. You're nothing but a by-product! The apartment house is the real devil in this pretty little play—the apartment house is responsible for Feminism and Socialism and Anarchism and Eugenics and pups like you. You're just a sort of bad substitute for the movies—that's all you are. The apartment house breeds the whole bunch of you—the apartment house and its artificial, lazy, good-for-nothing life.

(LIONEL *starts toward the door hurriedly, but stops as if shot when the telephone bell rings close to his ear. He comes back into the room and* MAXWELL *goes to the telephone.*)

MAXWELL

Hello! . . . What's that? . . . Yes, this is Mr. Johnson. . . . No, I don't think so. Hold the wire and I'll see. (*With his hand over the transmitter he looks into the room.*) Nellie!
HELEN (*coming into the living room with her hair in a long braid, wearing a blue tea gown*)
Yes, Max?

MAXWELL

What is your name?

HELEN

Why, Helen, of course, stupid.

[285]

MAXWELL

Helen what?

HELEN

Helen Johnson.

MAXWELL

Not Miss Helen White?

HELEN

No! No! No!

MAXWELL (*smiling*)

Well, that's all right, then. There's a cop down-stairs with a warrant for the arrest of a Miss Helen White and a Mr. Lionel Morris, charged with making incendiary speeches in Union Square. They think that Morris's taxicab stopped at this building, and the policeman is going through all the apartments. He'll be here in a minute. (*In the receiver.*) All right, Sam, it's all right. Thanks for tipping me off. (MAXWELL *reënters the room and sits on the pianola bench.* HELEN *reclines, with some dignity, on the chaise-longue.* LIONEL *crouches behind the purple statue.*)

MAXWELL (*meditatively*)

Satan finds some mischief still—

[286]

SOME MISCHIEF STILL

HELEN

What are you saying, Max?

MAXWELL

Oh, I was just thinking of the janitor. I had quite a talk with him after you left.

(*The doorbell rings, and* MAXWELL *admits a large policeman.*)

POLICEMAN

Excuse me, sir; it's just a matter of form. I'm looking for a couple of them Anarchist-Suffrage-I. W. W. bugs. It's just a matter of form. The man's name is Lionel Morris and the woman's name is Helen White. Are you Lionel Morris?

MAXWELL

No; my name is Maxwell Johnson. The janitor knows me, and so do a lot of people in the building.

POLICEMAN

Thank you, sir. It's just a matter of form. Now, madam—it's just a matter of form—are you Helen White?

HELEN

No, I am not Helen White. I am Mrs. Maxwell Johnson.

POLICEMAN

Thank you, madam, thank you; it's just a matter of form. You see these parties is incendiaries; they called me a mermaiden. Now, just two more questions—it's just a matter of form: Is Miss Helen White here?

HELEN

No, Helen White is not here.

MAXWELL

And I'm glad she isn't here, officer.

POLICEMAN

You may well be that, sir; you may well be that. Now, is Lionel Morris here?

(*There is a pause, during which the purple statue shakes slightly.*)

MAXWELL

Well, what do you think about it, officer? Take a look around the place. Want to look in the dumb waiter or down the kitchen sink?

POLICEMAN

Oh, I know he's not here, Mr. Johnson, and I'm sorry to have troubled you. Much obliged to you. Good night, sir.

SOME MISCHIEF STILL

MAXWELL

Have a drink before you go?

POLICEMAN

Well, I hadn't ought to, but I guess I will, thanks.
(*HELEN pours the whiskey and MAXWELL and
the policeman lift their glasses.*)

POLICEMAN

Well, here's how, sir.

MAXWELL

Here's Joplin!

HELEN

Oh, I'll drink that.
(*She takes a sip from MAXWELL's glass.*)

POLICEMAN

What's that, something new?

MAXWELL

No, it's old as Adam and Eve.

POLICEMAN

Well, it's a new one on me. Thank you, sir.
Good night.

MAXWELL

Good night. (*The policeman goes out. After*

the door slams shut, LIONEL *stands up, but remains behind the purple statue.*) Hadn't you better go to some other apartment house? The cop's gone down the elevator. He'll be gone by the time you get downstairs. (LIONEL *goes out and as he turns he brushes against the purple statue, which topples on its pedestal. He bangs the door shut after him violently, and the statue falls to the floor and breaks into several pieces.* MAXWELL *and* HELEN *look at it for a moment and then turn to each other and laugh.*)

HELEN

Oh, look what's happened to the "Emancipation of Woman"!

CURTAIN